DATE DUE			
OCT 2 6 1992			

Books by Robert C. Christopher

The Japanese Mind: The Goliath Explained
Second to None: American Companies in Japan

CRASHING THE GATES

The De-WASPing of America's Power Elite

ROBERT C. CHRISTOPHER

SIMON AND SCHUSTER

NEW YORK   LONDON   TORONTO   SYDNEY   TOKYO

Simon and Schuster
Simon & Schuster Building
Rockefeller Center
1230 Avenue of the Americas
New York, New York 10020

Copyright © 1989 by Kriscon Corporation

SIMON AND SCHUSTER and colophon are registered trademarks
of Simon & Schuster Inc.

Designed by Beth Tondreau Design/Gabrielle Hamberg
Manufactured in the United States of America

1   3   5   7   9   10   8   6   4   2

Library of Congress Cataloging in Publication Data
Christopher, Robert C., 1924–
Crashing the gates: the De-WASPing of America's power elite/
Robert C. Christopher.
p.   cm.
Bibliography: p.
Includes index.
1. Ethnicity—United States.   2. WASPs (Persons)   3. Elite (Social sciences)—
United States.   4. United States—Ethnic relations.
I. Title.
E184.A1C455   1989
305.8'00973—dc19   89-30008
                                                                      CIP
ISBN 0-671-47334-4

This book is for my children and grandchildren: Ulrica, Thomas, Valerie, Nicholas, Alistair, Gordon, and Shawn.

CONTENTS

CONTENTS

PREFACE

Though the process became a conscious one only a few years ago, I have in a sense been accumulating material for this book all my life. Since the onslaught of the Great Depression, which was the first national event to engrave itself on my consciousness, a kaleidoscopic succession of social, political, economic, and technological evolutions has transformed the United States into a very different country from the one in which I was born. Of all these changes none, in my view, has been more far-reaching in its implications nor more positive in its impact than the progress Americans have made in coming to terms with their ethnic diversity. Yet on a year-to-year basis, the decline of ethnic chauvinism in this country has been imperceptible enough that it is, I believe, difficult to appreciate how far we have come in the last half-century unless, as people of my generation do, you have firsthand memories of the attitudes that prevailed even among relatively enlightened Americans in the era immediately preceding World War II.

My own children, I know, can scarcely credit the fact that when I left it to enter the Army in late 1942, my hometown of New Haven, Connecticut, was a place where marriage between Irish and Italian Americans was still uncommon enough to occasion raised eyebrows on both sides, where social intercourse between WASPs and Italian or Jewish Americans was still minimal and generally awkward, and where no one of Polish or Greek heritage could sensibly hope ever to win the presidency of a local bank or brokerage house.

All that, of course, is totally at variance with the social patterns that prevail in the world my children inhabit. For them, as for most Americans of their age and educational background, the notion of "sticking to our own kind" in the choice of marriage partners, friends, or business associates is a totally foreign one. That an archetypical WASP such as George Bush should have grandchildren who are half Hispanic strikes my offspring as essentially unremarkable, and they cannot truly comprehend the fact that it is only a matter of a few decades—or less—since status and power in many areas of American life were largely reserved for the members of a single ethnic group.

It was, I suppose, the consciousness of this particular generation gap—a deepening fascination with the question of how we Americans got from where we were in my youth to where we are now and what that portends about where we are going—that originally inspired me to start work on this book. But while it may have been personal in its genesis, the book bears the stamp of many minds and many experiences other than my own. I am, in fact, indebted to literally dozens of people for generously sharing with me their ideas and information on the enormously complex subject with which I have attempted to deal.

I have, I hope, credited all—or nearly all—of these people by name in the body of the book. However, there are a few whose assistance was invaluable yet who are either unmentioned or perhaps insufficiently acknowledged in the chapters that follow. Though they will all surely take issue with at least some of my conclusions, Professors Herbert Gans, Nathan Glazer, and James Shenton helped immeasurably to clarify my thinking on numerous aspects of my subject. My longtime boss and cherished friend, Kermit Lanser, imparted insights concerning the graphic arts, a field in which I have lamentably little background. Howard Johnson and Harry Haskell provided enlightenment on the museum scene in Boston and Kansas City respectively.

Waldemar Nielsen and Dr. Lydia Brontë performed the same service with regard to the world of the great foundations, while Lt. Col. Joseph Collins, U.S.A., opened doors in the Pentagon that might otherwise have been closed to me.

Beyond all this, I owe very special thanks to Brian Rogers and the staff of the Charles E. Shain Library at Connecticut College for graciously providing me not only with research facilities but with a peaceful retreat in which to write. In the early stages of the writing Alice Mayhew of Simon and Schuster supplied much-needed enthusiasm, and Bob Bender of the same house discharged with notable patience and efficiency the unenviable task of editing an ex-editor. Finally, my agent, Melanie Jackson, was as always an inexhaustible source of just the right blend of encouragement, sound critical judgment, and common sense.

Old Lyme, Connecticut
September 1988

1

ROOM AT THE TOP

On July 21, 1988, when a dark, compact man of vaguely Mediterranean appearance stepped up to the podium in Atlanta's Omni Coliseum to accept the Democratic nomination for the presidency of the United States, it seemed to some that American history had entered a new era. On the face of things that reaction was natural enough: never before in modern times had a child of immigrant parents been a serious candidate for America's highest office. Yet in their concentration upon Michael Dukakis's role as the embodiment of the American ethnic dream, convention orators and the nation's press either ignored or paid only passing attention to some significant facets of the Dukakis story.

For one thing, Michael Dukakis could not aspire to be the first U.S. president of immigrant parentage; that distinction had been captured more than a century and a half earlier by Andrew Jackson, whose parents were born in Ireland. Of considerably more practical importance, however, was the fact that in certain aspects of his life and character Dukakis had clearly been much more heavily influenced by his American upbringing than by his Greek heritage.

Indeed, in the early stages of his political career Dukakis had placed so little stress on his ethnicity that when he became a presidential candidate, *New York* magazine's Joe Klein, a veteran observer of Massachusetts Democratic politics, was moved to comment: "I knew Michael Dukakis before he was Greek." No one, to be sure, could legitimately accuse the immigrant's son from Brookline of ever seeking to pass as a WASP, yet both in behavior and in outlook he undeniably had more in common with his fellow New Englander George Bush than with Greece's mercurial premier, Andreas Papandreou.

That, of course, is neither in any sense to his discredit nor difficult to explain. The son of a successful doctor who left an estate of some $2 million, Dukakis was endowed by his parents with what most middle class Americans of liberal persuasion would regard as one of the finest educations money can buy—undergraduate work at Swarthmore College and final polishing at Harvard Law School. And the uniquely American social and intellectual tone of those elite institutions was clearly reflected in his subsequent life, both personal and professional. Though he is quick to capitalize upon his command of spoken Greek when facing a Greek-American audience, Dukakis had not hesitated to imperil his formal membership in the Greek Orthodox Church, an affiliation that the majority of Greek Americans regard as a key ingredient in their ethnic identity. (Though his marriage to a woman of Jewish background would not necessarily put him outside the Greek Orthodox fold, the fact that he did not marry her in a Greek Orthodox ceremony should have done so.)* And while there were a number of Greek Americans in his immediate political entourage, his close advisers also included WASPs, Irish Americans, Jews, an Italian American, and a foreign policy expert of Czech birth.

There was, of course, very good reason why none of these things stimulated any great degree of public discussion—and that was that

---

* Under Greek Orthodox canon law, someone who marries outside the church is not entitled to receive its sacraments, but in Dukakis's case, as in a number of others, church authorities have tempered orthodoxy with ethnic pride and chosen not to make an issue of the matter.

---

there was nothing very remarkable about them. They simply reflected the fact that in the closing years of the 1980s the role that ethnicity and religion played in the lives of successful Americans had become extremely subtle and complex.

Less than thirty years earlier when another man from Massachusetts had been the Democratic nominee for president, the fact that he was a non-WASP had been perceived as a potential political liability of major proportions. In almost every visible respect—education, manner, tastes and lifestyle—John Fitzgerald Kennedy had borne the imprint of the traditional American elite to a far greater extent than Michael Dukakis. Yet both at the convention that nominated Kennedy and throughout the campaign that followed it, serious doubts had been expressed that the nation was prepared to accept even so establishmentarian a Roman Catholic as its president—doubts sufficiently persistent and widespread that JFK felt obliged to offer public assurances that his ancestral faith in no way diminished or impinged upon his adherence to historic American political values.

In 1988, however, no such demeaning assurances were expected or required of Michael Dukakis. Instead, political wisdom dictated that he flaunt his immigrant heritage, which was almost universally seen as an electoral asset, something which established him as being more in the true American grain than his well-born WASP opponent. Rather than constituting the harbinger of a new era, in short, the nomination of Michael Dukakis was a manifestation of patterns already solidly established in the upper reaches of the American power structure.

Indeed, one of the most striking social trends discernible from even the most cursory survey of the U.S. press in the years immediately preceding the Dukakis nomination was the progressive disintegration of ethnic barriers—most notably those against whites of non-WASP origin. Among the countless news stories documenting this development were several of uncommon piquancy. Items:

- In July 1986 when the Kennedy clan assembled at the family compound in Hyannis Port for the wedding of John Kennedy's daughter, Caroline, suitable obeisance was paid to ethnic tradition: the ritual was Roman Catholic and the bride's gown and veil were both heavily embroidered with shamrocks. But the white wooden church in which the ceremony was held was pure New England Congregational in inspiration, and the groom—author and exhibition planner Edwin Schlossberg—was Jewish. As for the guest list, it was ethnically eclectic as well: along with such fixtures of WASP society as Mrs. Paul Mellon and the bride's grandmother Mrs. Hugh Auchincloss, those in attendance included society designer Carolina Herrera and her husband, Reinaldo, Mrs. Abe Ribicoff, and Maurice Templesman, the Manhattan metals magnate who had become the constant companion of the bride's mother.

· April Fools' Day, 1987, saw an even more eclectic gathering of the elite in Manhattan. On hand for this occasion were a clutch of the rich and social such as Consuelo Crespi, Ann Bass, George Plimpton, and man-about-Manhattan Jerome ("The Social Moth") Zipkin. In the wake of these eminences came fashionable designers like Halston and Calvin Klein, artists and writers such as Jamie Wyeth and Tom Wolfe, and whole platoons of showbiz types including Liza Minnelli and Yoko Ono. What brought this glittering company together was a memorial service at St. Patrick's Cathedral for a Czech coal miner's son—artist Andy Warhol (né Warhola).

· A month after the Warhol memorial, *Business Week* presented a waiting world with its list of the twenty-five most highly paid corporate executives in America for the year 1986. Solidly ensconced on top of the heap was Italian-American Lee Iacocca with total compensation of just under $21 million. The No. 2 and No. 3 slots were both occupied by Jewish Americans—Paul Fireman of Reebok International (just over $13 million) and Victor Posner of DWG ($8.4 million). No. 4, with $6.3 million, was an Irish American, John Nevin of Firestone. The top WASP on the list, Charles Exley, Jr., of NCR, ranked fifth and took home a trifle under $6.3 million—or less than one-third as much as Iacocca.

· By long-standing custom New York's august Council on Foreign Relations holds a Christmas party each year for the high-powered businessmen, lawyers, journalists, academics, and other heavyweights who make up its membership, and in mid-December 1987 that tradition was duly observed. But this time the hostly responsibilities that fall upon the Council's board chairman and president on such occasions were not, as they had been for most of the 1980s, discharged by those twin pillars of WASPdom David Rockefeller and Pillsbury heir Winston Lord. Instead, thanks to a 1986 change in the Council's leadership, arriving guests were greeted by chairman Peter Peterson, a Greek-American financier, and president Peter Tarnoff, an ex–Foreign Service officer of Jewish birth.

· In May 1988, Miss Sarina Rosaria di Bonaventura, the daughter of a Boston University music professor of Italian ancestry, was married to Mr. Philip S. Birsh, a Wall Street executive specializing in mergers and acquisitions. The ceremony, a civil one since Miss di Bonaventura was gentile and Mr. Birsh Jewish, was held at Greentree, the elegant Long Island estate of Mrs. John Hay Whitney. To anyone unacquainted with the couple that might have seemed a somewhat surprising locale for their wedding, but in fact it was a very natural one: Sarina di Bonaventura Birsh is, as it happens, Mrs. Whitney's granddaughter—and the great-granddaughter of President Franklin D. Roosevelt.

IN ONE WAY or another, all of these events mirrored a sea change in life in the United States: the replacement of a power elite historically almost exclusively composed of WASPs or assimilated WASPs by one in which it has become commonplace to be of patently non-WASP heritage. And while it is clearly the result of long-simmering processes, this change has achieved its present proportions within a remarkably short space of time; even in the 1960s most of the news items I have cited would have struck the average newspaper reader as unusual, and at least one of them—the transfer of authority at the Council on Foreign Relations—would have been inconceivable as late as the 1970s.

There is, moreover, still another phenomenon that these stories reflected—one that must be accounted both a cause and a consequence of the rapid ethnic diversification of the nation's leadership group. By the 1980s, two decades after some of the most prestigious sociological gurus in the United States had proclaimed the extinction of the melting pot, Americans in unprecedented numbers were opting to "melt" in the most basic possible manner—intermarriage with the members of ethnic and religious groups other than their own.

In one sense at least, none of these developments can accurately be said to have escaped public attention. They are, in fact, so ubiquitous that the great majority of middle class Americans have repeatedly been exposed to them in their personal and professional lives. Yet as a general proposition the reality that all across the top levels of American society power is now dispersed among people drawn from diverse ethnic backgrounds is one that is often overlooked and seldom accorded the importance it deserves as a portent of the nation's future.

The reasons for this are easy to see. There are other and far less encouraging realities in contemporary American life as well: brutal attacks on blacks by working class white youths, racial conflict on college campuses, overt or at best thinly disguised anti-Semitism on the part of numerous blacks, violence against Vietnamese immigrants in Texas, attempts to restrict admission of Asian Americans by prestigious educational institutions, hostility between Hispanic and black political leaders in major cities—and so on and on through a long unhappy litany.

These, of course, are the ethnic realities that are most assiduously reported in the press and that are most often invoked by our politicians —whether for reasons of personal ambition, genuine hatred of injustice, or a combination of both. And that is not surprising. For these things *are* realities, and there is a sensible human tendency to devote more attention to something that needs repair than to something that is already functioning satisfactorily.

Where ethnic relations are concerned, moreover, that tendency is reinforced by the weight of history. All of us inevitably are in greater or lesser degree prisoners of our own pasts, and any American now in late middle age remembers a time when the children or grandchildren of Southern and Eastern Europeans were as unlikely to be found in positions of power and authority in the United States as blacks and Hispanics are today. Worse yet in some ways, we remember that in those not-so-long-ago days, the best hope a "white ethnic" had of achieving such a position lay in accepting what Norman Podhoretz, the brilliant, acerbic editor of *Commentary* magazine, has trenchantly labeled "the brutal bargain." That is to say that in many fields the down payment that a Jewish, Italian, Greek, or Slavic American was obliged to make on success consisted of obliterating all public manifestations of his ethnic heritage and remolding himself into a facsimile WASP.

Such things are not easily forgotten—nor perhaps should they be. And it would surely be not only morally blind but dangerous to the health of our society to shrug off as unimportant the many ways in which ethnic and racial discrimination still disfigure American life. Yet to focus almost exclusively upon the areas in which discrimination persists and to minimize the significance of those areas where we have made solid progress in combatting it is also unhealthy. For what that does, among other things, is to give continued life to social attitudes that have in large part ceased to reflect reality and as a result are more likely to obscure our national problems than point the way to any solution of them.

One of these psychological survivals is the stubbornness with which many members of ethnic groups that are now heavily represented in the American Establishment cling to the belief that "somebody else is running the country." Among Jewish Americans this sometimes manifests itself in what journalist Peter Schrag in his book *The Decline of the WASP* labeled "the goy complex"—the assumption that "at the heart of things there is a WASP patriciate which, if it so desires, can manipulate all the lesser goys (Italians, Irishmen, whatever) to make them do its bidding." And gentile versions of essentially the same illusion abound. In the very late 1970s, at a time when both the secretary of state and the national security adviser happened to be Polish Americans, I was bemused to hear a highly educated and influential New Yorker of Polish origin blame what he regarded as the ineptitude of U.S. policies toward Poland upon "Ivy League cookie pushers." And nearly a decade later, shortly after *Fortune* magazine disclosed that there were now more Catholics than Episcopalians serving as chief executive officers of major U.S. corporations,* an otherwise well-informed Italian American of my acquaintance assured me that U.S. industry's loss of international competitiveness was largely attributable to the poor management of "all those WASPs in the big corner offices."

A rather more idealistic version of the "somebody else is running the country" syndrome is the belief that ethnic discrimination is fundamentally a crime committed by the prosperous and powerful against the poor and powerless. This is an assumption that at least by implication underlies the pronouncements of many populist politicians and writers and has given rise to the seductive notion that all that is required to redress the evil consequences of discrimination is a coalition embracing all of the nation's dispossessed groups.

The difficulty with this thesis, as I see it, lies in a reality pointed out by the distinguished Columbia University sociologist Herbert Gans. "By and large," Professor Gans has written, "American ethnicity today is working class ethnicity." To put it somewhat differently, it is the less privileged members of American society who, out of a sense of vulnerability and the need for a mutual support group, cling most obdurately to their ethnic identity and are most apt to display hostility toward other ethnic groups. By contrast, successful Americans tend to have greater confidence in their ability to cope with a multiethnic environment and hence, broadly speaking, to attach somewhat less importance to their own ethnicity as well as that of their colleagues or competitors.

Even to some who do not share them, the attitudes I have been describing may seem understandable and relatively harmless quirks of

---

* Though Episcopalians account for only 3 percent of the total population, they supplied one-third of the chief executive officers of the nation's 500 largest industrial corporations as recently as the 1950s.

---

opinion. Like all ideas, however, they have consequences. The notion that it is the members of some shadowy and exclusive in-group who have created such problems as the United States currently confronts enables far too many Americans to ignore the immortal observation of Walt Kelly's Pogo: "We have met the enemy and he is us." Similarly, the myth that discrimination is primarily a device employed by the upper class to protect its status obscures the fact that in the contemporary United States it is not so much the rich and powerful who perpetuate ethnic tensions as it is those on the lower rungs of the social and economic ladder.

In short, there is compelling reason for Americans to pay greater attention than they now do to those segments of our society in which ethnic discrimination is no longer rampant and to seek to determine as accurately as possible what forces conspired to bring about change in these areas. For unless we do that, we are in danger of misunderstanding the nature of the ethnic problems that still afflict us and, as a result, of resorting to inappropriate remedies for them.

To my mind, the most striking evidence of the reality of this danger is to be found in the dominance that the concept of "cultural pluralism" has achieved in American intellectual circles. In the most obvious sense, of course, cultural pluralism is an undeniable fact of American life: ethnic enclaves that perpetuate the cultures of other societies abound in this country, and our own national culture now incorporates elements stemming from places as diverse as Germany (the Christmas tree), Africa (jazz), and East Asia (karate).

But for many of those who so enthusiastically embraced the cause of cultural pluralism in the 1960s and still proclaim it to be the only acceptable course for the United States to follow, the phrase carries connotations going well beyond the obvious one. To its most ardent partisans, such as Michael Novak (*The Rise of the Unmeltable Ethnics*), cultural pluralism implies the conscious pursuit of a national order in which Americans find their identity primarily as members of ethnic and/or religious blocs and only secondarily as individuals engaged in carving out a position in the general society.

Despite the eminence and evident sincerity of some of its advocates, however, the suggestion that this brand of cultural pluralism constitutes either a logical or feasible goal for American society strikes me as mistaken. Its fatal flaw, I believe, lies in the fact that it rests upon a misreading of both past and present trends in ethnic relationships in the United States.

Almost from the time Europeans first began to settle on this continent, ethnic prejudice and its use to promote or protect particular social and economic interests have been prominent features of the American landscape. And two of the first ethnic groups to fall victim to this tragic reality—American Indians and blacks—continue to be victims of it to this day. Yet despite these conspicuous and indefensible offenses against human dignity, the overall long-term thrust of American life has from the first been more inclusionary in ethnic terms than that of any other major nation. Perhaps more to the point, it has been far more inclusionary than most contemporary Americans assume. And in our time this trend has accelerated and broadened to such an extent that the interlocking elites that effectively manage our nation's affairs can no longer legitimately be characterized in either an ethnic or a cultural sense by any single word more restrictive than "American."

To trace just how, when, and why this came about is the aim of this book.

2

THE MYTH
OF THE WASP

Though it was certainly in conversational use well before then, the acronym "WASP" had never appeared in print so far as I can discover before 1962.* I can still recall, in fact, how puzzled one of my mother's Yankee aunts was when sometime in the late 1950s I applied the term to her. Once she had learned what it meant, however, she embraced the word with delight. "How nice!" she said. "I mean, unpleasant epithets like that are only used about minorities, so it must be people recognize that we are now a minority, too. And that means they won't be able to go on blaming us for all the things that make them unhappy."

* Credit for coining the term "WASP" is often given to Prof. E. Digby Baltzell of the University of Pennsylvania, and it was indeed Baltzell's use of the acronym in his 1964 book *The Protestant Establishment* that did most to launch it on the road to general acceptance. The first use of the term in print, however, actually appears to have been in an article that E. B. Palmore published in *The American Journal of Sociology* in 1962 in which he carefully explained that "for the sake of brevity, we will use the nickname 'WASP' for this group, from the initial letters of White Anglo-Saxon Protestant."

As a piece of sociological prediction, of course, this was 180° off target. Nearly twenty years later in an interview with Charlotte Curtis of the *New York Times*, former New York mayor John Lindsay pointed out that "WASP" was the only pejorative ethnic term that it is still permissible to use in enlightened social circles in the United States. By the same token, where Polish, Puerto Rican, or Jewish jokes are widely and quite properly held to be in bad taste, even the most ardent foe of ethnic prejudice is unlikely to raise any objection to WASP jokes. ("How can you tell the bride at a WASP wedding?" a staunch liberal of my acquaintance recently inquired of me—and then triumphantly chortled: "Easy; she's the one kissing the Golden Retriever.")

Where this double standard is most strikingly visible, however, is in the movies and television shows that constitute the only art forms to which millions of Americans are exposed on any regular basis. In one episode of the TV series *St. Elsewhere*, to pick an example at random, the villain was a ruthless, anti-Semitic United States senator named Endicott. In reality, of course, any politician of such stature in Massachusetts, where this particular series was set, would be far more likely nowadays to bear an Irish or possibly a Greek surname than a distinctively Yankee one. But quite likely without even giving conscious thought to the matter, the producers of *St. Elsewhere* adhered to a tried-and-true rule of modern American mass entertainment: if you want to avoid coming under fire for ethnic slander, the only safe course is either to give your villains no identifiable ethnicity at all—or else to make them WASPs.

The phenomena I have just described are of trivial importance in themselves and would not be worthy of notice except for one fact: they reflect a cast of mind that is widespread in today's United States and that also manifests itself in far more consequential ways.

The attitude to which I refer is a profound sense of resentment against WASPs founded upon fear and distrust of them. In its most respectable form it is summed up in Michael Novak's proposition that "American democracy operates as a shield for WASP hegemony"—in other words, that the most important institutions in American society and all other groups in the American population are manipulated by WASPs to serve their own clannish ends.

At times this resentment of WASPs verges on paranoia. In the

February 1986 issue of *Manhattan inc,* for example, an able and often perceptive journalist named Ron Rosenbaum offered as a kind of back-handed apologia for the Mafia the following observations: "For a hundred years before the Sicilians reached Ellis Island, America was run by two notoriously vicious and murderous WASP gangs—the southern plantation owners and the northern factory owners. And until very recently, descendants of those WASP gangs ran a kind of mafia of their own that was involved in murder, heroin, and corruption. It was known as the Central Intelligence Agency or, in the colorful slang of that ethnic group, 'The Company.' "

Even some dedicated WASPophobes would, I suspect, find it difficult to subscribe fully to that remarkable piece of rhetoric. Yet on a more rational level of discourse, it remains commonplace to find Americans of non-WASP background instinctively inclined to ascribe political, economic, or social developments of which they disapprove to WASP skulduggery. As percipient an observer as Nathan Glazer, for example, has suggested that it was the fact that John F. Kennedy was Irish "as well as a Democrat, Catholic, and intellectual" that explained the antipathy to his administration displayed by "such a large part of the big business establishment, the seat of the old Americans, the WASP power." And there are surely millions of other Americans who would unhesitatingly accept that thesis, ignoring the fact that in pursuit of what it perceived as its class interest the big business establishment displayed equal or greater antipathy to the administrations of Franklin Roosevelt and Harry Truman, both of whom were WASP, and conspicuously nonintellectual.

Though it is not characteristic of his thinking in general, Glazer's analysis in this particular instance is reminiscent of a common American attitude—namely a strong aversion to the notion that class plays any significant role in our national life. What WASPophobia actually reflects more often than not is a deep-seated distrust and/or resentment of the motives and behavior of those who through birth, achievement, or a combination of the two enjoy privileged positions in American society. But because they are so reluctant to concede that class differences have any fundamental importance in this country, Americans almost automatically tend to express their social, political, and economic grievances in terms of ethnicity.

On balance, that probably has more positive effects than negative ones; rejection of the concept of class conflict as a central public concern has, I believe, clearly helped to promote political stability in the United States. But in at least one respect the surrogate we have found for class conflict has muddied the waters of national debate. Specifically, it has served to reinforce two propositions offered in a single sentence in Norman Podhoretz's autobiographical book *Making It*. These are that WASPs are "an ethnic group like any other" and that they enjoy "majority status" in the United States.

Both these assumptions are, of course, solidly entrenched in the American psyche—and both are demonstrably wrong.

AS I SUSPECT most people do, I always find it irritating when, in the midst of a lively discussion, some pedantic killjoy intones: "Now wait a minute! Before we go any further, let's define our terms." Yet the awkward fact is that while virtually all Americans blithely assume that everyone knows what a WASP is, hardly any of us can produce a definition of the term that will stand up to serious scrutiny. And so, reluctantly, I will now play the pedantic killjoy's role myself.

In a sense, the general sloppiness in use of the word "WASP" is completely understandable. No two of the numerous dictionaries I have consulted define the term in exactly the same way. Worse yet, the meanings that they offer range from the strictly literal ("white Anglo-Saxon Protestant") to the ludicrously general ("a person whose native language is English").

All of the dictionaries I have looked at, however, agree on one point: the word has special reference to people variously described as being of "Anglo-Saxon," "English," or "British" ancestry. And that, in my experience, is the sense that most people implicitly give the word in ordinary conversation.

It is right here that the confusion begins to set in. People whose forebears were Welsh, Scottish, or even, in many instances, Irish are undeniably of British ancestry. But unlike the English they have no significant amount of Anglo-Saxon blood, their ethnic heritage being predominantly Celtic and/or Scandinavian. In the eyes of most present-day Americans, to be sure, this seems a distinction without a difference insofar as the Welsh and the Scots are concerned—though it emphatically does not appear so to the Welsh and the Scots. But even in the United States the word "Irish" is not generally considered synonymous with "Anglo-Saxon" or "British."

As a practical matter, then, most Americans operate on the rather vague premise that the term "WASP" basically refers to people whose ancestors originally came from England, Scotland, or Wales; it doesn't really matter which. And along with that generally unspoken assumption goes another one: that there continue to be more WASPs in the United States than people of any other ethnic background.

For the second of these propositions, there is what might at first blush seem to be strong statistical support: of the 227 million Americans counted in the 1980 census, nearly 49.6 million were classified as being of English ancestry and another 10 million as being of Scottish heritage. (By comparison 49.2 million people were classified as "German" and 40 million as "Irish.")

On closer inspection, however, these classifications prove to be highly imprecise. Specifically, they lump together everyone who claims to be "solely or partly" of a particular ancestry and thereby convey an impression of uniform ethnicity among the self-styled members of each ethnic group. In reality, however, roughly one-third of all the people included in the 1980 census were either undecided or confused about their ethnic affiliation—so much so, in fact, that they chose to identify with a different ethnic group on this occasion than they had in the previous census. Even more to the point, nearly half of all Americans who reported a single ethnic identity in 1980 were actually the products of intermarriage between members of two, three, or even four different ethnic groups.*

In short, by the Census Bureau's own admission, the general census of 1980 is less reflective of the true state of ethnicity in the present-day United States than the so-called Current Population Survey (CPS) that the bureau conducted by means of personal interviews in 1979.

---

* One striking evidence of the frequency of multiple ethnic heritage among contemporary Americans is the fact that there are 17 different triple ancestry patterns so common that the Census Bureau has precoded them for survey purposes. The precoded groups range from Indian-German-Irish to Dutch-French-Irish—and partial English ancestry is a constituent element in fewer of them (9) than either Irish (12) or German (10).

And the picture that emerges from the latter study is a very different one from that suggested by the general census: in the CPS, only 11.5 million Americans professed to be purely English by ancestry and only 1.6 million Scottish. This was substantially smaller than the number (17 million) who claimed to be of exclusively German ancestry. It was also smaller than the 1980 census figure for Hispanics (14.6 million), roughly the same as that for Italian Americans (12 million)—and only a little more than twice the accepted estimate at that time for the nation's Jewish population (5.7 million).*

But statistically sound as they may be, the CPS figures are in their own way just as unsatisfactory as those in the general census. In fact, they fly in the face of common sense: everybody knows that there are more WASPs than Italian Americans in the United States—and certainly far more than twice as many WASPs as Jews. And that raises an interesting problem in logic: if the number of Americans of unalloyed "Anglo-Saxon" ancestry is so relatively small, where did all the WASPs come from?

ANY SERIOUS INQUIRY into the origins of WASPdom must begin, I believe, with a cold-eyed look at one of our great national myths, a myth neatly capsulized by Charlotte Curtis of the *New York Times* in a 1985 column noting the near disappearance of WASPs from seats of power in New York City. "White Anglo-Saxon Protestants," Ms. Curtis wrote, "invented America. They tamed the wilderness, built its steel mills, produced its assembly lines, governed its people, grew and harvested its wheat, baked its apple pie, waved its flag, praised the Lord and passed the ammunition."

Regardless of their own antecedents, a surprising number of today's Americans—probably the majority—would, I believe, accept Ms. Curtis's statement as a reasonably accurate characterization of our history over the first 250 years or so after the Pilgrims came ashore at Plymouth Rock. Yet, in fact, it seriously misrepresents the way in which the American nation developed—and has been developing ever since colonial times.

---

* There are no census statistics on the number of Jewish Americans because census takers are legally forbidden to require people to state their religious affiliation.

The reality is that America was invented and built not just by Anglo-Saxon Protestants but by people of diverse ethnic origins and religious beliefs. And in so saying I am not simply joining in the long-overdue acknowledgment of the role that blacks have played in American history, indefensible as the long night of national silence on that subject was. My point is a broader one: namely that the culture and institutions we generally think of as WASP creations were from the start very heavily influenced by people whose ancestors had never set foot in England, and that we owe many of the most cherished symbols of the American past to ethnic groups whose heritage was emphatically not Anglo-Saxon.

It was, after all, Dutchmen and not Englishmen who founded what was to become America's greatest city and whose descendants, as a consequence, played a role in the nation's economic and political development out of all proportion to their numbers. Though the fact is less often remembered, the so-called Kentucky rifle and the Conestoga wagon were not introduced by Anglo-Saxons either: they originated with the Pennsylvania Germans. And the legendary tamers of the wilderness—the first great wave of Indian fighters and Western pioneers—consisted in overwhelming measure of Scotch-Irishmen.

As for waving the flag and passing the ammunition, that, too, was far from being an Anglo-American monopoly even at the dawn of our independence. Irishmen, both Catholic and Protestant, comprised so large a part of General Washington's army—more than 40 percent by some estimates—that while his troops were encamped at Valley Forge the Father of His Country saw fit to issue a special ration of grog on St. Patrick's Day. The Irish, moreover, were not the only "minority group" heavily represented in the fight for independence: German-speaking volunteers from Pennsylvania and Maryland made up one entire regiment of the Continental Army, and the core of the American force that repelled the British invasion of New York's Mohawk Valley consisted of four battalions of German-American farmers.*

All this has long since faded from public memory in the United

---

* Ironically, the American Loyalist forces that fought with the British almost certainly contained a higher percentage of men of English and Scottish heritage than the Continental Army—and though the fact generally goes unmentioned in U.S. history textbooks, there were

---

States, however—and besides, any American whose ancestors fought in the Revolution is nowadays automatically regarded as being "of the old stock." But that was by no means how things appeared to eighteenth-century Americans themselves. The quarter-million Scotch-Irishmen who poured into this continent in the first seventy-five years of that century and who made up an estimated 15 percent of the total population of the American colonies at the start of the Revolution encountered precisely the same kind of hostility the Catholic Irish did when they began to arrive in large numbers a few generations later. Indeed, the brand of bigotry that would one day manifest itself in "no Irish need apply" ads was visible in Boston as early as 1729 when, according to a contemporary account, "a mob arose against ye landing of Irish." The fact that the Irish in question happened to be a shipload of indentured servants from Protestant Ulster made no real difference. Protestant or no, the Scotch-Irish were seen by eighteenth century Americans of English, Dutch, or German provenance as undesirables —ignorant, uncouth, quarrelsome, and unduly addicted to strong drink.*

The Scotch-Irish were not the only immigrant group to face prejudice in pre-Revolutionary America, and in one lamentable respect their experience foreshadowed a pattern in ethnic relationships that has repeatedly been duplicated ever since. As I have already noted, the large numbers of Germans who settled here in the eighteenth century fully shared in the general antipathy to Ulstermen. Yet they themselves were also frequently regarded with suspicion and dislike by Anglo-Americans. In this respect, in fact, even Benjamin Franklin failed to display the tolerance and common sense for which he is famed. "Why," Franklin angrily demanded in 1751, "should the Palatine boors be suffered to swarm into our settlements and by herding together establish their language and manners to the exclusion of ours? Why should Pennsylvania, founded by the English, become a colony of

times during the Revolution when British commanders had more American volunteer regiments at their disposal than Washington did.

* Since I am partially of Scotch-Irish ancestry myself, I feel free to note that the last of these charges was not totally without foundation. That ultimate expression of American defiance of authority—the illicit whiskey still—was introduced to this continent by the Scotch-Irish, and their descendants to this day predominate in the production of moonshine.

aliens who will shortly be so numerous as to Germanize us instead of our Anglifying them?"

In retrospect, to be sure, all this seems irrelevant and more than a little ridiculous. Today the descendants of savage Ulstermen and boorish refugees from the Palatinate alike are among the WASPiest of WASPs, and WASPdom has even retroactively been conferred upon great figures from our national past who in reality had scant claim to it. Who any longer knows that Paul Revere's father was christened Apollos de Revoire, that both Andrew Jackson and Henry Ford were the sons of Irish immigrants, or that the quintessential American *beau sabreur* George Armstrong Custer was the great-grandson of a Hessian officer named Kuester? And even those who are aware of it tend to attach scant importance to the fact that the first Astor and the first Rockefeller came from Germany, that the Drexels of Philadelphia were originally Austrian Catholics, and that the Mellons still know the precise location of their ancestral homestead in Northern Ireland. For all of these families are now indisputably WASP—as are many others with such patently non-Anglo-Saxon surnames as du Pont and Zabriskie.

Yet esoteric as it may seem to dwell on the national origins of their progenitors, the early history of these great WASP clans (and of thousands of lesser ones as well) actually has great bearing on the current American scene. Specifically, it helps to explain why there are so many more WASPs than there are Americans of exclusively or even predominantly British ancestry. It is, in short, a useful reminder that today's WASPs are the product of a great genetic blender, an amalgam of many diverse strains.

That fact, to be sure, is not necessarily fully apparent to the casual observer of contemporary WASPdom. One reason for this is that many "old stock" families that bear distinctively WASP names are in a sense flying under false colors. The Anglicization of one's surname in order to "Americanize" it is often thought of as a fairly recent practice and one largely confined to people whose forebears originated in Eastern or Southern Europe. But in reality it is a time-honored expedient tracing back at least to the eighteenth century and often one adopted so long ago that the change is now scarcely remembered even by the family directly involved, much less the general public. Not only did Kuester become Custer, but Pfoerchin turned into Pershing and Huever into Hoover. And on a less exalted level the nation is full of Prices whose ancestral name was Preus, Smiths who were once Schmidts, Millers who were Muellers, Blacks who were Schwarzes, etc.

As the foregoing list suggests, name-changing in eighteenth and early nineteenth century America was particularly notable among German Americans, presumably because they then constituted the largest segment of the population with conspicuously "foreign" names. But it also cropped up among every ethnic group that was not of Anglo-Saxon origin. Among my acquaintances, for example, have been Donalds who were originally O'Donnells, Bakers and Bellingers who started out as Boulangers, and Christophers whose forebears arrived in North America under the name Kristofferson, Kristof, Christophe, Cristoforo, or Cristofilos.

Whatever their original ethnic roots, however, families that Anglicized their names relatively early in American history have almost invariably tended over the succeeding generations to acquire WASP coloration and to intermarry with WASP families and/or other assimilated WASPs. In a sense, in fact, the primary importance of name-changing may have been that it helped to facilitate marriage between persons of diverse ethnic backgrounds. And it has been such intermarriage, perhaps more than anything else, that accounts for the otherwise improbably large percentage of the contemporary American population that is today regarded as WASP.

Perhaps the most striking recent manifestation of the role of intermarriage in swelling the ranks of WASPdom was supplied by a well-publicized dispute that arose in 1986 over control of the St. Louis *Post-Dispatch* and its affiliated publications. With the sole exception of New York corporate takeover specialist Alfred Taubman, all of the major participants in this contest were descendants of the first Joseph Pulitzer, a half-Jewish Hungarian who arrived in the United States during the Civil War period. Yet as a result of intermarriage most of them bore names such as Moore, Elmslie, Weir, and Quesada. And all of them, including those who still carried the Pulitzer surname, were perceived by the general public and by their social peers as members of the WASP plutocracy.

As a piece of social history, the WASPification of the Pulitzer clan is, to my mind, fascinating in itself. But the most important thing about it is that it is neither unique nor reflective of any new departure in American patterns of behavior. Just how long the process it represents has been going on and how totally absorptive it can be is clearly revealed by a look at the family trees of two eminent Americans who in their day enjoyed national prominence. One of them, the late Sen. Leverett Saltonstall of Massachusetts, was universally regarded as an archetypical Yankee patrician; the other, William C. Bullitt, whom Franklin Roosevelt appointed as the first U.S. ambassador to the Soviet Union, was inevitably described in the press as a "Philadelphia blueblood." Yet Saltonstall could—and did—claim membership in the Ancient Order of Hibernians on the strength of his descent from a colonial governor of Massachusetts named James Sullivan, while Bullitt counted among his ancestors Haym Solomon, the greath eighteenth century Jewish merchant who helped to finance Washington's army.

The family histories of Leverett Saltonstall and William Bullitt do more than simply illustrate the antiquity of the practice of ethnic intermarriage in America, however. No less than those of Generals Custer and Pershing, they are reminders of the degree to which the perceived ethnic identity of an American depends on the surname that he or she happens to bear. Consider, for example, the case of Nathan Hale Shapiro, a young man who in early 1986 was earning his living as a carpenter and painter in Jamaica Plains, Massachusetts. On his mother's side, Mr. Shapiro is a seventh-generation descendant of a sibling of the martyred Revolutionary War hero—which, genetically speaking, makes him every bit as WASPy as the children of the late congressman Jonathan Bingham (of the Connecticut Binghams) or the late governor John Davis Lodge (of the Boston Lodges), both of whom married women of Jewish ancestry. For that matter, in a purely ethnic sense, Nathan Shapiro is no less an Anglo-American than Manhattan lawyer Oren Root, Jr. (of the New York Roots), one of whose grandmothers was Italian and whose maternal grandfather was the Greek-American theater magnate Spyros Skouras. Yet, quite obviously, someone named Shapiro is less likely to be perceived as a WASP than someone named Bingham, Lodge, or Root regardless of the genetic facts of the matter.

In our rebellious age, to be sure, even when they bear WASP

surnames, the children of ethnic intermarriage sometimes choose to disavow WASP identity—or at least to make a point of proclaiming their mixed heritage. But historically, as I noted earlier, such people have mostly tended to be absorbed into the ranks of WASPdom, and partly for that reason no doubt, the diverse ancestry of today's WASPs is generally overlooked or discounted by Americans of more recent immigration origin. "Listen," a Polish-American friend told me a few years ago, "wherever they came from originally, the folks that got here early have been in bed with each other, figuratively as well as literally, for a long, long time, and as far as I'm concerned, they're all WASPs now." In short, in my friend's view—and, it is clear, in that of most contemporary Americans—WASPdom today, regardless of its diverse origins, is a closed shop.

HERE AGAIN, however, the conventional wisdom is demonstrably invalid. Not only is the number of Americans who are perceived as WASPs still expanding as a result of intermarriage, it is also expanding as a result of acculturation. On occasion, indeed, these two processes reinforce each other—as they notably have in the case of former secretary of the treasury C. Douglas Dillon. On his mother's side Dillon is of such old American stock that one of the many affiliations he lists in *Who's Who* is membership in the Society of Colonial Wars. His paternal grandfather, however, was a post–Civil War immigrant who was born Sam Lupowski, the son of a Polish Jew and a Frenchwoman named Dillon.

Because of his partly Jewish ancestry, Dillon in the 1950s reportedly had some difficulty in winning admission to Washington's Chevy Chase Club—a circumstance that today would be not merely offensive but inconceivable. For in the world of 1988, C. Douglas Dillon is unquestionably one of the leading lights of the WASP establishment.

It is, in fact, difficult to imagine anyone more quintessentially WASPy than Douglas Dillon. Born to wealth—his father once bought control of an automobile company with a personal check for $146 million—Dillon was educated at Groton and Harvard and thus acquired not only the caste marks but the cast of mind of the WASP plutocracy. This, in turn, has led him to adhere rigorously to classic, even somewhat outdated WASP patterns in both his personal and professional life: a Republican who has pursued mutually reinforcing careers in Wall Street and Washington, he belongs to a number of the nation's most prestigious men's clubs, has played a major role in the affairs of New York's Metropolitan Museum of Art, and, as was once far more characteristic of rich Americans than it is today, has developed family ties to European aristocracy through the marriage of his daughter, the current Duchesse de Mouchy.

Given all this, Douglas Dillon's emergence as one of the presiding chieftains of WASPdom may in retrospect seem to have been foreordained. But in reality achievement of that status is neither insured by nor dependent upon possession of inherited wealth, a St. Grottlesex diploma, and a couple of ancestors who served in the French and Indian wars. Shrewdly pursued ambition and outstanding accomplishment can by themselves turn the trick within the space of a single generation.

For evidence of that, it is only necessary to cite the example of John McCloy. Back in the 1970s when *Time* anointed him "the head of the WASP establishment," I recall hearing McCloy himself protest that he did not understand how "a poor Irish boy from Philadelphia" could qualify for that title.

In so saying, however, McCloy was being somewhat disingenuous; as he was certainly aware, the circumstances of his birth had long since become irrelevant. Rather, he was top WASP because he had transformed himself into that, step by well-calculated step. Starting off as a "scholarship boy" at Amherst College,* he successively established himself as a brilliant attorney, influential government official during World War II, postwar American proconsul in occupied Germany, senior partner in a premier Manhattan law firm, director of a clutch of the nation's most powerful corporations and foundations—and as the

---

* Incredible as it must seem to today's student generation, anyone who attended a "good" Eastern college on a scholarship prior to World War II tended to be regarded with a certain degree of social condescension. Over lunch a few years ago I mentioned to a wealthy WASP in his late fifties the latest accomplishment of one of our mutual friends—a man who was an outstanding athlete at an Ivy League university in the late 1920s and went on to achieve considerable eminence both professionally and socially. "He's a remarkable man all right," my luncheon companion agreed—and then, as conclusive evidence of that, pointedly added: "You know, of course, that he was a scholarship boy originally."

---

ultimate accolade, chairman of the Council on Foreign Relations. And whether as a cause or consequence of his eminence, he also became an embodiment of the crisp, authoritative personal style characteristic of America's traditional ruling elite.

It is, of course, true that John McCloy sprang from an ethnic group whose members when they so chose have always blended easily into the WASP scene. But to assume that his ancestral background was an indispensable condition of his acceptance as a superWASP would be wrong—a fact that is amply demonstrated by the experience of his most recent successor as chairman of the Council on Foreign Relations, New York financier Peter Peterson.

Not long ago I asked an eminent New York intellectual with notoriously keen ethnic sensibilities what ancestry he would ascribe to "Pete" Peterson. "Hmm," said this gentleman. "I've never really thought about it. Offhand, I'd be inclined to say WASP, but now that you raise the point, I suppose that, given his name, his family must have been Scandinavian originally."

My friend's presumption was on the face of things thoroughly justifiable: the name "Peterson" does have a Scandinavian ring, and like many Americans of Scandinavian heritage, Peter Peterson is a Midwesterner whose accent, appearance, and manner offer no clear clue as to his ethnicity. Moreover, his résumé is as unrevealing, ethnically speaking, as his persona: a protégé of former Sen. Charles Percy of Illinois, he succeeded Percy as chief executive of Bell and Howell, served for a time as Richard Nixon's secretary of commerce, and having been fired from that post for what Nixon apparently considered the disloyal practice of socializing with members of "the Georgetown crowd," moved into the top job at the prestigious New York investment banking house of Lehman Brothers.

External evidence notwithstanding, however, Peter Peterson is of neither British nor Scandinavian descent: both his mother and father, a small-restaurant owner, emigrated to the United States from Greece.

Despite his Americanized surname—which his parents adopted in place of Petropoulos—Peterson does not conceal his Greek background; when I interviewed him for an article some years ago, it was one of the first personal facts that I learned about him. Yet somewhat ironically, on a notable occasion when his minority origin might have stood him in good stead, he derived no benefit from it at all. In his book *Greed and Glory on Wall Street* journalist Ken Auletta speculates that in the corporate infighting that ultimately destroyed Lehman Brothers as an independent entity, one source of tension between Peterson and his chief opponent, Lewis Glucksman, was almost certainly Peterson's WASP style and the fact that he moved so extensively in WASP circles.

Because of his goals and lifestyle, in other words, Peter Peterson has become in the eyes of friend and foe alike if not a full-fledged WASP at least a WASP in the making. And in that he is by no means unique. On the contrary, as later chapters of this book will demonstrate, there are numerous budding WASPs in American business and public life today.

THERE IS, THEN, one fact that emerges inescapably from any realistic analysis of American society, past and present: it is not biological inheritance that exclusively or even primarily determines which of us are considered WASPs. To be sure, blacks, Asian Americans, and members of the diverse groups lumped together under the catchall term "Hispanics" continue to be excluded from WASPdom solely on the basis of ethnicity. But the opposite, so to speak, does not hold true. There is one body of Americans of almost undiluted British ancestry and long residence on this continent that today outstrips all other such groups both in present size and in rate of growth: it consists of the people commonly called "Appalachian whites." Yet for all their ethnic credentials, the poor whites of Appalachia cannot be described as WASPs unless the term is redefined to strip it of all connotation of favored economic or social status.*

The reverse side of this particular coin is that, while Anglo-American Protestants aren't necessarily WASPs, high economic and social status can confer WASPhood on people who either in ethnic origin or

---

* To a limited degree such redefinition has apparently occurred in the Midwest, whose industrial centers have attracted many migrants from Appalachia. According to the 1985–86 edition of the *Dictionary of Acronyms, Initialisms and Abbreviations*, some Chicagoans mockingly assert that what WASP really signifies is "White Appalachian Southern Protestant."

---

religion clearly fail to conform to the literal meaning of the acronymn. There are, in fact, members of such great Bostonian WASP clans as the Lodges and the Gardiners who are Roman Catholic, and some of the old-line Maryland Catholic families that still live the horsey life and move in Baltimore's most rarefied social circles can scarcely be considered anything but WASP. Even more revealing perhaps is the present state of affairs in Darien, Connecticut, a preppy New York exurb that a generation ago not only systematically excluded all Jews (it was, in fact, the model for the town in Laura Z. Hobson's *Gentleman's Agreement*) but was also distinctly inhospitable to Catholics. Today, a fair number of the blazer-loving, tennis-playing residents of Darien are parishioners of a church called St. Thomas More,* and as one of them remarked a year or so ago: "Catholics are WASPs in this town now."

That, of course, does not hold true for great numbers of Catholics in the United States, including many wealthy and well-placed ones. But what applies to Darien's Catholics is true of more and more American Catholics all the time, a notable case in point being conservative journalist and author William F. Buckley; despite Buckley's strong public identification with Catholicism and his Irish heritage, the combination of inherited money, elite education, and languid quasi-British manners surely make him seem the very model of WASPdom to most Middle Americans.

Indeed, the fact that Bill Buckley has stressed rather than downplayed his non-Protestant, non-Anglo-Saxon provenance yet bears the caste marks of the upper-class WASP serves to illustrate a central fact about WASPhood in the contemporary United States. This is that it is acquired in precisely the same ways Shakespeare asserted that greatness is: some people are born to it, some achieve it, and some have it thrust upon them.

There is, then, only one infallible standard by which to determine whether someone is or is not a WASP nowadays: if you behave like a WASP and are so regarded by others, you *are* a WASP. And even if you don't think of yourself as a WASP but are perceived as one by

---

* This particular saint, whose name was also given to the Catholic chapel at Yale, appears to have special appeal for preppy American Catholics—conceivably because his memory evokes Catholicism with an English flavor.

---

others, you can effectively be saddled with WASP status, willy-nilly. When it comes to WASPhood, all of us today, consciously or not, are driven back upon the position that the late justice Potter Stewart confessed to occupying with regard to pornography: "I can't define it, but I know it when I see it."

IN CERTAIN RESPECTS exploring the evolution and composite nature of present-day WASPdom is a highly useful exercise: it not only helps to dispel a good deal of misleading pop sociology but also, I believe, offers clues as to the probable future evolution of the American elite.

Yet in another sense the study of WASPdom is increasingly irrelevant to any attempt to determine the overall thrust of American society. It can, in fact, become an active impediment to understanding by exaggerating the role of the WASP in these waning years of the twentieth century.

Ever since 1924 when H. L. Mencken proclaimed that the day of the Anglo-Saxon was over in this country, observers of the American scene have periodically announced the end of the long era of WASP dominance. And even to some non-WASPs this has not seemed cause for unalloyed rejoicing. In a conversation we had in mid-1986, *Commentary* editor Norman Podhoretz told me: "The decline of the common culture, which in this country is inescapably associated with the WASPs—admittedly not a very good term but I can't think of one that better suits the case—carries great dangers . . . In terms of political stability I'd say that the loss of WASP self-confidence has been damaging . . . I'd also say, perhaps with a touch of nostalgia, that the WASP ruling class was a good ruling class not a bad one. But you can't put Humpty-Dumpty back together again."

In so saying, Podhoretz was offering a variation on a theme sounded fifteen years ago in *The Decline of the WASP* by journalist Peter Schrag, himself of German-Jewish birth. "The WASP ethic and culture," wrote Schrag, "were the essential elements of our Americanism. We are losing them and therefore losing ourselves."

Both Podhoretz and Schrag make their case with great effectiveness, yet their regrets nonetheless seem to me misplaced. To begin with, WASPdom is by no means a totally spent force. As the careers of people ranging from Cyrus Vance to T. Boone Pickens attest,

WASPs in great number are still solidly entrenched at high levels in all of the most prestigious and/or profitable fields of endeavor in America. And to be born and raised a WASP is still an undeniable asset in this country if only because WASP children typically start out with a certain degree of economic and social advantage.

What is of central significance, however, is that WASP identity is no longer as important or as reliable an asset as it was even a generation ago. Indeed, under certain circumstances it can become a positive handicap. It is, for example, debatable whether George Bush is intrinsically any more "preppy" or strongly establishmentarian in his values than John F. Kennedy was. Yet many people who were dazzled by Kennedy's aristocratic aura scorn Bush as a child of privilege—which suggests that Bush's offense in their eyes lies not just in his moneyed background and more overt political conservatism but in the fact that he is a WASP aristocrat rather than an Irish-American one.

Prejudice against WASPs is, of course, nothing new in American politics; in parts of my native New England it has been a distinct political liability to be a WASP for half a century and more. What *is* new, though—and infinitely more significant—is that in areas of American life that remained almost entirely WASP preserves fifteen or twenty years ago, ethnicity no longer cuts much ice one way or the other. As one of my colleagues at Columbia University observed recently: "For sociologists, it's interesting to consider whether most people perceive [former secretary of defense] Frank Carlucci as an assimilated WASP or as an Italian-American. But the important point to remember is that today that has become a question of academic rather than practical significance. In the Foreign Service, CIA headquarters, the boardroom at Sears, the White House, and all the other places where Carlucci has spent his career, it hasn't mattered which he was."

3

IN THE HALFWAY HOUSE

Uuniversity of Pennsylvania professor E. Digby Baltzell, a man considered by many to be the preeminent student of WASPdom, has long stressed the point that an upper class is not necessarily also a ruling class. But such a state of affairs, he warns, can only be a transient phenomenon. "If [an upper class] is not a ruling class," he insists, "it will soon be replaced by a new upper class."

Assuming that thesis to be valid, the WASP in America is now a threatened species—at least in so far as upper class status is concerned. For within the last twenty years the de-WASPing of the ruling elite in America has proceeded at a breathtaking pace.

The most obvious manifestation of this process is that with each passing year more and more of the movers and shakers in American society are neither WASPs nor even facsimile WASPs by anybody's reckoning. As I shall show in later chapters, this particular sea change has now occurred in virtually every major professional and occupational elite in the United States. But there is no single symptom of it more dramatic than one cited by Charles Silberman in his book *A Certain People*.

In the 1924–25 edition of *Who's Who in America*, Silberman reports, people of English descent were more than twice as likely to be listed as those of Jewish ancestry. By the time the 1974–75 edition of *Who's Who* appeared, however, that ratio had been almost exactly reversed: relative to their overall numbers, Jewish Americans had now become more than twice as likely to be listed as those of English heritage. And since the access that Jews enjoy to top positions in certain important professions has notably increased since 1975, their relative representation in the current edition of *Who's Who* is presumably even greater.

As Digby Baltzell sees it, the decline of WASPdom is essentially a self-inflicted wound: WASPs have been losing power, he asserts, because they have been unwilling to absorb into their ranks the most talented and successful products of other elements of the American population. But although this view has predictably found favor with many non-WASPs, it has one great flaw: it does not adequately take into account the fact that, exclusionary as the WASP community has invariably seemed at any given moment, its actual history is one of continual absorption and assimilation of successful "outsiders."

This is not to say that Baltzell is totally wrong; it is quite true that the initial WASP reaction to the arrival upon the American scene of people of different heritage has characteristically been reluctance to share power with the newcomers. In justifiable resentment, the children or grandchildren of those newcomers have not infrequently retaliated by banishing WASPs from positions of authority once they were strong enough to do so. But very often it was through the use of institutions and practices established by WASPs that the descendants of the newcomers acquired the power to do that.

In the broad sweep of our history, in short, the role WASPs have played in the emergence of a new American elite has been positive rather than negative, inclusionary rather than exclusionary. To great extent, in fact, the WASP establishment has conspired in its own undoing because historically it has been dominated by an ethic that did not permit the indefinite and absolutely consistent practice of discrimination against outsiders.

This ethic, to echo an observation of Nathan Glazer's, was embodied in nascent form in the beliefs professed by the Founding Fathers and in the political institutions that their beliefs prompted them to create. For those institutions and the psychological climate that they established paved the way for something akin to institutionalized social revolution in America—a process that began to become visible early in the history of the Republic. It can, in fact, be argued that in a sense the ultimate collapse of Anglo-American hegemony in this country was clearly foreshadowed on the day in 1832 when Scotch-Irish frontiersman Andrew Jackson got himself reelected president by running, in effect, against proper Philadelphian Nicholas Biddle, then the nation's top banker.

The social mobility fostered by America's political institutions was, moreover, mightily reinforced by the opportunities created by the nation's explosive economic growth following the end of the Civil War. The latter part of the nineteenth century and the early years of the twentieth saw the rise to tycoon status of all sorts of outsiders: men born to social obscurity on the Eastern seaboard (Commodore Vanderbilt, Thomas Fortune Ryan, Henry J. Heinz), immigrants from Europe (Joseph Pulitzer, Andrew Carnegie), and nonestablishment types from the Midwest, West, and South (John D. Rockefeller, Henry Clay Frick, James B. Duke). Notable, too, among the new rich were a number of Jewish families, among them the Schiffs, the Rosenwalds, the Lehmans, the Morgenthaus, the Guggenheims, and the Warburgs.

Within a generation or two, of course, the new rich became old rich, and in most cases their descendants were absorbed into WASP-dom socially and through intermarriage. (Though he got his fortune from old John D., the late governor Nelson Rockefeller got his given name from the socially pretentious Yankee who was his maternal grandfather, Sen. Nelson Aldrich of Rhode Island.) And even some of the great Jewish families, so Richard Zweigenhaft and G. William Domhoff argue in their book *Jews in the Protestant Establishment*, came to feel "primary identification . . . with the corporate and social elites, not with their Jewishness." Crediting the phrase to a student of ethnicity named Peter Rose, Zweigenhaft and Domhoff term such people JASPs (for Jewish Anglo-Saxon Protestants) and assert that "they are Jewish in the same way that multimillionaire scion John F. Kennedy was Irish."

THAT STATEMENT, however, overlooks one highly significant point: unlike a great many Jewish and Irish Americans in times past, the Morgenthaus, Lehmans, and Kennedys of today have remained avowedly Jewish or Irish and have not let themselves be absorbed into WASPdom. Yet they have enjoyed access to power and to some of WASPdom's most cherished institutions—as for a very long time now have great numbers of talented non-WASPs from less privileged backgrounds. (The first member of the Kennedy family to attend Harvard, it is worth recalling, was John F. Kennedy's father—who was the son of a Boston saloon keeper.) And that access was conceded, however grudgingly at times, by the WASP establishment itself.

This last fact is one that is widely disregarded because the opportunities extended to non-WASPs have so often been flawed by social exclusiveness—and even more often by the evident assumption of social superiority—on the part of the classic WASP aristocrat. Though the late Jim Farley was probably wrong in thinking that the nation was ready to elect an Irish Catholic president in the 1940s, he was certainly right in believing that Franklin and Eleanor Roosevelt regarded him as a social inferior. In a similar vein, Henry Kissinger, who taught at Harvard while McGeorge Bundy was dean there, subsequently recalled that Bundy "tended to treat me with the combination of politeness and self-conscious condescension that upper-class Bostonians reserve for people of, by New England standards, exotic background and excessively intense personal style." And as a scholarship student at Yale at the beginning of the 1940s, I myself resented what I perceived as the disdain of "white-shoe boys" such as John V. Lindsay (who, in fairness, was probably utterly unaware of my existence).

Yet whatever their unspoken attachment to the social standards of their class, Roosevelt, Bundy, and Lindsay all in one way or another contributed to the opening up of American society. It was, after all, FDR who forged the first national political alliance critically dependent upon religious and ethnic minorities; it was Mac Bundy who as head of the Ford Foundation fostered public policies so subversive of WASP power that Henry Ford II publicly disassociated himself from them;

and it was John Lindsay who defused New York's racial tensions with a sensitivity and skill conspicuously unmatched by his successors, Abraham Beame and Edward Koch.

Embodied in the careers of all three of these men was, I believe, the saving grace of the WASP ethic—a set of priorities described to Charles Silberman in another context by one of Bundy's successors at Harvard, Dean Henry Rosovsky. Said Rosovsky: "When you look at Harvard and Yale and see how the established aristocracies have changed those institutions, you *have* to believe America is different. Some of them surely preferred things the old way; a few may still feel that Jews lack manners or are too careerist, but they believed their responsibilities went beyond being comfortable. They recognized that the university would become a dinosaur if it stayed closed, and so they opened it up. Their values transcended their solidarity with class."

EVEN GIVING WASPS THEIR DUE, it would surely be naïve to portray the long process that has culminated in the ethnic diversification of the American establishment purely as a consequence of the more admirable aspects of the WASP value system. In even greater degree, that process has clearly reflected a necessary accommodation by the nation's ruling class to the realities of economics, politics, and population mix. And whatever the proportions of altruism and cold pragmatism involved, it was not until World War II that the most notable and far-reaching changes in the role of ethnicity in the United States began to become apparent.

The first manifestation of these changes was a kind of patriotic circling of the wagons in support of the long-standing public mythology that portrayed the United States as a uniformly successful exercise in cultural integration—a place where, as in a *tableau vivant* featured at an English language school established by the first Henry Ford, arriving immigrants marched off the boat wearing their national dress, entered an enormous pot stirred with long ladles by WASP instructors, and emerged wearing American clothes and waving Old Glory. The most pervasive World War II version of Ford's tableau, however, was somewhat more tolerant of a modest degree of diversity: it took the form of the idealized Hollywood infantry platoon in which soldiers of a variety of clearly identifiable ethnic backgrounds—Irish, Italian, Jewish, WASP, Polish, and what-have-you—all fought and wisecracked together in defense of such sacred American institutions as democracy, baseball, hot dogs, and the girl next door.

Even this more sophisticated version of *e pluribus unum*, to be sure, involved a certain amount of poetic license. The World War II American Army still contained many units that were intentionally or unintentionally ethnically segregated—not only the traditional all-black ones but also National Guard and other geographically based units that were wholly or predominantly composed of Japanese Americans, Puerto Ricans, white Texans, etc. Yet if it did not reflect the reality of the time with complete accuracy, the Hollywood platoon did foreshadow the reality of the future* and had validity in the sense that World War II did throw millions of Americans of different social and ethnic backgrounds into enforced intimacy.

Still another unifying by-product of World War II was the discovery by many American servicemen overseas that they had far more in common with other Americans, even those of notably different ethnicity than their own, than they did with the current inhabitants of their ancestral homelands. In my own case, I had grown up with the assumption, largely inspired by my father's Canadian birth, that I had some special if imprecise tie to the people of Great Britain. Yet when I was assigned to a unit that included a considerable number of British Army personnel, I quickly found that they were foreigners to me and much less congenial on the whole than fellow Americans with whom I had previously thought I had little in common. And years later when I mentioned that fact to an Italian-American veteran of World War II, he replied: "You know, it's funny, but I had the same feeling when my outfit got shipped to Italy. It was the most screwed-up place I ever saw, and for my money the people were just a bunch of losers."

---

* As a matter of policy, of course, ethnic segregation is today religiously avoided in U.S. military and quasi-military organizations, and where diversity does not occur naturally, it is sometimes deliberately imposed. Only a bit over fifteen years ago author Peter Schrag could ask with seemingly justified skepticism whether it was possible to imagine the United States "sending a Negro, a Jew, or a woman" into space. Yet by 1986 the selection of personnel for the ill-fated final launch of the space shuttle *Challenger* was transparently rigged to ensure that the crew included a black, a Japanese American, and two women, one of them Jewish and the other of Irish descent.

Important though they surely were, it is admittedly impossible to quantify the impact of the phenomena I have just been discussing. But it is quite possible to do so in the case of what was, in terms of ethnic relationships, probably the most seminal single development of the World War II period: the passage of the G.I. Bill of Rights.

Quite properly the G.I. Bill is universally credited with having made it possible for large numbers of veterans to attend college who could never have afforded to do so otherwise—and it is self-evident that, given the generally lower economic status of non-WASPs at the time, this inevitably had a certain leveling effect in terms of opportunity. What is less often recognized is that the G.I. Bill also helped to break down among certain ethnic groups such as Polish Americans and Americans of southern Italian background a traditional tendency to regard education as an impractical frippery. For along with rendering college attendance a viable financial alternative to acceptance of a low-level job, the G.I. Bill also served to give veterans drawn from such groups greater freedom to disregard the wishes or attempted dictates of their immigrant parents.

This was notably true in my hometown in Connecticut where I know of at least half a dozen Italian Americans of my age who took advantage of the G.I. Bill in defiance of parental advice—and thereby totally altered not only their own outlook on education but that of their children. And this impressionistic evidence drawn from a single community is solidly supported by the national statistics. In his invaluable book *Italian Americans: Into the Twilight of Ethnicity*, sociologist Richard D. Alba notes that among people born in the United States between 1914 and 1929, WASPs were four times as likely to graduate from college as Italian Americans; among those born since World War II, however, the college attendance rate of WASPs and Italian Americans is virtually identical.

The net result of the G.I. Bill then was that in the two decades following World War II the pool of Americans with the educational qualifications for managerial and professional careers steadily became a more accurate reflection of the overall ethnic composition of the population. And where—as was still frequently the case—people of non-WASP background did not progress as fast or as far as they felt their talent and educational attainments warranted, resentment was inevitable. Inevitably, too, people of demonstrable ability and professional qualifications became less ready than their proletarian parents had been to accept exclusion from positions of status purely because of their ethnicity or lack of WASP veneer. An ethnic assertiveness based less on the consciousness of vulnerability and more on self-assurance began to raise its head.

With the arrival of the 1960s, moreover, two new climacterics in the American saga conspired to erode still further public acceptance of WASP hegemony. The first of these was the black civil rights movement, which, though far too late and to far too limited a degree, nonetheless won a greater measure of participation in our national life for that group of Americans who had suffered exclusion from it most completely and for the longest time.

Sadly, the fact that it failed to remedy fully the historical injustices done American blacks was not the only negative aspect of the civil rights movement. When those at the bottom of the ethnic heap asserted the right to acceptance into the mainstream of society on their own terms, it should have served as an inspiration to other groups that had suffered discrimination to go and do likewise—and to some extent it doubtless did so; it seems probable, for example, that it helped to quicken the pace of Hispanic claims on a more influential role in American society.

But in the eyes of observers as ideologically incompatible as avowed progressive Herbert Gans and neoconservative Norman Podhoretz, the predominant reaction to the civil rights movement among many ethnics was essentially a negative one. Just as whites in the South had historically felt threatened by blacks, so blue collar ethnics elsewhere in the country now came to see the new assertiveness of blacks and the affirmative action policies that it inspired as a peril to their own economic and social interests. And though it essentially reflected a defensiveness based on class considerations, this fear expressed itself overtly in an unprecedented surge of aggressive ethnicity among non-WASPs of nearly every description.

THE SECOND GREAT BLOW WASPdom suffered in the 1960s was dealt it by the Vietnam conflict. The political elite that presided over the conduct of the first war in which the United States was incontestably defeated included some eminent non-WASPs such as presidential adviser Walt Rostow and his brother, onetime under secretary of state Eugene Rostow. But the great majority of the officials whom David Halberstam bitterly immortalized as "the best and the brightest" were products of the WASP Establishment, and it was that establishment that became inextricably identified with the whole Vietnam fiasco in the public mind.

More subtle in its effects but nonetheless, I believe, at least subliminally corrosive was the fact that it was essentially the children of the disproportionately WASP middle class who ultimately destroyed public support for the Vietnam War by refusing to fight in it. It is a cliché that the burden of service in Vietnam fell in undue measure upon working class Americans, but it is a cliché that is given new life in the pages of *Crisis in Command*, a look at the latter-day U.S. Army published in 1978 by Richard A. Gabriel and Paul L. Savage. "The Harvard class of 1968," these authors report, "had 1,203 members . . . Of these, available statistics indicate that 36 served in the armed forces, only 26 in Vietnam, and not one died in action [there] . . . Indeed, of the 33,468 members of Harvard classes between 1941 and 1971, just 30 (including dropouts) died in Korea and Vietnam."

In the ultimate sense, how one judges such behavior on the part not only of Harvard men but of the majority of the nation's college population depends upon whether it is seen primarily as a manifestation of high principle or rather of narrow self-interest and civic irresponsibility. But in the context I am concerned with here the question of whether the Vietnam War was a just or unjust one is not paramount. To argue that the almost universal refusal of America's most privileged young people to serve in Vietnam was morally justified cannot alter the fact that it aroused bitterness and cynicism among many of the less privileged. By the same token, to argue that Lyndon Johnson, the Bundy brothers, Robert McNamara, Dean Rusk, and their colleagues mired the United States ever deeper in the Vietnam morass out of thoroughly patriotic motives cannot alter the fact that they grievously mismanaged the enterprise.

Justifiably or not, moreover, these two phenomena combined to induce not only a marked decline in the public prestige of the WASP elite but a perceptible erosion of its traditional self-assurance. When I first became a member of the Council on Foreign Relations at the beginning of the 1960s, the unspoken assumption in its commodious headquarters on Manhattan's East 68th Street was that it was the function of the foreign policy establishment to instruct the mass of Americans as to how the nation's interests could best be advanced in its international dealings. But in the wake of Vietnam a new theme began to be heard in the CFR's high-ceilinged halls: no foreign policy, however desirable in theory, could any longer be considered workable unless it rested on a solid public consensus.

I do not want to exaggerate the importance of the Vietnam War in the diminishing acceptance of the WASP as the role model for all Americans: the relative degree to which Vietnam, the civil rights movement, and the democratization of higher education each contributed to that process is, I believe, impossible to assess with precision. But there can be no doubt that by the end of the 1960s these three factors between them had radically changed the way Americans looked at themselves. To quote Richard Alba: "In the twinkling of a historian's eye, the 'ethnic mosaic' replaced the 'melting pot' in the prevailing image of American society, and the very concept of assimilation fell into disrepute."

As is commonly the case with even the least defensible political and social theories, it was intellectuals who initially promoted the notion that the melting pot had always been essentially a fiction or, alternatively, had ceased to be an apt metaphor for social and political realities in present-day America. And as is also usual, this intellectual current, which reached flood tide in the 1960s, was by no means monolithic in character: there were major variations in the degree of revisionism espoused by the new theorists on ethnicity and in the substantiality of their work as well. Some, such as Nathan Glazer and Daniel Patrick Moynihan in their immensely influential *Beyond the Melting Pot*, presented carefully qualified and reasoned arguments in objective fashion. Others, such as Michael Novak and Father Andrew Greeley, seemed as much influenced by what they wished reality to be as by any concrete evidence as to what it actually was.

Balanced or not, however, the intellectuals' new emphasis on the persistence and importance of ethnic diversity was clearly in tune with a growing popular mood and rapidly won widespread acceptance. Just how widespread that acceptance had become was dramatically illustrated on the day in the late 1970s when, in a speech to a predominantly Italian-American audience in Baltimore, Jimmy Carter ringingly declared that the United States was not a melting pot but a minestrone— by which he apparently meant a mixture of ingredients each of which clearly manifests its original identity and contributes distinctively to the overall flavor of the whole.

Whether this was a particularly felicitous image or even entirely valid in culinary terms may be questioned. But it is not at all farfetched to suggest that public use of it by the president of the United States in a sense marked the moment that cultural pluralism finally supplanted cultural assimilation in American mythology as the avowed national objective.

WARMLY AS many Americans embraced it, though, the analysis of the role of ethnicity and cultural pluralism that came to prevail in the 1960s was flawed in one critical respect: it failed to allow for the fact that in one of the most basic aspects of life the melting pot, far from being inoperative, was bubbling away more strongly than ever before. With each passing decade Americans were marrying across ethnic and religious lines in ever increasing numbers.

To be sure, as we have already seen, marriage between people of different ethnic and religious backgrounds has been going on since the beginning of American history and had long since become commonplace among the descendants of the various immigrant groups that arrived in this country before the mid-nineteenth century; by the 1950s, in fact, more than half the marriages being made by Americans of British, German, and Irish ancestry were to people of different ethnicity from their own. But nothing in previous American experience totally foreshadowed a phenomenon that began to become apparent in the 1960s and reached extraordinary proportions in the seventies and eighties—a massive increase not only in the frequency of intermarriage but in the range of ethnic groups among which it is widely practiced.

It is still a common assumption that those Americans whose forebears came to this country from Southern and Eastern Europe after the middle of the nineteenth century are characterized by great ethnic cohesion and reluctance to marry outside their own groups. But while that was once the case, it has emphatically ceased to be so in this generation. By the mid-1960s, according to Richard Alba, the overall rate of ethnic intermarriage among Polish Americans, for example, had reached 60 percent and no fewer than two-thirds of all third-generation Polish Americans were married to people of non-Polish origin. By that same period, Greek-American sociologist Charles Moskos has noted, nearly one-third of all marriages performed in Greek Orthodox churches in the United States involved one partner not of Greek ancestry—and by the 1970s this figure had risen to nearly 70 percent in the Greek Orthodox archdiocese of New York, the largest in the nation.

Even more revealing, perhaps, are statistics presented by Richard Alba in his 1985 study of the Italian-American population. As of 1979, Alba reports, the intermarriage rate among Americans of exclusively Italian ancestry was running more than 50 percent. And Americans of only partial Italian ancestry were "marrying out" in even greater numbers: 75 percent of them, in fact, were choosing husbands or wives with no Italian blood at all.

The inevitable result of all this is that the number of Americans of purely Italian heritage is diminishing at a startling rate. The Current Population Survey published in 1979 shows that nearly 90 percent of Americans between the ages of 55 and 64 who reported having any Italian ancestry at all were of exclusively Italian descent. But among "Italian Americans" between the ages of 18 and 24 in 1979, only 40 percent were of unmixed ancestry—and among those under 14 a mere 20 percent were of wholly Italian ethnic background.

The potential implications of this last statistic are, of course, enormous. What it clearly suggests is that in the absence of any new mass migration from their ancestral homelands, it is entirely possible that such conspicuous elements of the American ethnic mosaic as Italian Americans, Polish Americans, and Greek Americans will sooner or later cease to exist as true ethnic groups in the biological sense.

That is far from saying that these "ethnic groups" will totally disappear or that people with Italian, Irish, Polish, or Greek roots will no longer feel any sense of ethnic identity at all. In a conversation we had at Columbia University in the summer of 1986, historian James Shenton, half-English and half-Slovak by ancestry, noted that there are a great many variables that affect the way in which Americans of mixed heritage resolve the question of their ethnicity. "The perception of ethnic identity," Shenton pointed out, "may be in some degree determined by the surviving surname . . . And it is often determined by which side of the family is most concerned with its ethnicity."

But whatever ancestral strain they may identify with most strongly, people of mixed ancestry inevitably tend to reflect their multiple heritage in their behavior patterns. "To emphasize one ethnicity at the expense of another," Shenton remarked, "can cause problems —so children of intermarriage tend to cling to those aspects of ethnicity which cause the least disruption among the various elements of the family." And in considering the social behavior of people of mixed Italian and non-Italian ancestry, Richard Alba reached essentially the same conclusion. Such people, he wrote, "have been raised by and large outside the bosom of the ethnic community" and as a result "can be expected to show only tinges of ethnic identity."

If Shenton and Alba are right in their generalizations—and my own observation convinces me that they are—the overall effect of the rapid increase in interethnic marriage can only be to reduce cultural differences between white Americans regardless of ancestry. But ethnicity in the strict sense is not the only source of cultural diversity in this country: religion, too, has historically been an important divisive factor. In fact, to a number of sociologists, religious differences once appeared an even more intractable barrier to cultural integration than ethnic differences. Their conclusion—which seemed to be strongly supported by a study carried out in New Haven in the early 1940s by Ruby Jo Reeves Kennedy—was that while ethnic intermarriage might be on the rise, Americans would largely continue to marry within their own religious groups, and that what would ultimately emerge would be three primary marriage groups: Protestant, Catholic, and Jewish.

But in this respect, too, the last generation has seen a dramatic change in American behavior patterns. When I was growing up in New Haven in the 1930s, marriages between Protestants and members of the city's large Italian-Catholic population were rare, and when they did occur, they caused raised eyebrows in both communities. Yet today such marriages are commonplace not only in New Haven but throughout the country. Indeed, according to Richard Alba, roughly half of all American Catholics of Italian or partly Italian ancestry born since

World War II have married non-Catholics, and in the great majority of such marriages the other partner has been Protestant.

A similar change—if somewhat slower in pace—has also been occurring in the behavior of another group long notable for resistance to marriages outside the faith. When *Beyond the Melting Pot* was published in 1963, its authors accurately reported that "intermarriage . . . remains low among Jews." Exactly twenty-five years later, however, the *New York Times* reported that the number of Jewish-Christian couples in the United States already stood at 375,000 and that the percentage of Jewish Americans who chose to marry gentiles had soared from only 6 percent in 1950 to 40 percent in the 1980s.

The chances seem strong, moreover, that this figure will continue to increase in the years ahead as a result of a substantial shift in attitudes toward religious intermarriage on the part of both Jewish and non-Jewish Americans. In 1965, Charles Silberman reports, 70 percent of all Boston Jews declared that they would oppose a marriage between one of their children and a non-Jew, but by 1975 only 34 percent still held to that position. Similarly, polls taken in 1940 showed that a majority of non-Jewish Americans disapproved of marriage between Jews and Christians, but by 1983 only 10 percent still did. And significantly, these changes in attitude were most marked among those whose age made them the most likely candidates for marriage; in the 1975 Boston survey 84 percent of Jews between 18 and 25 said they were prepared to accept or at worst take a neutral stance toward intermarriage, and on a national basis the number of non-Jews under the age of 30 who openly professed disapproval of intermarriage between Jews and gentiles had dwindled to a mere 4 percent.

At bottom, what all this obviously implies is the increasingly rapid development of cultural patterns that are common to all Americans regardless of religion. Yet as with ethnic intermarriage, the impact of religious intermarriage is neither uniform nor easily predicable in any particular instance. There are, for example, some indications that the number of gentiles who convert to Judaism because they have married Jews has grown in recent years, but I find no evidence that there has been a parallel increase in the conversion of Protestants who marry Catholics. And I am aware from my own acquaintanceship of a number of mixed marriages in which neither partner has converted, and the children have wound up adhering to no organized religious body at all.

That, of course, is not to say that the maintenance of different faiths by the partners in a marriage precludes a traditional religious upbringing for their children: in one case with which I am familiar, a woman who was raised as a Catholic and is now married to a Protestant faithfully sees to it that her children by her Jewish first husband attend synagogue and Hebrew school. And while such training may not always "take" completely, it almost always has some lasting effect: James Shenton, who although raised as a Catholic now considers himself "not devout," nonetheless says that he can generally divine without being told if someone he is dealing with was also brought up as a Catholic. What's more, Shenton adds, because of his Catholic upbringing the notion that an evangelical Protestant preacher such as the Reverend Pat Robertson might conceivably emerge as a presidential candidate renders him "incredibly uncomfortable."

Professor Shenton's unease at the new assertiveness of evangelical Protestantism is clearly shared by most Jewish Americans and many mainstream Protestants as well—a fact that might seem to suggest that, intermarriage or no, religion has actually become a more divisive factor in American life in recent years. Yet offsetting the greater activism of evangelical Protestants, in my view, is the fact that there has been a marked decline in traditional religious practice among some other elements of the population. In 1940, for example, some three-quarters of all nominal Catholics in the United States regularly attended Mass on Sunday; today, only about one-third do so. And while a number of factors have conspired to produce that outcome, it is hard to escape the conclusion that at least one of them is less intensity of faith on the part of children of religious intermarriage.

Even the most optimistic interpretation of the integrative effects of ethnic and religious intermarriage, of course, cannot disguise one unpleasant fact: the process does not yet significantly extend to Hispanic Americans and has done even less to bring black Americans into the mainstream of our society. This is a reality almost universally ascribed to racism, and that charge can scarcely be refuted: in January 1987, to choose an ugly example at random, the *Wall Street Journal* published an article reporting that in the relatively sophisticated city of Nashville, Tennessee, 24 percent of the male population and 28 percent of females still believed that "interracial marriage" should be outlawed.

Yet deeply ingrained as prejudice against blacks is in the psyche of white America, I believe it would be excessively pessimistic to regard it as ineradicable. As the Japanese relocation camps that were established in the wake of Pearl Harbor demonstrated, the prejudice against Japanese Americans in the pre–World War II United States was deep, especially on the West Coast. And Chinese Americans, while less unpopular, were certainly not accepted as being on a social or political par with Caucasians at that time. Yet as of 1981 more than a third of the marriages made by third-generation Japanese Americans were with Caucasians. And according to political scientist Andrew Hacker, the number of marriages between whites and Asian Americans generally increased by more than 70 percent in the ten years ending in 1986.

All this leads Hacker to suggest that it will not take more than two generations before there will be a Eurasian segment of the middle class that Americans will take wholly for granted. Some other social scientists including Nathan Glazer think Hacker is too sanguine about this, but their quarrel is more with the time frame that he sets than with his basic proposition. In short, even if the process takes longer than Hacker anticipates, it seems clear that in due course the experience of Asian Americans will reproduce that of Americans of Southern and Eastern European origin. And that, in turn, seems to support the notion that where economic and cultural differences cease to be acute, racial differences too diminish in importance.

THE MARXIST ECONOMIST Paul Sweezy once asserted that "a social class . . . is made up of freely intermarrying families." Even by that standard, which strikes me as somewhat simplistic, the composition of America's ruling class has also undergone notable change in the space of the last two decades.

I do not know of any way to document this point statistically since class status is not officially recognized nor a matter of public record in modern America, and even on a personal basis it is generally much less freely discussed than ethnicity. But in the absence of more scientific data, it is, I think, instructive to study the society pages of the *New York Times* on the assumption that anyone whose wedding or engagement is announced there is likely to be relatively "upscale" in economic and social terms.

What emerges from such a survey, I have discovered, is a fascinating microcosm of what might be called the new American gentry. Out of 94 weddings and engagements reported in the *Times* in one two-week period in June 1986, roughly 40 percent involved couples obviously of different ethnic backgrounds. There were, to be more specific, 25 weddings or engagements clearly involving white Christians of different ethnicity, eight Jewish-gentile unions, and five Asian-Caucasian ones. Yet despite the diversity of ethnic and religious backgrounds, most of these marriages, judging from the educational and professional histories supplied, were between people of similar socioeconomic status: in one of the Asian-white marriages, for example, both partners were recent Harvard graduates, and in another, both were on the staff of Yale University.

The particular two-week period just mentioned, moreover, did not appear in any way unusual except for the obvious fact that more people tend to get married in June than at other times. Over a six-month stretch of 1986 during which I forced myself to read the *Times* society pages faithfully, the ratio between all marriages reported and ethnic or religious intermarriages did not vary notably from week to week. And in many cases the individuals involved came from very privileged backgrounds indeed. The Jewish-gentile marriages reported, for example, included those of Caroline Kennedy, the son of one of the nation's leading authorities on child psychology, an heiress to a major mining fortune, and the great-grandchildren of two of the most famous figures in American financial history, one of them Jewish and the other not. Similarly, the participants in the Asian-white marriages included the son of a onetime chairman of one of the nation's biggest banks, the son of a retired army general, the scion of a distinguished publishing family, and the granddaughter of a wealthy Asian diplomat.

Perhaps because people who take the trouble to have their marriages announced in the *Times* are almost by definition conventionally inclined, most of the weddings I have referred to were religious ones.

Inevitably, the nature of the ceremonies employed often reflected religious concessions by one partner or the other: there were Asians married in Catholic and Episcopal churches, Jews in Catholic and Congregational services, and Protestants in Jewish or nondenominational ones. But in a significant minority of cases neither partner made such a concession and the wedding service was jointly conducted by a two-man team consisting of a Protestant minister and a Catholic priest, a rabbi and a Protestant minister, or a rabbi and a Catholic clergyman.

In such cases, of course, the evidence of intermarriage is indisputable. But the full extent of ethnic and religious integration reflected in the *Times* society pages is certainly even greater than can be determined by reliance on such externals as interfaith ceremonies, genealogical claims, or the evident ethnicity of some surnames. This was sharply driven home to me when in the space of a single month recently I noted the announcements of three Protestant weddings involving young people with English or Scotch-Irish surnames who had attended fashionable prep schools and universities. Had I not been acquainted with the families involved, nothing in the *Times* announcements would have alerted me to the fact that one of the young people involved was half-Jewish, another was half-Italian, and the third had one Jewish and one Irish grandfather. (Let me emphasize that I do not mean to suggest any deliberate concealment here; in all three cases the families involved have become so *déraciné*, so to speak, that WASPhood is the only identity really open to them.)

There is also another—and quite different—criticism that could be made of my unscientific survey of the *Times*: New York, as non–New Yorkers never tire of pointing out, is not all of America, and ethnic and religious integration may well be rather more prevalent among prosperous and privileged New Yorkers than among people of similar status in most other American urban centers. Still, a Harvard professor of my acquaintance has assured me that his longtime surveillance of wedding announcements in the *Boston Globe* indicates that in this respect things are following much the same course in the Athens of America as in New York. Perhaps even more relevant is the fact that similar patterns are visible in the Los Angeles area. And much as it may gall the rest of us to admit it, it is New York and southern

California that ultimately set the cultural tone in this country nowadays.

FROM THE TIME it first began to become evident that the composition and mores of the American elite were changing with unprecedented speed, that fact aroused apprehension in many observers—and such apprehension was not exclusively confined to those with a strong vested interest in the old social order. "America," Peter Schrag lamented in *The Decline of the WASP*, " . . . is becoming a nation of outsiders for whom no single style or ethic remains possible."

But the fear of a kind of cultural disintegration, however justifiable it may have seemed in the late 1960s, has not been borne out by what has happened since. On the contrary, in what might be called the boot camps of the Establishment—the colleges and universities where the nation's future leaders receive the civilian equivalent of basic training —a trend almost diametrically opposed to the one feared by Schrag is increasingly visible. "The students with whom I deal get more and more diverse [in ethnicity] all the time, yet more and more alike," said Columbia's James Shenton in mid-1986. "If I couldn't see them and didn't know their names, I wouldn't have a clue to their ethnic origins in the way they respond."

A few weeks later Harvard's Nathan Glazer offered a version of the same proposition that was only slightly more qualified. "Among Jewish undergraduates here," he told me, "you find maybe ten percent who are very orthodox or have a passionate interest in things Jewish. At the other extreme, you find a similar percentage of WASP undergraduates with distinctively WASP culture aspiring to clubs and the like. But with most of the student body—and this is true not only of WASPs and Jews but of Italian Americans and all the others—you really can't tell the difference."

What Shenton and Glazer were describing involves far more than just a similarity in the superficialities of social behavior. There is certainly significance in Andrew Hacker's observation that virtually all second-generation Asian Americans now pass "the telephone test"— by which he means that their ancestry is in no way discernible from their speech. But there is much greater significance in the kind of basic commonality that I have detected in my own students at Columbia's Graduate School of Journalism—the fact that while there are inevitably great personality differences among them, their values and aspirations tend to fall within the same broad parameters and certainly are not predictably affected by their ethnic or religious backgrounds. And perhaps even more important, the career choices that they regard as open to them are not significantly affected by those considerations either.

The same attitude is visible in every professional school at Columbia with which I am familiar and in the undergraduate college as well. Unlike their grandparents—and very often their parents, too—the "white ethnics" and Asian Americans who now throng college classrooms in America do not automatically regard their ethnicity as an overwhelming impediment to success in certain prestigious or economically attractive occupations. Today, for example, young Italian Americans have the reassuring knowledge that they will not be breaking fresh ground if they enter a field such as commercial banking, which used to be a WASP preserve, or areas of merchandising that were once largely Jewish enclaves.

This is by no means to say, of course, that young Americans now enjoy equality of opportunity regardless of background. Attending "the right schools" and having well-connected parents are still powerful reinforcements to native talent. As one evidence of that, Robert Sam Anson reported in the January 1987 issue of *Manhattan inc.* that among the fledgling lawyers appointed to coveted openings on the staff of Manhattan District Attorney Robert Morgenthau in recent years have been "the progeny of Mario Cuomo, Cyrus Vance, Dan Rather, [New York labor leader] Victor Gotbaum, Robert Kennedy, and the dean of the Harvard Law School." That observation was manifestly not intended as a pat on the back and might reasonably be held to imply that "the old boy net" still carries weight in Morgenthau's office. Still, it is worthy of note that, if so, this particular net includes not only prominent WASPs but Italian, Jewish, and Irish-American heavyweights as well.

Just how drastic a change in American society this last fact reflects is a subject of argument. Specifically, there are many who believe that the apparent ethnic diversity of the contemporary U.S. Establishment is in considerable degree vitiated by an unspoken pro-

viso that in order to win acceptance into the elite it is necessary to practice what Andrew Greeley has labeled "Anglo-conformity."

This quite clearly is just another way of asserting that Norman Podhoretz's "brutal bargain" is still imposed on ambitious non-WASPs, albeit in substantially less harsh form than in earlier times. And Podhoretz himself remains convinced that this is the case. "Very few people who have achieved national prominence bear the stigmata, if you like, of their immigrant backgrounds," he said during the course of a conversation that we had in 1986. "You don't have raw, unprocessed white ethnics coming into these positions. The personalities of highly successful ethnics may reflect their origins to some extent: [Ambassador Philip] Habib with his Lebanese background has a kind of jauntiness you don't generally find in State Department people. But overall his behavior and manner are congenial to that kind of world."

On one level, Podhoretz's generalization clearly holds true. Conformity to certain broad behavioral patterns undeniably still characterizes most people who achieve power and influence in the United States. But to argue that what is involved can be accurately described as Anglo-conformity or continues to reflect WASPification in any traditional sense seems to me to fly in the face of observable realities.

One of those realities is that nowadays even the children of successful and thoroughly "assimilated" ethnics not infrequently take pains to proclaim their ethnic heritage rather than disguise or downplay it. Common as this attitude now is, there is a particular instance of it that stands out in my own memory. Following Columbia's 1986 Commencement Day exercises, I observed two sets of proud and obviously prosperous parents strolling off to nearby restaurants with their newly graduated sons. In both cases the father of the graduate was bareheaded and attired in a three piece suit that looked as if it had been made by Brooks Brothers. The graduates themselves, however, presented a different picture: one had already replaced his mortarboard with a yarmulke, and the other, a handsome, olive-skinned youngster, wore the black bombazine jacket and white cotton trousers widely favored in India and Pakistan under his academic robe.

If such assertions of non-WASP origins among relatively privileged Americans were confined to people in their teens and twenties, they might conceivably be written off as nothing more than symptoms of youthful rebelliousness. But that explanation clearly does not hold good for Lee Iacocca or the chief executive of New York's Galesi Group, a polished, highly sophisticated man in his late fifties who in his undergraduate years at Princeton went by the given name of Francis. Since his Princeton days, Galesi—who is a real estate developer and venture capitalist—has acquired a wife who traces her ancestry back to Russia's royal Romanovs, a duplex at Manhattan's posh River House, a country place on Long Island, a 1,900-acre estate in Jamaica, and other assets that as of 1986 were estimated to exceed a quarter of a billion dollars. But along the line, he also reverted to his baptismal name of Francesco and took up the study of Italian, a language that his immigrant parents made a point of using as little as possible.

In a sense, what has made behavior such as Galesi's unremarkable is that just as today's successful ethnic is not the ethnic of yesteryear, today's WASP is not the WASP of yesteryear either. Despite his belief that it is still virtually mandatory for anyone who wants to become a national figure to adopt a personal style that is "roughly speaking WASP," Norman Podhoretz concedes that "WASP culture itself has changed; the famous reserve is pretty well gone."

But it is not only WASP reserve that is pretty well gone; it is also such classic WASP traits as a horror of "living beyond one's means" and a preference for drably conservative clothing, "plain" food, and public adherence to strict standards of sexual morality. And on a very different plane, the once nearly universal WASP assumption of innate superiority to all those of other ethnic and cultural heritages has been greatly eroded. So much so, in fact, that as an undergraduate at Yale in the early 1980s, a young woman named Laura D'Antonio pridefully reported: "I am the only one-hundred-percent Italian in my dorm, but I know at least a dozen people who *wish* they were Italian."

That claim will surely sound incredible to the great majority of WASPs or Italian Americans born before World War II, but I can offer at least one piece of corroborative evidence for it: though he has no known Italian ancestors, is thoroughly WASP in appearance and has lived nearly all his life in the United States, my eldest son derives enormous pleasure from the fact that he happens to have been born in Italy. Indeed, so great is his pride in this accident of birth that he went to the trouble of learning to speak Italian as an adult and at thirty still cherishes his right to Italian as well as American citizenship.

I do not for a moment mean to hold my son up as the prototypical young WASP—or indeed young American of any background. Still, I think it accurate to say that in social behavior, ambitions, and cultural values he does not depart in any radical way from patterns widely observable among people of his generation and educational attainments in this country. And in no aspect of his life is that more true than in the very peripheral importance that he attaches to the ethnicity of his friends and associates and in his essentially sportive attitude toward his own ethnicity.

The phenomenon that I am trying to describe is, I believe, implicit in the term "yuppie."* Though it has justly been described as glib and imprecise, that instant cliché nonetheless has one positive aspect: it is pan-ethnic—or perhaps more properly, cannot be said to carry any particular ethnic connotation.

Happily, "yuppie" now appears to be headed for the lexicographical ash heap, but what it implies about the diminishing role of ethnicity in American life today cannot be gainsaid. As a Jewish American of my acquaintance, himself the child of immigrants, remarked about his own children and grandchildren: "In the third and fourth generations in this country, people aren't facsimile anything anymore. Then they're just American."

Carrying the same proposition further, Nathan Glazer has observed that among privileged and upwardly mobile young Americans nowadays what is going on is not a continuation of the process under which "people become facsimile WASPs; it's the emergence of a common culture." In other words, while conformity may as a rule still be a prerequisite for acceptance into the elite, the standards by which conformity is measured are no longer what they were even a generation ago. Rather they are the standards of an establishment that, while generally unreceptive to displays of ethnicity so extreme as to be dis-

---

* In the interest of retaining their filial affections, I feel compelled to note that "yuppie" is not a description that could conceivably be applied to any of my children, emphatically including my eldest son.

---

ruptive, has nonetheless almost insensibly absorbed behavioral, social, and ethical nuances from a variety of sources and no longer simply reflects the values of a single dominant ethnic group.

To put the matter more concisely, successful Americans now live in a kind of halfway house between the old myth of the total eradication of diversity by the melting pot and the newer one of rampant cultural pluralism. When it is stated in so abstract a fashion, that proposition may seem excessively vague and ethereal. But when, as I now propose to do, one examines how and by whom power is actually exercised in today's United States, the new American formula for dealing with ethnic diversity proves very concrete and pragmatic indeed.

4

WHERE THE POLS ARE

"I am a product . . . of a dream that brought my father to this country seventy-six years ago, that brought my mother and her family here one year later—poor, unable to speak English, but with a burning desire to succeed in their new land of opportunity.

"My friends, the dream that carried me to this platform is alive tonight in every part of this country . . ."

—Michael Dukakis before the Democratic National Convention, July 21, 1988

If the "all-American" Army squads so prevalent in World War II movies were still a Hollywood staple, a contemporary screenwriter trying to concoct one might well come up with a roster something like this:

Adams, Boschwitz, Cohen, D'Amato, DeConcini, Durenberger, Inouye, Kassebaum, Kerry, Lautenberg, Leahy, Levin, Matsunaga, Mikulski, Murkowski, Sarbanes, Zorinsky.

As anyone with even a passing interest in politics will recognize, however, this is not a list of fictional GIs but a sampling of the members of the United States Senate as of early 1987.

When it first occurred to me, this device for dramatizing the ethnic and religious diversity that now characterizes what is occasionally somewhat pompously described as "the best club in the United States" seemed so neat that I proudly inflicted it on a friend who comes from an old and moneyed WASP family. "Cute," she said. "But what does it really prove? Politics isn't where the power really lies; it's the people who control the purse strings who actually call the tune."

That, of course, is a proposition that the very wealthy in this country sometimes advance to console themselves for their relative political impotence and that, ironically enough, is also an article of faith with many at the opposite end of the economic spectrum. But it is at best a half-truth. Because the goals of the various great economic interests are frequently in conflict with each other, because the press is incessantly sniffing around for signs of malfeasance, and because the opinions of ordinary voters cannot safely be totally ignored, American politicians on the national level are not as a general thing for sale nowadays; usually they can only be rented. And while outright corruption is always with us, surprisingly often the payoff on attempts, direct or indirect, to purchase the favor of an influential politician is either marginal or illusory. "With a lot of these jokers in the Congress," a veteran Washington lobbyist told me, "it's essentially a negative thing. What they're saying to my clients in not-so-thinly disguised terms is 'Pay up and I won't screw you.'"

There are, in other words, important constraints upon the ability of vested economic interests to call the tune in the United States; broadly speaking, it is the politicians who establish the rules under which the economic game is played, and they do so primarily to serve their own ambitions and ideological predispositions. And for that reason among others it seems to me impossible to talk intelligently about the exercise of power in late twentieth century America without taking into account the changing role of ethnicity in our politics.

Simply to observe that ethnic diversity is a hallmark of American politics invites the weary question: "So what else is new?" It was in the political arena that WASP hegemony in this country was first successfully challenged: Irish Americans won significant political influence in New York City as early as the 1820s, and the people of Boston started electing Irish mayors a century ago. And in a great number of

American communities, of course, the original revolt against WASP political dominance proved to be only the first in a series of power seizures by one newly assertive ethnic group after another.

That, in fact, is the manner in which I, like millions of other Americans, was raised to expect that ethnicity would always express itself politically. By the mid-1930s when I first became conscious of such matters, the Yankees who had once ruled my hometown of New Haven, Connecticut, had been relegated to political oblivion. The first mayor of New Haven whom I can remember was a former official of the local cigar-makers union known as "Honest John" Murphy, and I learned early to take it as a fact of life that anyone who aspired to a top elective or appointive job in the city (or for that matter, to a senior position in the local Catholic hierarchy) had better be Irish-American.* Then, during a mayoralty election shortly before World War II, New Haven streets blossomed with signs urging Italian Americans, who by then had become the city's largest single ethnic group, to "arise and avenge the wrongs of forty years." Not too long thereafter New Haven did in fact elect its first Italian-American mayor, and as I write this, the mayor's office is occupied by a gentleman named Biaggio DiLieto. But like "Honest John" Murphy in his day, Mayor DiLieto represents an ethnic constituency now waning in power; over recent decades New Haven's black community has grown greatly in size—so much so that black politicians have openly begun to assert that it is time for one of them to have a turn on center stage.

There is, as I have noted, nothing at all remarkable about any of this; it reflects a classic pattern in American urban politics. And precisely because it is a reality with which so many of us are personally familiar, it tends, I believe, to dim our perception of the emergence of a more complex set of realities that increasingly characterizes the interaction between ethnicity and politics in this country.

These are realities perhaps best epitomized by citing a seemingly disparate set of facts; as of 1960 no non-Protestant had ever been

---

* This was so conspicuously true that it generated vast amusement among New Haven's non-Irish citizens when the Board of Education passed over all local candidates for a city job in favor of an out-of-towner with an extravagantly Irish name—only to discover too late that the appointee was, in fact, a Southern Baptist.

president of the United States nor had any black or Italian American ever served on the Supreme Court or in a presidential cabinet. And as late as 1970 no one of Jewish or Eastern European ancestry had ever been secretary of state, and no Jew or black had ever headed the national committee of a major political party.

The fact that none of these statements any longer holds true is a concrete manifestation of a snowballing process of change in our national political life—a process symbolically if indirectly acknowledged in the somewhat perfervid observances of the hundredth anniversary of the Statue of Liberty in 1986. The more or less official enshrinement of Ellis Island alongside Plymouth Rock as one of the cradles of the American nation that occurred then was not an exaltation of any particular ethnic group or groups; it was, in fact, the exact opposite—a tacit assertion that as a people we are no longer prepared to accept the proposition that any element of the population is most "truly American" or has any special claim to leadership because of ethnicity or religion.

It is, of course, easy to find situations that fly in the face of this principle in our current political life—most particularly in local politics. The looming emergence of blacks as the dominant political force in New Haven will simply replicate a development that has already occurred in a number of other American cities such as Newark, Atlanta, Chicago, and Detroit. It is difficult to conceive that a non-Hispanic can be elected mayor of Miami in the near future. And it is equally difficult to imagine the Mormons losing their grip on Salt Lake City.

But even in local politics the kind of unalloyed and unabashed ethnic hegemony once enforced by James Michael Curley in Boston, Boss Crump in Memphis, or Frank Hague in Jersey City has become increasingly hard to maintain over the last twenty years or so. An interlocking complex of factors—increased voting by once effectively disenfranchised minorities, altered immigration patterns, and changes in the population mix in many urban and suburban areas—now obliges local politicians in a growing number of communities to pay greater attention than they once did to the interests of ethnic groups other than their own. When I first settled in the then overwhelmingly blue collar community of Hoboken, New Jersey, in the early 1970s, for example,

Italian Americans had run the city virtually without challenge for some thirty years. Now, barely fifteen years later, anyone who wants to govern Hoboken must also accommodate to a large Puerto Rican minority and a host of yuppies of no strong ethnic coloration at all.

As an easily accessible bedroom community for people who work in Manhattan but can't afford to live there, Hoboken is admittedly a rather special case. But even in communities where one ethnic group is still clearly in the political saddle, multiethnic support is now often crucial to a politician's success, and this inevitably tends to bring to the fore those who are not perceived as being overly obsessed with their own ethnicity.

This was quite clearly the case, for instance, in the 1986 mayoralty election in New Orleans, a city that is now more than 60 percent black. Of the two black candidates who ran in New Orleans that year, Sidney Barthelemy commanded far less support in the city's black community than his opponent, Ernest "Dutch" Morial. In fact, Barthelemy won only 35 percent of the black vote, but because he was seen by whites as being less inimical to their interests than Morial, he won 85 percent of the white vote—and that proved the key to victory.

A no less striking demonstration of ethnic accommodation in local politics was provided by the reelection that same year of Congressman Peter Rodino of New Jersey. Forty years earlier when the voters first sent Rodino to Congress, the population of his Newark district was predominantly Italian-American, but today it is more than half black, and in 1986 Rodino found himself running against a black city councilman who enjoyed the potent endorsement of the Reverend Jesse Jackson. Yet despite his race and advanced age (he was then seventy-six), Rodino was able to retain enough black support to win what he promised would be his final term—support that was given him largely because as chairman of the House Judiciary Committee he had used his power to defend and expand civil rights legislation.

Though it does not apply in the cases of Sidney Barthelemy and Peter Rodino, there is now still another powerful deterrent to excessively overt appeals to ethnicity on the part of ambitious local politicians: today in most of the United States, no one who hopes to win statewide office can afford to indulge in such behavior. The most familiar demonstration of this fact lies in the manner in which once notoriously segregationist Southern politicians such as George Wallace and Orval Faubus changed their tunes when black voters became a significant factor in their states. But there is another, related, phenomenon that is less often noted but which, I believe, is even more significant because it reflects a continuing geographic dispersion of various population groups that is making a high degree of ethnic diversity the norm in more and more regions of our country. In its most obvious form, this phenomenon is simply described: an increasing number of America's state governments are presided over by men and women who do not have an ethnic base in their states large enough to explain their political clout.

Examples of this abound in our recent political history and can be found all across the country. While there are a considerable number of Armenian Americans in California, Gov. George Deukmejian certainly did not reach the top of the pole in Sacramento because he can deliver "the Armenian vote." And it is equally clear that it was not "the Jewish vote" that accounted for Neil Goldschmidt's election as governor of Oregon in 1986, nor did Gov. Kay Orr owe her victory in Nebraska the same year primarily to the support of her fellow Swedish Americans.

While it is not confined to any particular region, however, the divorcement of statewide political success from ethnic constituencies has perhaps reached its fullest flower in New England. It is, of course, by no means a totally new story there: the fact that he was Jewish did not prevent Abraham Ribicoff from being elected governor of overwhelmingly gentile Connecticut as far back as the 1950s. But what might be called the deethnicization of Yankee politics reached extraordinary proportions in the mid-1980s when five of the six New England states boasted governors whose ethnic power bases ranged from limited to nonexistent. If Governors William O'Neill of Connecticut and John McKernan of Maine had been supported only by Irish-American voters, or Governor Michael Dukakis of Massachusetts only by Greek-American ones, none of them would ever have made it to the statehouse. As for Vermont's Madeleine Kunin and New Hampshire's John Sununu, it is only necessary to observe that she is of Swiss-Jewish origin and he is very likely the sole resident of his state who is Lebanese and Greek by ancestry and Cuban by birth.

If these were exceptional, handpicked cases, they would be of debatable significance. But that possibility is quickly dispelled by a look at the top opposition figures in most of the states to which I have just alluded. California's Deukmejian fought both his gubernatorial campaigns against Tom Bradley, the black mayor of Los Angeles. Kay Orr's Democratic opponent in Nebraska in 1986 was former mayor Helen Boorsalis of Lincoln, whose parents emigrated to this country from Greece. Michael Dukakis's opponent in Massachusetts that year was yet another Greek American, businessman George Kariotes. In Vermont, Madeleine Kunin beat out two rival candidates, one of whom —Mayor Bernard Sanders of Burlington—was, like Kunin herself, Jewish. As for Connecticut's William O'Neill, he was challenged in the 1986 state Democratic primary by ex-congressman Toby Moffett, who is of Lebanese ancestry, and in the general election by Republican Julie Belaga, who is of Spanish descent.

And that, as Walter Cronkite used to intone, is how it was in state politics in much of America by the mid-1980s.

INEVITABLY, the factors that have eroded the importance of ethnicity in state politics have had a similar effect on our national politics. And while the advent of Michael Dukakis served to spotlight this reality, it could not truly be said to have significantly altered matters. Well before the methodical man from Massachusetts appeared on the national scene, ethnicity had ceased to be a decisive factor in the unending contest inside Congress and the executive branch for control of the real levers of power in Washington.

So far as the Congress is concerned, this transformation in attitudes has been most notable in the traditionalist precincts of the Senate. When New York's Herbert Lehman was elected a U.S. senator in 1949, it was tacitly understood that as a Jew—and the only one then serving in the Senate—he would forever be excluded from its inner circles, and as late as the 1970s Jacob Javits remained something of an outsider. But by 1987 there were no fewer than eight U.S. senators of Jewish ancestry. And not only did half of them represent states in which Jews constituted less than one percent of the population, the more congenial and politically adroit among them enjoyed significant influence over their fellow senators. In fact, one of the eight, New Hampshire's Warren Rudman, even managed to make his name something approaching a household word—at least in politically conscious households—by cosponsoring perhaps the most controversial fiscal measure of the Reagan era: the allegedly self-enforcing scheme for federal deficit reduction that a Senate wag aptly described as "budget-cutting by anonymous consent."*

Indeed, though the Reagan years were marked in many respects by attempts to turn back the clock politically and economically, they produced no signs whatsoever of any ethnic counterrevolution in the Senate. During Mr. Reagan's first term, the key figures in the Republican Senate majority included at least one Italian American, Pete Domenici of New Mexico, and the senator with the most direct personal pipeline to the President was generally conceded to be Paul Laxalt of Nevada, who is of Basque ancestry.

More remarkable yet, when control of the Senate reverted to the Democrats in 1986, Washington buzzed with speculation that Hawaii's Daniel Inouye might challenge WASPish Robert Byrd of West Virginia for the post of majority leader. And while the stocky, self-contained World War II hero did not actually do so at that time, the fact that he was seen as a credible potential contender for the job (and was an active though unsuccessful candidate for it in 1988) reflected his emergence as one of the most respected of Senate "insiders"—a status that would not conceivably have been accorded any Japanese American as recently as the late 1950s when Inouye himself first entered Congress.

Essentially, the same process that has occurred in the Senate has also been at work in the House of Representatives, albeit in somewhat less conspicuous fashion. Because congressmen must answer to more localized electorates than senators, the membership of the House began to reflect the nation's ethnic mix strongly well before that of the Senate did. But in the last fifteen years or so, the influence exerted by "ethnic" congressmen has notably increased: the workings of seniority and a changing social ethic have transformed more and more non-

---

* Rudman's chief partner in this dubious enterprise, Phil Gramm of Texas, may also be said to have made a contribution to ethnic diversity in senatorial circles. That contribution, however, was the somewhat oblique one of having married a Korean-American economist— a lady who at the time her husband was pushing the Gramm-Rudman Bill appropriately enough occupied a senior position at the Office of Management and Budget.

WASPs from backbenchers into major power brokers in the House. Perhaps the most telling manifestation of this is to be found in the fact that the chairmanship of the potent Ways and Means Committee, long the domain of Southern WASP Wilbur Mills, passed in the mid-1980s to Polish-American Don Rostenkowski of Illinois.* But it is scarcely less noteworthy that at the beginning of Mr. Reagan's second term, the chairmen of the seventeen standing committees of the House included, in addition to Rostenkowski, three Italian Americans, a Hispanic, a French Canadian, and four blacks.

In the last analysis, of course, such developments in the Congress have reflected an evolutionary change in attitudes toward ethnicity on the part of the American electorate. And that change has inevitably had its impact on the entire federal establishment. The events of the 1970s and 1980s, in fact, have made it abundantly clear that, so far as ethnic considerations are concerned, Mr. Dooley's observation that "the Supreme Court follows the election returns" applies equally well to the executive branch of our government.

There is, to be sure, nothing particularly new about the presence of non-WASPs in important appointive positions in Washington: FDR's advisers, official and unofficial, ranged from "Tommy the Cork" Corcoran to Treasury Secretary Henry Morgenthau—and Jack Kennedy had his "Irish mafia." Still, the classic cabinet and subcabinet officer as late as the Lyndon Johnson years was of the type most recently personified by Cyrus Vance: a lawyer, financier, businessman, or educator drawn from the upper ranks of the Establishment. Which was to say in all probability a WASP—or if not, a facsimile WASP.

In this respect I believe a symbolic turning point is to be found in the apotheosis of Henry Kissinger, who was arguably the most powerful non-WASP cabinet officer this country has yet had—and who was certainly the first one whose immigrant origins were a central part of his persona. It may well be unfair to suggest that Kissinger deliberately cultivated his "foreignness" in the belief that it gave him a kind of exotic distinction. Yet it is a curious fact that his businessman brother,

---

* Power-brokering in a multiethnic environment was, of course, by no means an unfamiliar art to Rostenkowski, who originally won his political spurs as a lieutenant of that quintessential Irish-American pol, Chicago's late mayor Richard Daley.

73

Walter, though only a year younger than Henry and hence presumably no less set in his ways by the time the Kissinger family arrived in the U.S., nonetheless somehow succeeded in eradicating from his English any trace of a German accent. And there was, I thought, self-promotion as well as wit reflected in Kissinger's nonanswer to a question I put to him in his final months as secretary of state. Did he think, I asked, that he would be succeeded in that job by his longtime rival Zbigniew Brzezinski if Jimmy Carter won the upcoming presidential election? "So far as I know," replied Dr. K owlishly, "there is no Constitutional requirement that the secretary of state be foreign-born."

In the event, of course, America's first German-born secretary of state was not succeeded by one born in Poland. Somewhat ironically, however, Carter did eventually turn to Polish-American Edmund Muskie to fill the job—a development that inevitably prompted Washington wits to observe that Muskie and Brzezinski, who as Carter's national security adviser took a harder diplomatic line, were "Poles apart." And overall the born-again Baptist from Georgia established a new landmark in executive branch ethnicity by giving an unprecedented number of the senior positions in his administration to non-WASPs.*

On this score, Ronald Reagan's record never matched that of his predecessor. Yet not even Mr. Reagan's harshest critics could, I think, seriously charge him with making ethnicity a decisive factor in his choice of associates—or not, at least, where Caucasians were concerned. Anyone whose family friends include Frank Sinatra, Betsy Bloomingdale, and New York bon vivant Jerome ("The Social Moth") Zipkin is clearly less influenced by ancestry or religion than by celebrity, economic status, and personal compatibility. This cast of mind, moreover, has inevitably carried over to some extent to Mr. Reagan's official appointments: where Jack Kennedy's first choice for the rarefied post of chief of protocol was that quintessence of WASP aristoc-

---

* In addition to Muskie and Brzezinski, Carter's high-level appointees at one time or another included three Jewish Americans (Defense Secretary Harold Brown, Treasury Secretary W. Michael Blumenthal, Transportation Secretary Neil Goldschmidt), two Italian Americans (HEW Secretary Joseph Califano, Attorney General Benjamin Civiletti), and two blacks (U.N. Ambassador Andrew Young, HEW Secretary Patricia Harris).

---

racy Angier Biddle Duke, the first social arbiter named by Reagan was Mrs. Walter Annenberg, whose late father-in-law acquired a fortune as a publisher of horse-racing news and in the process cultivated what might most kindly be described as some rather ungenteel associations. And when Mrs. Annenberg returned to private life in 1982, the protocol post was promptly conferred upon another non-WASP: Selwa ("Lucky") Roosevelt, a lady of Lebanese Druze ancestry who acquired her illustrious surname by marrying one of Theodore Roosevelt's grandsons.

It would, though, do Mr. Reagan a great injustice to imply that it was glitz alone that explained why he showed so little disposition to confine his own associations, personal or political, to scions of "the old stock." Rather, the fact that in Antonin Scalia he named the first Italian American ever to sit on the Supreme Court and in Frank Carlucci the first one to head either the National Security Council or the Department of Defense reflects his acceptance of a cardinal rule of contemporary American political life: if you want to win—and hang on to—a regional or national political base you can't afford to let the ethnicity of your associates loom larger in your calculations than their talent, toughness, and political smarts.

BACK IN THE 1940s when he found himself confronted with a controversial question concerning Middle Eastern affairs at a political rally in New Jersey, Harry Truman allegedly turned to a local dignitary and asked in a loud whisper: "How many Arabs vote in this state?" That question is one that any American politician, no matter how lofty his principles, would still regard as relevant. For while state and national politics in the United States have become thoroughly multiethnic, that is by no means to say that they have become totally nonethnic or that even the most eminent political figures feel that they can safely ignore ethnic considerations.

In a society in which people of so many different ancestries are striving to win a place in the sun, this state of affairs is not only inevitable but no doubt up to a point desirable. As Herbert Gans has pointed out, "ethnic" politicians who achieve high office in the United States "become identity symbols for members of their group, supplying feelings of pride over their success."

The truth of this proposition was, of course, strongly demonstrated by the presidential campaign of Michael Dukakis. Of the $10-million war chest that Dukakis had acquired by the end of 1987, close to 17 percent had been contributed by Greek Americans, a group that at the time constituted only a little more than half of one percent of the national population. More telling yet, a substantial part of this money, according to the *New York Times*, came from Greek Americans who normally voted Republican. And, according to former Massachusetts senator Paul Tsongas, part of the reason for this abandonment of normal ideological preferences was that the rise of Michael Dukakis "helped to erase the sense of shame" instilled in Greek Americans by the disgrace of ex-vice president Spiro T. Agnew.

Valid as Gans's thesis about the importance of ethnic politicians as identity symbols clearly is, however, he seems to me to be on trickier ground when he asserts that the fact that "such politicians do not represent ethnic constituencies . . . only enhances their symbolic function." In many cases, of course, that is indisputably true: what made the Dukakis nomination doubly gratifying to Greek Americans, Jack Kennedy's election as president particularly sweet to Irish Americans, and Mario Cuomo's triumph in New York a special source of pride to Italian Americans was the endorsement of "one of our own" by predominantly non-Greek, non-Irish, and non-Italian electorates.

But while it is now generally impossible to rise to the very top of the political heap in this country without developing a multiethnic power base, there are still politicians on the national level—particularly in the House of Representatives—who *do* owe their office essentially to the support of a single ethnic constituency. And even those who have broader bases not infrequently seek to advance causes particularly dear to the hearts of their own ethnic groups. On everything from civil rights to the unending civil strife in Northern Ireland, politicians drawn from the ethnic groups most passionately concerned regularly play a significant role in shaping our national policies.* And so

* As the case of Northern Ireland demonstrates, however, the workings of ethnicity in our politics are not always totally transparent or predictable. Despite widespread sympathy for the IRA among working class Irish Americans, a number of leading Irish-American politicians, including Sen. Daniel Patrick Moynihan and former New York governor Hugh

completely is this state of affairs accepted that, in 1986, according to the *New York Times*, Indiana's Sen. Richard Lugar unabashedly advised Philippine president Corazon Aquino to urge American voters of Filipino ancestry to organize a political pressure group modeled after those that support aid to Greece and Israel. "Lugar," said one of his aides, "told Mrs. Aquino that [Filipinos] have to act like any other special interest group in American politics."

On the face of it, Senator Lugar's assertion that ethnic blocs still constitute a central factor in American politics is too obvious to dispute. But what is far less clear is the extent to which ethnicity—and its handmaiden, religion—any longer play the decisive role in voter behavior.

One person who rates the impact of ethnicity very highly indeed is Chicago's famed author-priest Father Andrew M. Greeley. "It's a very subtle, very subconscious sort of thing," says Father Greeley, who when not writing best-selling novels is a card-carrying sociologist at the National Opinion Research Center. Arguing that ethnicity can be expressed negatively as well as positively—that there is, in other words, an anti-Jewish vote, an anti-Italian vote, etc., etc.—Greeley asserts: "It doesn't have to do with issues . . . It has to do with the sense of 'they're not our kind of people' or 'they *are* our kind of people.' "

Almost any American, I suppose, can recall political campaigns whose outcome would seem to support Father Greeley's point. But it does not take a degree in sociology or political science to recognize that such campaigns are less numerous than they used to be, and that increasingly the prevailing phenomenon in American politics is the one pithily expressed by Democrat Sam Gejdenson, who in 1988 won a third term as congressman from the Second District of Connecticut. "The only people who care that I am Jewish," said Gejdenson on one occasion, "are bigots and Jews." What Gejdenson scarcely needed to add was that there were nowhere near enough Jews in southeastern

---

Carey, have publicly denounced that organization's attempts to shoot its way into power in Ulster. But perhaps precisely because he himself is not of Irish ancestry. Former New York congressman Mario Biaggi found it expedient to woo Irish-American support by taking a far more hawkish position on Ulster.

77

Connecticut (where they amount to less than one percent of the population) to contribute significantly to his election nor enough bigots to keep him out of office.

Indeed, within the last generation a strong ethnic identification has become more and more of a two-edged sword for a politician who aspires to anything more than a local role. It is, I think, undeniable that by emphasizing his Italian background Gov. Mario Cuomo of New York substantially enhanced his voter appeal not only with Italian Americans but with other "white ethnics" as well. But he clearly overplayed his hand somewhat when in early 1986 he proclaimed that the one thing that might lead him to run for the presidency would be "people talking about an Italian can't do it . . . Italians from the Northeast can't win."

Coming as it did at a time when polls showed Lee Iacocca to be the most popular potential candidate among Western and Southern voters, Cuomo's blast appeared disingenuous and self-serving to many of his fellow politicians—including, unsurprisingly, Anthony J. Colavita, who was then chairman of the Republican party in New York State. "The governor," charged Colavita, "uses the ploy of making an issue out of something, of being the one to create the issue, then turning it around to make it look as if . . . he is simply the victim who has to defend himself." And when, at about the same time, Cuomo angrily assured a press conference that "the Mafia . . . is nothing; it's a word that somebody made up," he incautiously exposed himself to open ridicule; in a skit staged by New York political reporters and writers not long afterward, he was portrayed as insisting "there's no such thing as pizza."

To be sure, none of this prevented Cuomo from winning a smashing victory when he ran for a second term as governor at the end of 1986. But there is no evidence either that it in any way served to strengthen his hold upon the one group of voters who might be assumed to be particularly responsive to such rhetoric—namely Italian Americans. And a similar but far more damaging refusal to respond automatically to ethnic rallying cries greeted Geraldine Ferraro when, during the 1984 presidential campaign, she attempted to discredit various allegations of impropriety leveled at her and her husband by attributing them entirely to prejudice against Italian Americans. In a bitter address to the Coalition of Italo-American Organizations after the campaign was over, Mrs. Ferraro declared: "I had expected unequivocal support from a community I had always considered my own . . . In fact, for those four months, most of the [Italian-American] community rolled over and played dead."

What Ferraro had failed to take sufficiently into account was not just that many people, including Italian Americans, were inclined to suspect that she and her husband had perhaps been involved in questionable financial practices. It was also that as Italian Americans have increasingly entered into the mainstream of U.S. society, their voting patterns have progressively lost ethnic predictability and come to parallel closely those of the overall national population.

Far from being confined to Italian Americans, moreover, this is a process observably at work in the majority of ethnic and religious groups in this country. In April 1987 pollster Marvin D. Field, a long-time analyst of political behavior in California, pointed out to the *New York Times* that his state's rapidly growing Asian and Hispanic populations were internally split by "a wide variety of tugs and pulls"—among them differences in age, education, income, and class. And an earlier *Times* article quoted a similar comment by Lee M. Miringoff, director of the Marist College Institute of Public Opinion, concerning the dwindling emphasis most New York voters now place on the selection of religiously "balanced" tickets, a practice that was considered indispensable to electoral success in the state as late as the early 1960s. "The traditional categories of voting are not what they used to be," Miringoff declared. "Jews don't draw the curtain on the booth and vote just for Jews—and Catholics don't vote just for Catholics."

Here again, the political career of Mario Cuomo is particularly instructive. In New York's closely contested 1982 gubernatorial election, Cuomo, though Roman Catholic, lost roughly half the state's Catholic vote to his then Jewish opponent, Lewis Lehrman. Offsetting that, however, Lehrman lost two-thirds of the Jewish vote to Cuomo.

Admittedly, both Cuomo and Lehrman were in certain respects unpalatable to the more inflexible of their coreligionists: Lehrman, whose wife is a WASP, had so tenuous an attachment to Judaism that he converted to Catholicism a few years after the election, and Cuomo's views on abortion—which he opposes personally but does not believe can legitimately be denied to those who hold different principles

—eventually earned him a public reproof from New York's John Cardinal O'Connor. None of those factors seems to have played a major role in the 1982 voting, however. Rather, it appears that politically conservative Catholics found Cuomo too liberal for their taste, while liberal Jews were alienated by Lehrman's highly conservative views.

The message inherent in the Cuomo-Lehrman election is, I think, obvious—and it is one that voters all across the United States have been transmitting with ever growing frequency. For me, that message was most succinctly expressed not long ago by novelist Thomas Fleming, whose fascination with politics dates back to his childhood in Jersey City where his father was a power in the then-ruling Irish-American machine. "The rules of the game have changed significantly since then," Tom Fleming remarked to me in 1986. "You can't rely just on ethnicity or religion anymore. Nowadays they're often outweighed by ideology.

IMPLICIT IN Tom Fleming's comment, of course, is the recognition that in the America of the late 1980s ethnicity and ideology are no longer as predictably linked as they once were. To many younger Americans this may seem a curious assertion in light of the strong relationship between the two forces exemplified by the political career of someone such as the Reverend Jesse Jackson. But if so, that is only because they are not familiar with the way politics operated in this country before World War II—and for that matter, for some years thereafter.

In the New England of my childhood, for example, it was broadly true that the kind of people now called WASPs tended to be Republicans, i.e., conservative, while "ethnics" tended to be Democrats, i.e., liberal. Indeed, in the Connecticut secondary school that I attended, an institution that catered primarily to the children of the local WASP bourgeoisie, only a dozen or so youngsters out of a total student body of more than 150 voted for Franklin Roosevelt in the mock presidential election that we staged in 1936. And except for two or three of us, all of the Roosevelt supporters were of Irish, Italian, or Jewish ancestry.*

---

* While I would like to pretend that my vote for Roosevelt reflected precocious independence of thought, the truth is that I was just as much a victim of parental brainwashing as the rest of my schoolmates. For reasons now lost in the mists of time, my mother's family,

All that, however, is now a thing of the past. Today in southeastern Connecticut the prime movers in such liberal causes as the nuclear freeze or the Jesse Jackson presidential candidacy tend to be drawn from the ranks of old-line WASPs. At election time, in fact, some of the preppiest Yankees in the area where I now live turn out to work for our extremely "progressive" and emphatically non-WASP Democratic congressman. On the other side of the coin, two of the three top contenders for the Republican gubernatorial nomination in Connecticut in 1986 were Italian Americans, and the only Republican state assemblyman with whom I am socially acquainted is of Greek ancestry.

The increasing disconnection between ethnicity and political philosophy is, I think, particularly interesting in staid Connecticut, whose inhabitants like to call it "the land of steady habits." But it is, of course, a nationwide phenomenon rather than a purely local one. At the highest levels of national politics—in the Senate and House of Representatives—WASPs and "ethnics" alike are to be found at both ends of the political spectrum. And the same diversity is to be found, as we shall see, in the great Washington "think tanks" that supply our political leaders with intellectual fodder: so far as their staff members are concerned, conservative think tanks tend to be somewhat less WASPy than liberal ones.

In terms of the prevailing intellectual fashions in American politics, in fact, there has been something akin to a reversal of ethnic roles in the last twenty years. Insofar as they can be said to represent any single element of the American population, such reformist lobbies as the Sierra Club and Common Cause speak for prosperous WASPs. Indeed, it is difficult to conceive of a figure who might more thoroughly embody the WASP establishment than Common Cause founder John Gardner, a man so incorrigibly patrician that in my few brief encounters with him in the late 1970s he quite innocently and unintentionally

---

though of Yankee stock, was traditionally fiercely Democratic—so much so that at the turn of the century a particularly unfortunate great-uncle of mine was christened Grover Cleveland Adams. "That poor child," one of his sisters indignantly remarked a half-century later. "So far as our friends were concerned, Mama and Papa might just as well have named him after Benedict Arnold."

induced in me emotions similar to those I had harbored toward "the St. Grottlesex crowd" during my years at Yale.

I do not, of course, mean to suggest that the patrician progressive marks a new departure in the United States; the careers of Franklin Roosevelt and Averell Harriman among many others stand as disproof of that. But what does reflect significant change in my opinion is the fact that within this generation the political stance adopted by many of the most articulate and prestigious of middle and upper class WASPs has altered so much that intellectual leadership of the conservative cause has to a large extent passed into non-WASP hands.

For what I suspect are not especially admirable reasons, this development has chiefly been reported by the media in terms of those Jewish converts from liberalism who have emerged as keepers of the conservative conscience—such people as Sidney Hook, Irving Kristol, Norman Podhoretz and his wife Midge Decter, and former Yale Law School dean and assistant secretary of state Eugene Rostow. But while the so-called neoconservative movement does include a number of Jews, that is only part of the story. For alongside the Jewish "neocons" are ranged other latter-day conservatives of a variety of ethnic origins: Irish Americans such as columnist Patrick Buchanan and R. Emmett Tyrrell of the self-consciously iconoclastic *The American Spectator*, Slavic Americans such as supply-side propagandist Jude Wanniski, black Americans such as economist Thomas Sowell, Italian Americans such as Justice Antonin Scalia, and even the Lebanese-American Baroody family, which for a quarter century treated Washinton's American Enterprise Institute as a kind of hereditary monarchy.

Intellectuals, to be sure, often tend to take more extreme and doctrinaire political positions than nonintellectuals, and it would be absurd to argue that traditional patterns of ethnic and religious voting are likely to disappear entirely from the American political scene in the foreseeable future. Jews, no matter how prosperous, still tend to be more liberal politically than other Americans of high economic status; fundamentalist and evangelical Christians remain predominantly conservative; and the privileged WASP who clings to the Republican or conservative Democratic faith of his fathers is far from becoming an extinct species. Most important of all, in the classic tradition of American politics, ethnic voting remains the rule among the members of groups on the lower rungs of the socioeconomic ladder: as Jesse Jackson never loses a chance to remind his party's power brokers, blacks still vote overwhelmingly Democratic—and most often for black candidates where possible. And while it is harder to generalize about Hispanics—there is considerable disparity in interests and attitudes among voters of Cuban background and those of Mexican or Puerto Rican heritage—the voting behavior of each of the subgroups within the overall Hispanic population continues more often than not to be significantly influenced by its ancestral ties.

But all that being said, the fact remains that for a very large and steadily increasing share of the American population, ethnicity now plays second fiddle to other considerations in determining political behavior. Here again the case of Geraldine Ferraro is revealing: her most ardent supporters were feminists rather than Italian Americans, and there can be no question but that her sex cost her the support of a substantial though unquantifiable number of Italian-American males.

AS CITIZENS OF WHAT IS, with the possible exception of Japan, the world's most overpolled nation, Americans might reasonably expect that changes in their electoral outlook would almost instantly be registered on political radar screens. Yet in reality many allegedly sophisticated observers of our public affairs, including a surprising number of professional politicians, continue to operate on assumptions concerning ethnicity that range from increasingly shaky to totally out of date.

Consider, for example, the New York gubernatorial race of 1986. As election day approached, no one doubted for an instant that Mario Cuomo would easily win a second term; the only question was whether he would succeed in piling up the biggest majority in the state's history. If that was his ambition—as it evidently was—it is extremely doubtful that the governor did anything to advance it by picking for the No. 2 position on the Democratic ticket an upstate United States congressman named Stan Lundine. Outside of his home district, only a small minority of New Yorkers had ever heard of Mr. Lundine—and presumably fewer still were aware that he is a WASP and an Episcopalian. But in Mario Cuomo's eyes those last two attributes were apparently key. For they meant that Lundine's nomination as lieutenant governor satisfied the hoary tradition that a statewide ticket in New York must be "balanced" not only geographically but ethnically and religiously as well.

Though it did him no visible harm—he did, in fact, win reelection by a record vote—this concession by Cuomo to presumed WASP and Protestant sensibilities was surely totally unnecessary. But to do him justice, Cuomo is far from being the only politician who, in my judgment, incorrectly assesses the role WASPs play in contemporary American politics. Even more notable in this respect is New York City's Mayor Edward Koch, who clearly retains at least partial belief in the myth of the WASP—a breed embodied for him by his predecessor John Lindsay, whose Ivy League assurance Koch plainly resents and whose "general coziness with the richies and powerful in this town" draws Koch's scorn. In an evident attempt to explain away Lindsay's political appeal to New Yorkers, Koch irritably asserted in his book *Politics* that "Jews . . . love to vote for someone whom they consider to be an FDR, a WASP with power and money who they think loves them. And they'll vote for an FDR in preference to a Jew because they much prefer to get someone they can think of as more classy, see."

Where Koch exaggerates the electoral appeal of WASPhood, however, there are probably even more political "experts" who subscribe to the opposite fallacy—namely that WASP political candidates are doomed to almost automatic rejection when facing a predominantly non-WASP electorate. This, in fact, is a myth sometimes invoked by WASPs themselves: following her obviously foredoomed mayoralty campaign of 1986, former New York City council president Carol Bellamy mused that perhaps "growing up as a WASP" had saddled her with a personal style too reserved to be politically effective. And it is one unquestioningly accepted by many non-WASPs such as Kevin Harrington, a former president of the Massachusetts senate who bluntly attributed the virtual demise of the Republican Party in his state to its slowness in discarding its Yankee image. "The old stock was marvelous," Harrington told *Wall Street Journal* reporter David Wessel in mid-1986. "But it can't win elections."

If Harrington really wanted to test that thesis, he would do well to take a closer look at neighboring Rhode Island. There an electorate that is overwhelmingly "ethnic" and Catholic has repeatedly sent to the U.S. Senate two WASPs of deepest dye, Republican John Chafee and Democrat Claiborne Pell, the latter of whom just barely escapes being a Hollywood caricature of a Yankee blue blood. As for Carol Bellamy, she might turn her gaze across the Hudson to New Jersey, where in 1986 Republican Thomas Kean was overwhelmingly elected to his second term as governor. Kean is not only a scion of one of his state's oldest and wealthiest families, but he compounds that offense by speaking in accents so plummy that a sharp-tongued friend of mine describes him as possessing "the high WASP honk." Yet in his reelection bid he outpolled his Democratic opponent among every one of the ethnic minorities, which, taken collectively, constitute the majority of the New Jersey electorate.

THOMAS KEAN'S across-the-board electoral success in New Jersey serves to underline what has now become an irreversible reality of public life in the United States: except in local situations where a single strongly cohesive ethnic group predominates, nobody—not even a WASP—is any longer automatically excluded from political leadership in our society simply because of ethnicity. At the same time, no office—not even the presidency with all its historic overtones and symbolic significance—is any longer reserved for WASPs or assimilated WASPs.

Because this state of affairs has come about through evolution, no particular event or moment can possibly be described as marking the turning point in the process. But I find it instructive to recall that in 1964, upon learning that Barry Goldwater had captured the Republican presidential nomination, the late Bruce Barton, Jr., wryly remarked: "I always knew that the first Jew to run for president would be an Episcopalian." In so saying, Barton was not indulging in anti-Semitism but merely reflecting a dispassionate appraisal of the interaction of ethnicity and voter behavior he had absorbed while growing up in a political household in the 1930s.* And it is a measure of how much the nature of American politics has changed in the quarter century since Barton delivered that line that his statement now sounds not just prejudiced but irrelevant.

---

* Barton's father, a New York advertising tycoon, was one of three Republican congressmen whom FDR tirelessly pilloried as symbols of reaction with his derisory campaign chant of "Martin, Barton, and Fish"—or more literally, "Mah-tun, Bah-tun, and FISH!"

Here once again Michael Dukakis serves as the perfect exemplar. The fact that he had not chosen to mitigate his ethnicity by becoming an Episcopalian or Congregationalist was clearly of scant importance to the mass of the electorate; if anything, it was probably an asset in the eyes of non-WASP voters. Similarly, the fact that his wife was Jewish undeniably enhanced his appeal for some Jewish voters—and that, in cold political terms, probably outweighed any impact it might have upon the vastly diminished ranks of anti-Semites in the contemporary United States.

In this respect, Dukakis—as in a sense was also true of Barry Goldwater—was plainly a harbinger of the future role of ethnicity in American politics. For like Goldwater and Dukakis, an increasing number of our political leaders these days have multiple ethnic ties—and given the great genetic blender now at work in the general society, that state of affairs will inevitably become even more common in years to come. "I suspect," Harvard's Nathan Glazer once remarked to me, "that Mike Dukakis's children, being half-Jewish, will probably be even less clearly affected by ethnicity than he has been if they go into politics."

That Glazer's observation is valid seems to me undeniable. And it applies with equal force to any political dynasties that might be established by Maine's Senator William Cohen (whose mother was of Irish Protestant stock), by Texas's Senator Phil Gramm (whose two sons are half Korean by ancestry), or by New York's Senator Alfonse D'Amato (whose first grandson was baptized Gregory Daniel Murphy).

Virtually any informed American could surely expand the list I have just offered by adding to it the names of politicians in his own state or city who have multiple ethnic affiliations stemming from inheritance, their marriage to people of different ancestry, or simply public perception. (In New York City there are at least two local political figures who are of Italian ancestry and bear Italian surnames but who are regarded as members of the Hispanic community because they are descended from people who originally emigrated from Italy to Puerto Rico.)

What we are seeing in American politics today, in other words, is not just increased mutual tolerance by members of the nation's various ethnic communities, but a progressive blurring of clearcut ethnic distinctions—and that inevitably will prove a self-reinforcing process. As a result, it is entirely conceivable that the first president of the United States who can boast of having Polish or Portuguese blood will be named DeAngelis or Kelly.

5

THE REWARDS OF
INDUSTRY

Though most people took little no-
tice of them, two vital clues as to who now sets the economic pace in
America appeared in the nation's press in the mid-1980s:

- In April 1985, Prof. Thomas J. Stanley of Georgia
  State University told *Forbes* magazine that a twelve-
  year study he had made of the American rich indicated that no more than 40 percent of the nation's
  first-generation millionaires at that time were
  WASPs. The bulk of the new American fortunes, he
  asserted, were being amassed by people of Eastern
  European, Italian, and Irish Catholic background.
- In early 1986, the *New York Times* reported, an executive search firm called Korn/Ferry International surveyed 4,300 managers holding positions just below
  the CEO level in the nation's biggest companies and
  found that 58.3 percent of them were Protestants.

Since the comparable figure in a survey Korn/Ferry
had conducted in 1979 had been 68.4 percent, this
suggested that more than 10 percent of the senior
management jobs in major U.S. corporations had
passed out of WASP hands and into non-WASP ones
in a period of less than seven years. And even this
seemed to mask somewhat the real rate of change:
among the total executive population surveyed, for
example, Jewish representation increased from 5.6
percent in 1979 to 7.4 percent in 1986—but when
older executives were excluded and the survey was
confined only to those under the age of forty, the 1986
figure for Jews jumped to 13 percent.

What clearly underlay both these reports was a development of
central significance for our society: control of the levers of economic
power in the United States, long primarily confined to WASPs, has
now ceased to be the prerogative of any particular ethnic group. To
some outside observers of the American scene, this new reality has
become strikingly apparent. In 1986, for example, French-Canadian
tycoon Robert Campeau, embittered by the hostility he had encountered in his own country's English-speaking business establishment,
shifted the focus of his entrepreneurial interests to the United States
with the candid explanation: "It's such a refreshing atmosphere,
compared to Canada. It doesn't matter what your name is down
there. It can be Italian; it can be whatever." Yet the process that
led to this state of affairs, though it has deep historic roots, only
began to bear fruit in a highly visible way in the 1970s—and as a result, its implications often are not yet fully apparent to Americans
themselves.

One thing that has tended to obscure the increasing dispersal of
economic power among Americans of diverse ethnic backgrounds is
almost certainly the fact that when it comes to possession of truly
immense personal wealth, WASPs still predominate in this country. Of
the fourteen billionaires who headed *Forbes* magazine's 1985 listing of
the four hundred richest Americans, nine were WASP or at least not
conspicuously non-WASP. And of the seventy-five family fortunes

listed by *Forbes* the same year, only about a quarter were in the hands of clans readily identifiable as non-WASP.

But as indicators of the long-term national trend, these figures were more than a little deceptive. For one thing, wealth and the passage of time, as we have seen, tend to confer WASPdom where it did not originally exist: the founders of the Heinz and Coors fortunes, for example, were of recent German ancestry, and the oldest of American fortunes, a cornucopia that has survived for eight generations and whose bounty is now shared in greater or lesser degree by some 1,700 of the nation's WASPiest citizens, was originally established by French immigrant Samuel du Pont.*

More to the point, however, possessors of "old money"—clans such as the Roosevelts and Rockefellers of New York, the Pews and Scrantons of Pennsylvania, the Lodges and Lowells of Massachusetts —tend over the generations to become conservators of wealth rather than entrepreneurs. And more often than not, the loss of the entrepreneurial spirit ultimately renders even successful conservation of extraordinary wealth impossible. Of the families included in the first national listing of rich Americans that B. C. Forbes, the founder of *Forbes* magazine, published in 1918, fewer than ten were still to be found on the list that the magazine published sixty-six years later. And of the thousand rich New York families identified by Moses Yale Beach in 1845, not a single one showed up in the *Forbes* 1985 rankings.

In short, in the United States at least there is considerable historic support for the adage "Three generations from shirtsleeves to shirtsleeves." Indeed, Georgia's Professor Stanley, whose research indicated that there were more than 830,000 millionaires in this country as of 1985,† estimates that some 80 percent of them were self-made. And since, as I noted earlier, Stanley also concluded that WASPs constituted a distinct minority of these emerging tycoons, it seems inevitable that if *Forbes* is still publishing its annual list of the richest Americans

---

* Whose admission to the United States was strongly opposed by President John Adams on the grounds that the last thing the country needed at that particular point was another "French philosopher."

† This, interestingly, was more than twice the number of millionaires that the Internal Revenue Service succeeded in tracking down in that year.

---

fifty years from now, even the "old money" families included will reflect a significantly different ethnic mix than prevails today.

PERHAPS THE most important single fact to note about the majority of Thomas Stanley's millionaires who are self-made is that they constitute the leaven in the American economy. As James Burke, the chairman of Johnson & Johnson remarked in 1986: "The large established companies are not the ones creating jobs. We are not the entrepreneurs." It is, as Burke implied, the self-made men—the entrepreneurs—who supply not only a disproportionate share of the new employment but also of the new ideas and new products that keep American industry vital. And there are obvious reasons why so large a share of the nation's entrepreneurial ventures, past as well as present, have been launched by people drawn from the ranks of disadvantaged or formerly disadvantaged ethnic and religious groups.

It is, of course, a truism that entrepreneurship has particular attraction for people impatient with corporate bureaucracy and determined to be masters of their own destiny. But what is less often acknowledged is that going into business for yourself can also be a matter of necessity: it is one of the few roads to prosperity open to someone who lacks the educational qualifications to win a management-track position in the corporate world.

This, of course, was a reality that in the first half of this century tended to have its greatest impact upon newly arrived white ethnic groups whose members in general were far less likely than WASPs to receive a college education. But until quite recently in our national life entrepreneurship was also one of the few promising recourses open to an "ethnic" who in fact possessed better than average educational attainments but was unable or unwilling to make himself over into a facsimile WASP.

It was primarily because of this consideration, I believe, that prior to World War II the most able and ambitious of America's newer immigrants and their immediate descendants showed an uncommonly strong propensity to go into business for themselves. In any case, among the Italian-American youngsters with whom I grew up, those from the most prosperous homes were virtually all the sons of men who had established successful local enterprises—contracting firms, an electroplating concern, a shirt factory, a small private bus line, etc. As for my Jewish contemporaries, they were more likely than my Italian ones to be the sons of lawyers and doctors, but a fair number of them, too, came from families that owned retail shops, movie houses, or other small to medium-sized businesses.

If in all this I seem to be indulging in stereotypes, it is because in economic terms the America of the 1930s was in fact characterized by considerably more ethnic specialization than obtains today. In my part of the country, such phrases as "German bakery" or "Italian contractor" came close to being tautologies, while tobacco farming—a highly risky business then of primary economic importance in the Connecticut River valley—attracted a disproportionate number of Polish Americans. Other patterns of this kind were equally common in other regions and in some cases were even nationwide. Wherever they had settled, for example, Jews tended to be prominent in retailing, clothing manufacture, and the various branches of the entertainment industry, and in the late 1930s more and more Jewish entrepreneurs began to move into real estate development and building.

To imply that all this is merely ancient history would, of course, be highly misleading. Indeed, one notable aspect of economic life in the United States since World War II has been an enormous increase in the size of the ventures that non-WASP entrepreneurs conduct in some of their traditional fields of specialization. To cite perhaps the most striking case in point, close to forty of the four hundred superrich identified by *Forbes* in 1985 were Jewish, Italian, or Greek Americans whose fortunes were basically founded upon real estate and real estate development. But what has been even more notable in my view has been the ever increasing variety of fields in which non-WASP entrepreneurs have come to play a significant part and the growing diversity of the ethnic groups represented on the upper rungs of the entrepreneurial ladder.

In making these observations, I don't want to fall into the trap of understating the entrepreneurial contribution of WASPs to the contemporary American business scene. The "old stock" has undeniably supplied some of the most dynamic of postwar U.S. economic pioneers —men such as David Packard of Hewlett-Packard, who helped to usher in what the Japanese like to call "the information age," and Robert O. Anderson, who in addition to putting together Atlantic Richfield managed to make himself the biggest individual landowner in the nation.* But the self-made tycoons who for one reason or another have impinged most strongly on my own consciousness are of a different stripe. Among them:

- An Wang, the Shanghai-born computer magnate who created the first Fortune 500 company to be headed by an Asian American and who on one memorable occasion startled Harvard president Derek Bok by responding to a request that he contribute to an ambitious university project by forking over the entire multimillion-dollar sum needed to complete it.
- Andrew Grove, a refugee from the 1956 Hungarian uprising who graduated with honors from New York's City College four years after he first began to learn English and who went on to become a founder of Intel, one of the nation's leading producers of microchips.†
- Dr. Sheldon Weinig, a witty, hard-driving onetime metallurgy professor at New York University who developed a process vital to the manufacture of semiconductors and parlayed it into a company that now produces its complex and costly ($300,000 or so a

---

* A status that, while highly advantageous financially, also involves certain complications. Back in the 1970s, in response to a polite inquiry from a luncheon campanion, Mrs. Robert Anderson somewhat wearily indicated that with half a dozen other residences to worry about she had not yet had a chance to familiarize herself with a Mexican hacienda recently acquired by her husband.

† Perhaps because the time of their arrival in the United States coincided with the emergence of the new information technology, veterans of the Hungarian revolt have shown a special affinity for the computer and semiconductor industries. In addition to Grove, other ex–Hungarian freedom fighters prominent in those fields as of 1986 included George Erde, a cofounder of California's Linear Technology; Thomas Klein and Andrew Vasadi, cofounders of California's Sierra Semiconductor; and Erwin Klein, president of Minnesota's Datamyte.

---

copy) machines in Europe and Japan as well as in the United States.

· Daniel J. Terra, an Italian immigrant's son who started manufacturing specialty chemicals for use in printing ink with a borrowed $2,500 in 1940, subsequently acquired a fortune of over $350 million, and in 1986 opened Chicago's Terra Museum of Art to accommodate his personal collection of more than 500 paintings. (Though his favorite Chicago eating establishment is rumored to be a hot dog stand, Terra likes to be addressed as "ambassador"—a style to which he became entitled when, in recognition of his services as a leading fund-raiser for Ronald Reagan in 1980, he was appointed to the specially created post of ambassador-at-large for cultural affairs.)

· Jeno Paulucci, another Midwestern boy who had only limited success peddling Italian-American specialities based on family recipes but who made it big after he hit upon the idea of canning Chinese—or more accurately, pseudo-Chinese—dishes under the brand name of Chun King.

· Mortimer Zuckerman, a brilliant but not infrequently abrasive native of Montreal who first built himself a U.S. real estate empire—he is one of the few people ever to outbid the flamboyant Donald Trump for a desirable chunk of Manhattan—and then, through his acquisition of Atlantic Little Brown, *The Atlantic* monthly and *U.S. News & World Report*, established himself as a publishing power as well.

· Kirk Kerkorian, a high school dropout from an Armenian immigrant family who started off as a commercial pilot, then launched his own airline (which he successively sold, bought back, and resold at a profit of more than $10 million). As of 1986, Kerkorian's net worth, most of it acquired by manipulating the assets of MGM and related entertainment enterprises, was estimated at $600 million or so.

Fascinating as all these men are, however, none of them is of quite so much interest to me personally as a figure who has been at various times both a partner and a rival of Kerkorian's in the entertainment business—a Jewish Bostonian named Sumner Redstone. As of 1988 Redstone was said by *Fortune* magazine to be worth some $1.8 billion, the first several hundred million of which he had amassed through vast expansion and highly intelligent management of a chain of movie theaters originally started by his father. And in early 1987 on the strength of his past successes he managed to raise a reported $3.4 billion with which to buy control of Viacom International, an entertainment conglomerate whose properties at the time ranged from television stations to the *Cosby Show*.

None of this by itself, though, explains my preoccupation with Sumner Redstone's career. What that really stems from is my vivid memories of him as probably the second most awkward member of my World War II Army drill platoon. (Incomparably the most awkward member of the platoon—so hopeless that our company commander in desperation eventually forbade him to march in ceremonial parades— was, I regret to say, a Yale classmate of mine.)

Given my recollection of Redstone as a rather pudgy and distinctly unathletic youth, I was somewhat startled by the news of him that I received from a mutual acquaintance in late 1979: trapped on one of the upper floors of a burning Boston hotel, Sumner, who by then was well into his fifties, climbed out a window and despite burns so severe that he later spent thirty hours in surgery, successfully managed to cling to a ledge until he was rescued. Reflecting on this, I concluded that there had to be a relationship between that remarkable exhibition of tenacious courage and the fact that, at least in terms of economic accomplishment, Sumner Redstone had so far outstripped all the parade ground stars who had mocked his awkwardness in our Army days. And so, years later when I read that the management of Viacom International was determined to block Sumner's takeover bid, there was no doubt in my mind about how the battle would end; I know an irresistible force when I see one.

THOUGH THEY PROVIDE the American economy with its cutting edge, entrepreneurs as I have suggested almost by definition are apt to be in greater or lesser degree outsiders—or at least atypical. What is generally perceived as the true U.S. business establishment consists of the senior executives of the nation's major corporations, and since they are, with relatively few exceptions, hired managers, these men necessarily tend to be more conformist than entrepreneurial. Precisely for that reason, they also mirror more accurately than entrepreneurs the contemporary standards of American society in general.

Until quite recently, the standards to which corporate executives conformed were, of course, unmistakably WASP standards. Traditionally, in fact, the great majority of American corporate executives actually *were* WASPs, and those who were not were obliged to abide by "the brutal bargain"—which in its most extreme form was personified by Gerard Swope, who even after he achieved the presidency of General Electric, a position he held from 1922 until 1940, continued to go to great effort to conceal the fact that he was Jewish.

But even if their principles allowed them to do so, the great majority of "ethnics" in pre–Pearl Harbor America found it impossible to achieve a persona sufficiently WASP-like to earn the toleration of the business establishment, and as a result, their hopes of corporate advancement were slim indeed. In a 1936 survey *Fortune* magazine found that only a small number of Jews had achieved top management levels even in investment banking and communications, and that hardly any had done so in more hidebound fields such as commercial banking, insurance, and manufacturing. And in this respect members of the other white "minority" groups—Irish Americans, Italian Americans, Slavic Americans, and Greek Americans—were only marginally better off if at all.

Like so many other traditional American social patterns, this one began to change somewhat in the decade after World War II. By the early 1950s an Italian American named Joseph Martino had become president of National Lead, a company chiefly known to the public for its Dutch Boy paint, and in 1954, Frank Petito, a Princeton graduate who had served on Dwight Eisenhower's headquarters staff in Europe, became the first Italian-American partner in the investment banking house of Morgan Stanley.* Shortly after the war, too, Philip Sporn, who made no bones about being Jewish, became head of the nation's largest utility, American Electric Power. And a few years later Rochester, New York, lawyer Sol Linowitz was appointed chairman of Xerox.

At the time they occurred, however, these developments were not generally seen for what they were: harbingers of a general process of change in corporate America's attitudes on ethnicity. In his book *Ethnicity in the United States*, which was published in 1974, Father Andrew Greeley insisted that "those with Slavic and Italian names are still systematically excluded from important corporate offices." Indeed, as late as 1986, G. William Domhoff, a University of California sociology professor who has written extensively on "ruling class" attitudes in the United States, told a *New York Times* reporter that "any male in America can rise" in business or the professions, but he added that "those who rise do so by becoming less and less Jewish or less and less Catholic or less and less something else."

In one sense, the cultural lag revealed by the pronouncements of Greeley and Domhoff is understandable; all of us, scholars and workaday folk alike, tend to be slow to allow visibly changing realities to force us into a reconsideration of long-cherished theories, and it was not until the 1970s—only yesterday in historical terms of reference— that the movement of non-WASPs into America's executive suites began to reach major proportions. Nonetheless, there were two events during that decade so notable that they should have alerted anyone to the fact that a new era had dawned in the nation's business life. One of these was the election of Irving Shapiro as chairman of E. I. du Pont de Nemours & Co. in 1973; the other was the appointment of Lee Iacocca as chairman of the Chrysler Corporation in 1979.

The choice of Shapiro, the son of a Lithuanian-born pants presser, to run what had traditionally been among the most aristocratic of America's major companies (until 1970 it had never been headed by anyone outside the du Pont family) marked a watershed in one obvious

---

* Nineteen years later, Petito, the son of an illiterate Sicilian immigrant, was named chairman of Morgan Stanley.

---

respect: it automatically ensconced a Jewish American in the inner-most sanctuaries of the nation's corporate elite—a state of affairs that received formal acknowledgment in 1976 with Shapiro's election as chairman of the Business Roundtable, a group composed of the chief executive officers of two hundred of America's most important corpo-rations. But even more significant than the exalted status Shapiro had achieved was the fact that he achieved it despite a consistent refusal to downplay his Jewishness in any way. Declaring "I am what I am," he not only rejected advice to change his name early in his career but remained publicly active in Jewish affairs throughout it. And in a final repudiation of any hint of the brutal bargain, he politely declined after becoming chairman of du Pont to join Delaware's most exclusive—and previously exclusively gentile—country club.

In its own way, Lee Iacocca's ascension was no less historic than Shapiro's. Whether Iacocca could have become a facsimile WASP even if he had tried to do so is debatable. But significantly, he never bothered to make the effort, choosing instead to treat his "minority" status as a professional asset. Thus, Iacocca's publicly expressed be-lief that it was at least partly his Italian background that precipitated his abrupt dismissal as president of the Ford Motor Co. by Henry Ford II served to suppress questions that might otherwise have been raised about his handling of that job. More important, his bravura performances in reviving Chrysler and in spearheading fund-raising for the rededication of the Statue of Liberty established him as an instant folk hero in the eyes of scores of millions of Americans, WASP and non-WASP alike. Indeed, even his unabashed exploitation of his Statue of Liberty role in Chrysler's advertising aroused scant criticism. And whatever that said about prevailing standards of taste, it reflected a positive development in our national life: in the United States of the mid-1980s, it seemed perfectly natural to most people that a man who emphasized rather than concealed his non-WASP origins should pre-sent himself as a preeminent corporate symbol of American chauvin-ism.

EVEN IF IRVING SHAPIRO AND LEE IACOCCA had been isolated cases, their triumphs would still be noteworthy. But in fact, as I have already suggested, they are merely the most conspicuous examples of a general ethnic diversification in the ranks of top executives over the past twenty years. One clear reflection of this phenomenon is to be found in the Harvard Business School class of 1949, which *Fortune* magazine some time ago dubbed "the class the dollars fell on." In addition to eminent New York investment banker Sidney J. Weinberg, Jr., the stars of the HBS class of '49 include James E. Burke of Johnson & Johnson, Sumner Feldberg of Zayre's, C. Peter McColough of Xerox,* Thomas Murphy of Capital Cities/ABC, and Marvin Traub of Bloomingdale's—all as of 1986 chairmen of their companies and all non-WASP. But perhaps even more telling than this roster is the fact that just over half the heavy hitters who made *Business Week*'s 1987 list of the twenty-five most highly paid U.S. executives were non-WASPs. (No. 1 on the *Business Week* list was Lee Iacocca with total compensation in 1986 of more than $20 million; No. 25 was Coca-Cola's Cuban-born chairman Roberto C. Goizueta with $3.1 million.)

Treading hard on the heels of these superstars, moreover, are serried ranks of other "minority" executives. This is not to say that corporate America's movers and shakers constitute a faithful cross section of the nation even yet. Though blacks with high public visibility such as Ford Foundation boss Franklin Thomas and former Carter cabinet officer Patricia Roberts Harris are increasingly sought after to serve as directors of major corporations, the impact of the civil rights movement on the top ranks of management itself is still barely detectable.

There are, to be sure, some notably successful black businessmen. Of these perhaps the most conspicuous is Reginald F. Lewis, a personable, self-assured Harvard Law School graduate who in 1987 paid $985 million for the international food division of the Beatrice Co. and thereby at one stroke transformed his TLC Group into a $2-billion-a-year enterprise—which made it by far the largest company owned by a black American. In terms of overall influence on the business establishment, however, Lewis has yet to match ex-educator Clifton Wharton, who as of 1988 was chief executive of the nation's largest private pension fund, TIAA-CREF, and as such responsible for overseeing the

---

* A Roman Catholic who, as my own sentimental attachments compel me to point out, was born in Nova Scotia.

---

investment of some $60 billion. And while Lewis and Wharton are clearly standouts, they are not alone: in 1986 *Black Enterprise* magazine published a list of twenty-five blacks who held senior positions in companies ranging from Xerox to Godfather's Pizza, and whose annual income ranged from $250,000 to more than $1.2 million a year.

Yet despite these scattered success stories, the reality is that black faces remain disturbingly rare in the nation's executive suites. It may well prove true, as some observers assert, that the widespread entry of blacks into the corporate world that began in the 1970s will become apparent in the composition of top management in the 1990s. But that hypothesis has yet to be tested, and as of the late 1980s the statistics were still dismal: a survey of four hundred of the biggest U.S. corporations conducted by Rutgers University in 1986 showed that less than 9 percent of the managers in such firms were "minorities"—and under that heading the Rutgers researchers included Hispanics and Asian Americans as well as blacks.

Where Hispanics and Asians are concerned, of course, it might be argued that there is a mitigating factor that does not apply in the case of blacks: both of the first two groups owe much of their present population share to relatively recent waves of immigration. Still, the bottom line is that both remain greatly underrepresented in the top ranks of corporate management. As of 1987, Shanghai-born Gerald Tsai, the chairman of the company that used to be American Can and is now mysteriously entitled Primerica, was the only Asian American who had succeeded in rising to the top of a Fortune 500 company as a hired manager. Similarly, senior executives of Hispanic background were still unusual in the mid-1980s, and it seemed possible to detect lingering overtones of the brutal bargain in the fact that two of the most notable Hispanics in top management—Coca-Cola's Goizueta and Morgan Guaranty Trust executive vice president Roberto G. Mendoza —both came of prosperous Cuban families and had been educated at Yale.

Deplorable as it is, however, the dearth of blacks, Asians, and Hispanics in the upper levels of the business establishment will, I am convinced, ultimately prove transient. And it does not alter the fact that in all other respects the upper strata of American business had by the 1980s become decidedly pan-ethnic. At Chrysler Corp., for example, Lee Iacocca's heir apparent as of 1987 was generally thought to be vice chairman Gerald Greenwald (who first earned his spurs in Detroit at the once notoriously anti-Semitic Ford Motor Co.)* That same year, another Jewish executive, fifty-two-year-old David Laventhol, seemingly took the lead in the long-term race to succeed Robert F. Erburu, a man of Basque ancestry, as chairman of the Times Mirror Co., the great media conglomerate created by Los Angeles's eminently WASP Chandler family. And as one glanced across the American corporate spectrum, an ever growing number of other non-WASPs were visible at or near the top of major public corporations. An essentially random selection of a dozen articles clipped from business publications during one four-week period in 1986, for example, produced the following list of corporate chief executives or senior operating officers:

American Express—P. A. Cohen; Bank of Boston—Ira Stepanian; CNA Financial—D. H. Chookazian; Data General—Edson deCastro; Disney—Michael D. Eisner; Eschlin—Frederick J. Mancheski; IBM—Paul Rizzo; Merck—P. (for Pindaros) Roy Vangelos; Metropolitan Property & Liability Insurance—Samuel F. Fortunato; Mobil Oil—William Tavoulareas; Unisys—W. Michael Blumenthal; Whirlpool—J. R. Samartini.

This roll call, moreover, does not fully reflect the results of my cursory sampling of a very small section of the business press for the period in question. I have, as recipe writers say, "reserved" at least as many names again for use in a somewhat different context. Still, fragmentary and impressionistic as it is, this list offers clear evidence of a major change in American society: within the space of a single generation, members of those ethnic groups that comprised the great waves of immigration that rolled into this country in the century before World War II have become an integral part of the nation's corporate establishment.

---

* Two other members of the top management team Iacocca assembled at Chrysler—executive vice president for manufacturing Stephan Sharf and corporate treasurer Frederick Zuckerman—were also Jewish, and Greenwald's most serious competitor in the succession stakes, President Robert A. Lutz, was born in Switzerland.

THE VASTLY INCREASED role now accorded non-WASPs at the highest levels of American business is at once a cause and a reflection of a parallel phenomenon: a marked decline in the domination of certain fields of enterprise by members of a single ethnic or religious group. To put the same basic point in a slightly different light, it is clear, as Columbia's Herbert Gans has pointed out, that among today's third- and fourth-generation Americans there has been a dramatic falling-off in ethnic occupational segregation—or self-segregation.

At first blush the proposition that the link between job choices and ethnic or religious background has greatly weakened is likely to strike many Americans—and particularly those who live in the nation's major cities—as highly debatable. For residents of New York, for example, it is a given that the diamond trade centered on a few blocks of mid-town Manhattan is "a Jewish business" and that the defendants in the city's highly publicized and seemingly interminable trials of organized crime bosses are almost without exception of southern Italian ancestry. And any Manhattanite would have to be singularly unobservant not to be aware that in addition to these familiar patterns of occupational specialization some new ones have appeared in relatively recent years —that the management of fruit stands, for example, is now a near-monopoly of immigrants from Korea, that the newsstand business in the heart of the city has largely been taken over by Punjabis, and that a disproportionate number of taxi drivers are now either transplanted Israelis or recently arrived Jewish émigrés from the Soviet Union.

But conspicuous as they currently are, most of these patterns of ethnic specialization will almost certainly prove to be ephemeral. For in its more rudimentary forms ethnic occupational specialization generally reflects the dictates of opportunity rather than conscious pursuit of exclusivity.* It is, in short, the same educational and cultural hand-

---

* The most notable exceptions to this rule are provided by fields of enterprise so risky that mutual trust becomes an overriding consideration for those engaged in them. Thus, according to sociologist Richard Alba, it is the castastrophic consequences that betrayed confidences can have for criminals that primarily explains why membership in Mafia crime families "has generally been restricted to men of southern Italian origin whose parents were

icaps that bring out entrepreneurship in the most able and aggressive members of each successive wave of immigrants. But as the children and grandchildren of immigrants move into the American main-stream educationally and culturally, the range of occupational oppor-tunities open to them widens, and the degree to which they feel any economic need for an ethnic mutual support group inevitably diminishes.

Though the fact is not often acknowledged, a classic example of this process at work can be found in the history of crime—a field of endeavor that, as Daniel Bell once noted, has served as "a queer ladder of mobility in American life." In individual terms, Bell's thesis has often strikingly been demonstrated: the first Annapolis graduate to win the Congressional Medal of Honor in World War II, Lt. Commander "Butch" O'Hare, was the son of a mob lawyer who was machine-gunned to death at the dog tracks in Cicero, Illinois. Similarly, pluto-cratic publisher Walter Annenberg—friend of presidents, former United States ambassador to the Court of St. James's, and founder of the University of Southern California's Annenberg School of Com-munications—is the son of the late Moses ("Moe") Annenberg, whose success in establishing a national monopoly on the dissemina-tion of horse race results back in the 1920s was allegedly facilitated by underworld figures.

In a sense, stories such as these can be seen simply as reminders, direct or indirect, of the fact that the evolution of organized crime in America has closely paralleled the evolution of immigration patterns: the Irish gangs that dominated the underworld of the nineteenth cen-tury were in due course supplemented by Jewish and Italian gangs. But today with the collective movement of Irish and Jewish Americans into the economic and cultural mainstream, Irish and Jewish gangs have ceased to be a major factor in organized crime—and it seems entirely probable that the same fate is in store for today's Italian gangs.

---

both Italian, and usually to those married to Italian-American women." And in an interview I had with him in 1986, Herbert Gans suggested that similar considerations accounted for the almost exclusively Jewish composition of the diamond trade, a business in which dealing with someone of unfamiliar background and hence unpredictable behavior involves exposure to great financial and physical risk.

Increasingly challenged by gangs composed of blacks,* Hispanics, and most recently, Hong Kong Chinese, the Mafia families are also confronted with an erosion of their recruiting base as younger Italian Americans find a full range of educational and career opportunities available to them.

To bigots, self-styled realists, and fans of Mario Puzo, the notion that the American Mafia is destined for history's dustheap will no doubt seem preposterous. But the record plainly indicates otherwise. When I was a child, the most highly publicized criminal organization in New York, Louis "Lepke" Buchalter's Murder Inc., was run by Jewish gangsters and its nemesis was a WASP—Thomas Dewey. Today, a half century later, the men who run New York's most highly publicized criminal organizations are Italian Americans—but so is Tom Dewey's reincarnation, U.S. Attorney Rudolph Giuliani.

Though crime is notoriously one of America's biggest businesses, I have dwelt upon it so heavily not because I hold the cynical belief that Mafia bosses and Merrill Lynch brokers are brothers under the skin or cherish the sentimental illusion that people consciously choose to become drug dealers because a career in banking is closed to them. Rather I have done so because it seems to me that in a collective sense the ethnic history of the American underworld serves to illustrate a crucial point about American society in general and American business in particular: where educational opportunity and attainment become broadly similar among groups of different ancestry, ethnic origin inevitably diminishes as a factor in personnel selection, and ethnic occupational ghettos or sanctuaries begin to break down.

This is a reality that was far harder to perceive a generation ago than it is now, and that, indeed, has become fully visible in some major sectors of legitimate business only within the last fifteen years. It is also a process that is often thought of exclusively as a matter of "the old stock" making room for Americans of more recent immigrant ori-

---

* While many of today's black gangsters are of West Indian background, more, like the majority of the nation's black population, are of long-standing American heritage. But the mass movement of blacks out of the rural South and into urban centers that has occurred in this century constituted a kind of internal emigration and may in some respects have had a psychological impact similar to that produced by moving from one country to another.

---

gin. But in fact it is sometimes considerably more complex than that—as is suggested by developments in recent years in the retail industry.

Though WASPs continued to retain a strong position in the field, large-scale retailing was one of the first areas of enterprise in which Jewish Americans achieved major success—and for a long time they were the only non-WASPs to do so in significant numbers. The last twenty years, however, have seen the emergence of a growing band of retailing executives who are neither WASP nor Jewish.

One of the first members of this new wave to achieve high visibility was Thomas M. Macioce (pronounced MASS-ee-oh-see), who was elected chief executive officer of Allied Stores Corporation in 1972. Though he steadily improved Allied's performance—in part through the acquisition of chains such as Brooks Brothers, Bonwit Teller, and Garfinckle's that had originally been established by WASP and Jewish merchandisers—Macioce ultimately departed under duress: he was ousted as chairman of Allied in 1986 when French-Canadian financier Robert Campeau won control of the company in a hostile takeover.*

By then, however, Macioce's ethnicity no longer made him in any way remarkable in the upper strata of American retailing. Nearly two years earlier the controlling interest in B. Altman & Co. had passed into the hands of a pair of profit-minded CPAs named Anthony Conte and Philip Semprevivo, and in early 1987, Joseph K. Antonioni, who had begun his career there as a stock boy, was named chief executive officer of the nation's No. 2 retailer, K mart Corp.

But while Italian Americans were increasingly prominent among top merchandisers, they by no means constituted the whole of the new wave. As of 1988, the management of two of America's most venerable merchandising empires represented a study in Irish-American sibling rivalry: while Edward A. Brennan presided over the fortunes of the nation's largest retailer, Chicago's Sears Roebuck & Co., his younger brother Bernard held sway at Sears' crosstown competitor, Montgomery Ward & Co. And among the more recently created retailing giants, the $2-billion-a-year Toys "R" Us chain stood out for ethnic catholicity;

---

* Presumably the painfulness of Macioce's fall was alleviated somewhat by the size of his golden parachute, which, at more than $13.5 million, represented the biggest consolation prize taken home by any displaced U.S. executive that year.

---

there, as of 1987, the president for U.S. operations was Robert Naka-
sone—a thirty-eight-year-old University of Chicago MBA whose family
still makes occasional use of a blanket originally issued to his mother
at one of the "relocation" camps into which Japanese Americans were
herded during World War II.

IN A SOCIOLOGICAL SENSE, there is nothing surprising about the emergence of retailing as an ethnically diversified occupation. Because it is
a field in which someone who starts off with little capital can, with
intelligence and hard work, relatively quickly transform a small operation into a very large one, retailing has never been a truly "classy"
business. In this respect, in fact, it has traditionally been almost the
polar opposite of commercial banking—a business in which, historically speaking, entrepreneurial aggressiveness was considerably less
important than access to large amounts of capital and close ties to the
social and economic elite. And given that difference, there is nothing
surprising either about the fact that as of the early 1980s a pair of Yale-
educated brothers named Paul and William Moore were respectively
Episcopal bishop of New York and chairman of what was then the
nation's eighth-largest bank, Manhattan's venerable Bankers Trust Co.
For in few other areas of American economic life did WASP dominance
remain so complete for so long as it did in big banking.

That assertion will no doubt be greeted with jeers by anyone be-
nighted enough to accept that classic anti-Semitic canard that "the
Jews own the banks." But while Jewish Americans have been prominent in investment banking for many decades now, what most people
have in mind when they use the unmodified word "banking" is commercial banking. And there the reality for virtually all of our national
history was the one bluntly stated in 1974 by Wisconsin's Sen. William
Proxmire: "There is probably no industry in this country that has more
consistently and cruelly rejected Jews from positions of power and
influence than the commercial banking industry."

But in fairness—if that is the word I want—it must be conceded
that it was not only Jews who were discriminated against. With the
exception of California's Bank of America and Security Pacific Bank,
both of which were founded by immigrants, major commercial banks
across the country routinely excluded non-WASPs of every kind from

their senior executive ranks. Thus, while there are more people of Italian ancestry in New York than in any other state, no New York bank of any importance at all was headed by an Italian American until 1966 when Angelo Costanza, a Sicilian immigrant's son, became chief executive officer of Rochester's Central Trust. And even Costanza's rise seemed at the time more of a fluke than a straw in the wind.

Given this dismal history, what has lately occurred in the world of commercial banking has been startling both in its speed and its scope. One of the earliest and most conspicuous signs that the wind had changed came in the 1970s when the country's tenth-largest bank, the First National of Chicago, elected a chairman of Lebanese ancestry, A. Robert Abboud. (Abboud was subsequently succeeded in that job by a second-generation Irish American, Barry Sullivan.) And less than a decade later Joseph J. Pinola, a native of the Pennsylvania coal country and the son of an Italian-American mechanic, became CEO of the First Interstate Bancorp of Los Angeles, an institution that, with twenty-two banks in eleven states, is now the nation's ninth-biggest banking company.

The West and Midwest, of course, have always been less hidebound than the East Coast in most respects, and banking is no exception to that rule. As of the mid-1980s, in fact, no non-WASP had yet risen to be the chief executive of a major commercial bank headquartered in the sanctum sanctorum of American finance, New York City. But even a cursory look at the men on the next level down in New York banking made it plain that the old order was crumbling there, too. At Citibank, the nation's biggest, all three vice chairmen in 1986 were Roman Catholics, and the biggest operating division of Citibank's sibling Citicorp was headed by a Jewish American. Chase Manhattan, Citibank's biggest competitor, also had three Catholic vice chairmen, including an Italian American, and the No. 2 man in the Chase hierarchy, President Thomas G. Labrecque, was Catholic as well. Chemical Bank, Morgan Guaranty Trust, Irving Trust, and Manufacturers Hanover all had senior officers of either Jewish or Italian-American background. And even Bankers Trust, notoriously the preppiest of the banking sisterhood, now included among its thirteen executive vice presidents an Italian American and two Jews.

Among bankers themselves, the commonest explanation offered

for all this is that deregulation of their industry has forced the major commercial banks to renounce their once nearly exclusive focus on lending money to large corporations and to reinforce that activity with new ones such as securities dealing, investment banking, and credit card operations. And these new businesses, so the conventional wisdom has it, put a new premium on executives with special skills and aggressive commercial instincts. "Twenty years ago personal relationships were . . . how we got a lot of business," Bank of Boston first vice president Barry M. Allen told the *New York Times* in the spring of 1986. "Now, with all the competition, it is just much more complicated and requires much more of people than who their families were and where they went to school . . . Now we can't afford to keep out any talented person."

Clearly Mr. Allen knew what he was talking about; at the time he spoke, the heir apparent to the CEO's job at his own bank was Armenian-American Ira Stepanian. But that deregulation alone accounts for what has happened in the world of banking seems debatable. Surely the changing climate of American society in general has had its impact on banking, too—if only because even in their traditional speciality of corporate lending commercial bankers now have to reckon with the fact that a high percentage of the executives with whom they must deal will be non-WASPs.

JUST AS IT HELPS to explain the changes in commercial banking, the increasingly multiethnic composition of the corporate elite has also played a part in the even more dramatic changes that have overtaken that indispensable handmaiden of American business, the legal profession. Unlike banking, law has not been the exclusive preserve of any single ethnic group for a long time. Even before World War II there were Jewish and Irish law firms as well as WASP ones, but generally, all of the partners and a majority of the clients of any given firm tended to be of the same background.

In time, primarily in an effort to broaden their client base, more and more smaller law firms began to "integrate"—and thereby not infrequently acquired names that, as a whimsical friend of mine once noted, sounded remarkably like old-fashioned New York political tickets. (My particular favorite in this respect is a Manhattan firm with which I have had dealings: Herzog, Calamari and Gleason.) But until well into the 1960s the biggest and most prestigious American law firms —the ones that the titans of corporate America instinctively turned to —were nearly all WASP-run.*

This is not to say that these firms were exclusively WASP in their personnel: even the stuffiest of them such as Cravath or Sullivan & Cromwell sometimes recruited young Jewish graduates of the top Ivy League law schools as junior staff members. But they almost never granted partnership status to Jewish lawyers no matter how great their contribution to the firm; indeed, in at least one case with which I am personally familiar, the partners in a prestigious Manhattan law factory allowed an outstandingly able Jewish associate to be hired away by a corporate client rather than admit him to their company. Yet even so, Jewish Americans were better treated than other "ethnics"; as Mario Cuomo was so embittered to discover, the top New York firms did not recruit at all among Italian Americans or any of the other graduates of the "local" law schools primarily attended by ambitious first- and second-generation Americans.

The first of these barriers to crumble was the one that reserved partnerships for WASPs. In an interview that I had with her in the summer of 1986, Helene Kaplan, herself a partner in the Manhattan-based firm of Webster Sheffield and the wife of a partner in Skadden Arps Slate Meagher & Flom, declared that it was at the beginning of the 1960s that the new openness began to be visible. Back then, she recalled, "we used to know who was the first person to become a Jewish partner in any firm . . . It used to be a very compelling subject at cocktail and dinner parties." Then, with a faint smile, she added, "But it is no longer."

Understandably not. By the second half of the 1980s Jewish partners had become so commonplace in the blue ribbon law firms of New York, Los Angeles, Chicago, and Washington that any attempt to compile a list of them would be impossibly tedious. Meantime, in terms of

---

* Among the first notable exceptions to this rule was the high-powered firm of Paul Weiss Rifkind Wharton & Garrison, whose Chicago office was for a time headed by Adlai Stevenson—a circumstance rendered somewhat ironic by Stevenson's penchant for casual indulgence in anti-Semitic remarks.

recruiting, the barriers against ethnics of any description have also been disappearing—in part because of the interest the major firms now show in law schools they once regarded as unworthy of their attention. "I would say that this is something which has developed in the past five to seven years," Kaplan told me. "But the days when you went to just the Ivy League schools are completely gone now. You may not want to go below the fifth-ranking person at Brooklyn Law School, but by golly, you'll look at those first five and make offers to them—and you may not get them because you can be sure that Cravath and Sullivan Cromwell are doing the same. If Mario Cuomo were number one in his class at St. John's today, I think he could have a shot at any firm in this city."

Though it may smack a bit of Pollyanna, it is possible to see all this as the silver lining in what many people regard as a very dark cloud indeed—namely, the enormous and seemingly uncontrollable growth of the American appetite for litigation. For while she concedes that the increased ethnic diversity of law firms is in some degree a response to that of corporate America in general, Helene Kaplan argues that the change in their recruiting practice primarily reflects "a boom in the law business." Because of that boom, she says, law firms have such "desperate need for bright, talented people that . . . it's very much of a seller's market." And in this intense competition for talent it does not pay to be concerned with where the seller's father or grandfather came from, or what, if any, religious faith he or she professes.

SOME OF THE STATEMENTS I have made about contemporary American business might seem to imply that entrepreneurs and the hired guns of corporate America—salaried executives, lawyers, etc.—should be regarded as unrelated breeds. But that, of course, is not the case. The nature of corporate life in the United States has repeatedly been shaped by entrepreneurial individuals—men such as Commodore Vanderbilt, John D. Rockefeller, Henry Ford, and Thomas Watson. And almost certainly the most significant clues to the socioeconomic character of American business in the future are to be found in the activities of an extraordinary group of men who straddle the entrepreneurial and entrenched corporate worlds—the corporate raiders and takeover tycoons whose names now loom larger in the nation's business pages than those of the chairmen of General Motors, IBM, or Exxon.

No one, I think, can yet predict with assurance how constructive the impact that these men are having on American business will ultimately prove to be. Undeniably, the knowledge that no corporation, however well established, is immune to the threat of takeover has forced established managements to pay greater attention to the interests of their stockholders. And by demonstrating that it can be hugely profitable to dismember conglomerates composed of essentially unrelated businesses, the takeover artists have dealt a salutary blow to the diversification mania of the 1960s and 1970s—a trend that clearly tended to impair the manageability and competitiveness of many enterprises. But at the same time, it is hard to rebut critics of the takeover game when they argue that it has forced corporate managers to pay more attention to financial manipulation than to their basic business and has further intensified the emphasis on short-term profits that often puts American companies at a disadvantage in their competition with more patient Japanese rivals.

All of these, in my view, are arguments that possess at least some degree of validity. But there is another factor that, although seldom publicly voiced, clearly colors the attitude of those who most strongly oppose corporate raiding and the current wave of takeovers. This is the notion that the leading practitioners of these activities are ruthless outsiders who do not play by the traditional rules of the economic establishment and must hence be regarded as an essentially destructive element.

So far as the first part of that charge goes, there can be little argument. Its validity is, I think, adequately established by the following facts:

- Though he must certainly be accounted a WASP, the dean of corporate raiders, Mesa Petroleum's T. Boone Pickens, never loses a chance to dramatize his persona as a plain-talking country boy engaged in populist battle against an effete elite.
- Carl Icahn, who cleared $100 million on just two of his numerous corporate raids and along the way re-

stored Trans World Airlines to economic health, is
the son of a cantor from Queens, an area that vies
with Staten Island for the title of New York City's
most unrelievedly lower-middle-class borough.
· Frank Lorenzo, who put together the nation's largest
air carrier by means of a series of takeovers conducted within the space of just two years, is the son
of immigrants from Spain and emphasizes his ethnic
origin by listing his given name in *Who's Who* as
"Francisco."
· Irwin Jacobs, the perpetrator of multimillion-dollar
raids against such corporations as Disney, ITT, and
Phillips Petroleum, remedied what he saw as a serious shortcoming in the swank Minnesota suburb
where he resides by opening "a classic New York
deli" there.

None of these gentlemen—nor very many of their peers—can
legitimately be described as products of privilege, and none of them
seems to conduct his business affairs with the public weal as his paramount concern. But it is worth recalling that in their own time Cornelius Vanderbilt, the first John D. Rockefeller, and the first Henry Ford
were all also regarded—and rightly so—as ruthless outsiders. Yet the
enormous fortunes they built have made their descendants accepted
members of the country's social and economic elite. More important,
all three of them, devoid of altruism as they were, set loose forces that
helped to produce an economy upon which the prosperity of the entire
world now depends.

It is not, I think, unreasonable to anticipate that in the end the
historic role of today's multiethnic fortune-builders will turn out to be
very similar to that of their spiritual predecessors. What's more, I think
it entirely probable that a generation or two hence the descendants of
the corporate raiders of the 1980s will be intermarrying with those of
nineteenth century tycoons and staring down with disdain from their
seats of privilege upon whatever new crop of outsiders happens to be
reshaping American business by then.

6
ABOVE
THE BOTTOM LINE

In 1980 when George Bush re-
signed from New York's Council on Foreign Relations amid a
well-orchestrated flurry of publicity, his motivation was painfully transparent. In an effort to dispel the aura of elitism that clouded his presidential ambitions, he had decided to pander to a common populist
obsession: the belief that there is a nexus of power in the United States
that is even less responsive to the public will than big government or
big business. As devotees of this theory see things, vast and unhealthy
influence over the nation's affairs is exercised by a network of institutions that like to describe themselves as "not for profit"—which,
among other things, means that they are not, in fact, directly answer-
able either to stockholders or any general electorate.

In its more extreme form, this populist notion is simply another
conspiracy theory of history and reflects nothing more than the political
paranoia of its proponents: those who asserted that Jimmy Carter sur-
rendered control of the U.S. to the Trilateral Commission when he
gave sixteen of its members jobs in his administration credited that

high-minded but diffuse organization with a purposefulness that it conspicuously lacks. And the not dissimilar complaint that the great foundations constitute a kind of law unto themselves was clearly belied by the rapidity with which Washington cracked down when, in the 1960s, McGeorge Bundy showed signs of transforming the Ford Foundation into a kind of Camelot-in-exile for erstwhile Kennedy courtiers.

Nonetheless, it is not just paranoids who ascribe undue influence to the not-for-profit sector. More nuanced and moderate versions of that view enjoy the support of perfectly reputable intellectuals and academics. In a revision of his book *Who Rules America?* published in 1985, Prof. G. William Domhoff of the University of California at Santa Cruz declared: "Corporations and corporate leaders finance and direct a network of tax-free foundations, policy-discussion groups, think tanks, and other organizations that formulate policy alternatives and attempt to shape the social and political climate. The leaders of these groups, along with men and women active in high-level positions in the corporate community, are the core of the power elite that is the leadership group for the upper class as a whole."

Along with many like-minded observers, Domhoff to my way of thinking overemphasizes—at least by implication—the manipulative nature of this country's not-for-profit institutions. From the start of our history, successful Americans have shown a stronger inclination than most national elites to see in their personal good fortune an obligation to contribute in some manner to the general welfare. To ignore or minimize the role that disinterested altruism has played in the extraordinary proliferation of American institutions avowedly dedicated to advancing the public interest in one way or another seems to me not only unduly cynical but misleading as well. To argue, for example, that the Rockefeller Foundation was primarily concerned with the welfare of privileged Americans when it promoted the "green revolution" in Third World agriculture involves more than misreading a particular situation; it requires the employment of logic and semantics so fundamentally distorted as to rule out rational analysis of public affairs in general.

Yet it would be equally foolish to pretend that altruism is the sole or even the decisive motivation of many movers and shakers in America's not-for-profit sector. As often as not, I am convinced, there is also a substantial measure of calculation at work—not so much in terms of class interests as of purely personal ones. For anyone who wishes to win full acceptance as a member of the American Establishment, financial success is not enough; it must be reinforced by demonstrations of public spirit and the achievement of leadership positions in what are generally considered worthy public enterprises. In one of its more transparent manifestations, this reality is embodied in the persistence of lavish charity balls; the management of such affairs is a time-honored device through which the wives of the nouveaux riches improve their social status. On a more substantial level, the search for status also helps to explain why busy men and women of affairs are prepared to devote so much time and energy to service on the boards of hospitals, universities, museums, foundations, public policy groups, and the like.

But it is more than a yearning for caste marks that underlies the attraction for the titans and would-be titans of corporate America of what are sometimes rather pompously described as *pro bono* activities; such activities have a very practical utility as well. Specifically, they open the way to a degree of influence over political and social affairs that financial power alone can never ensure.

A recent demonstration of this is provided by the role that Edgar Bronfman, the Canadian-born chairman of Seagram, played in helping to visit well-merited international obloquy upon former United Nations secretary general Kurt Waldheim. Intelligent, tough, and the possessor of a great inherited fortune, Bronfman is one of the heavyweights of the American business world; besides being top dog at the nation's largest liquor company, he has a major voice in the management of du Pont, nearly a quarter of whose shares were held by Seagram as of 1986. But it was not any of this that led the media to give such prominent attention to his denunciations of Waldheim; it was the fact that he was at the time president of the World Jewish Congress—and that, in turn, was in keeping with Bronfman's long history of involvement in not-for-profit bodies ranging from the Council on Foreign Relations to the United Negro College Fund and the Salk Institute for Biological Studies.

A second great practical benefit of participation in not-for-profit organizations lies in the cross-fertilization between the economic and intellectual establishments that they promote. For businessmen such participation offers not only exposure to new ideas but the opportunity to identify academics, journalists, and other cerebral types who possess the potential to play active—or at least advisory—roles in the world of affairs. The opposite side of this coin, of course, is that talented and ambitious idea-manipulators find in the not-for-profit sector access routes to psychologically and financially rewarding niches in the governmental and corporate worlds.

To anyone who regards the existing order in the United States as fundamentally deplorable, the interaction I have just been describing will certainly seem to boil down to the co-optation and corruption of the intelligentsia by the vested interests. Yet so far as I can see, there is nothing inherently sinister in it—and a total absence of cross-fertilization between the country's economic and intellectual elites would be far greater cause for concern.

Still, it is impossible to deny that for those who labor in the not-for-profit vineyards the indirect rewards of virtue frequently include enhanced career prospects and improved financial status. Government appointments, handsome fees for consulting services, corporate directorships that may pay $20,000 a year or more apiece for a limited investment of time and energy—these and other tangible benefits are potential by-products of the prestige and contacts that can be acquired through participation in the activity of foundations, policy discussion groups, and the like. Just how tangible these benefits can be, in fact, is made apparent by the case histories of some especially active and able fixtures of the not-for-profit universe. Items:

- A native of Omaha, Martha Redfield Wallace was educated at Wellesley and the Fletcher School of Diplomacy. After a brief stint as an instructor in economics at Tufts, she became successively an economist for the Department of State, an editor of *Fortune*, assistant director of corporate development at Time Inc., and director of the Henry Luce Foundation. After sixteen years with the Luce Foundation, during which time she was active in the affairs of a dozen other not-for-profit groups ranging from the Council on Foreign Relations to the New York Racing Association, Ms.

Wallace launched her own management consulting firm in 1983. As of 1986, she was on the board of directors of American Can, American Express, Bristol-Myers, and the Chemical New York Corporation. (In earlier years she was also a director of the New York Telephone Co. and the New York Stock Exchange.)

· With a B.A. from Harvard, an M.A. from Johns Hopkins, and a Ph.D. from the University of Michigan, Boston-born Clifton Wharton first made a name for himself running research programs on agricultural economics—which helps to explain the fact that he sat for seventeen years on the board of trustees of the Rockefeller Foundation. In 1978, after a successful stint as president of the University of Michigan, Dr. Wharton was named chancellor of the State University of New York. But despite the burdens of administering the sprawling SUNY system (from which he retired in 1986), he continued to find time for service with a clutch of not-for-profits, which, in addition to the Rockefeller Foundation, included the Council on Foreign Relations, the Asia Society, the Aspen Institute, and the Carnegie Foundation. As of 1986, Wharton was a director of the Ford Motor Co., Time Inc., Federated Department Stores, and the Federal Reserve Bank of New York. (He is also a former director of Equitable Life and the Burroughs Corp.) That same year he was named chairman and chief executive officer of TIAA-CREF, the mammoth pension system that handles the retirement funds of most professional educators. His reported salary in that position: $500,000 a year.

A product of Columbia University and the Yale Law School, Franklin Thomas started out as an attorney for the Federal Housing and Home Finance Agency and first moved into the not-for-profit sector in 1967 when he became director of Brooklyn's Bedford-

Stuyvesant Restoration Corp. In this capacity he was thrust into intimate contact with the Ford Foundation and so impressed its board that in 1979 he was tapped to head that giant of the philanthropic world. As of 1986, Thomas was a director of Citicorp/Citibank, CBS, the Aluminum Co. of America, Allied Stores Corp., and Cummins Engine Co. His reported salary at the Ford Foundation: $250,000 a year.

THE FACT THAT one of the subjects of these thumbnail sketches is a woman and the other two are black is obviously no happenstance. Rather, it is intended to cast into bold relief a phenomenon that has come into full flower only in the last fifteen years: the opening up of leadership roles in the most prestigious nonprofit organizations to women and to non-WASPs of every description. But impressive as the records of Ms. Wallace and Messrs. Thomas and Wharton are, they do not, I think, constitute the most potent evidence of the ability "minorities" now have to penetrate and capitalize upon this particular locus of power. For that, one must turn again to the career of Henry Kissinger.

Clearly it requires uncommon talent and drive for a Jewish immigrant burdened with a pronounced accent and an unimpressive physical presence to attain the highest rungs of the American Establishment —and equally clearly Henry Kissinger possesses those requisites in abundance. But he also possesses another important attribute as well: uncommon skill at showcasing his abilities where it counts.

In 1955, on the strength of the outstanding academic reputation he had won as a member of the Harvard faculty, Kissinger was chosen by the Council on Foreign Relations to direct one of its prestigious study programs, and it was under CFR auspices that he published two years later his much-praised book on post-Napoleonic diplomacy, *A World Restored*. Given his own ambition and the close involvement with the CFR of David Rockefeller, all this helped to propel Kissinger into the Rockefeller orbit—first as director of a special studies program for the Rockefeller Brothers Fund and later as an adviser on international affairs to Nelson Rockefeller. And when in the so-called Treaty of Morningside Heights, Governor Rockefeller conceded the 1968 Republican nomination to Richard Nixon, the victor's spoils included, fittingly enough, Henry Kissinger.

It would be unpardonable hyperbole to claim that Kissinger's association with the CFR was directly responsible for his ultimate rise to power—and thus for the fact that his income as a business consultant is now adequate to maintain an apartment in one of Manhattan's swankest residential buildings, a country home in the fashionable precincts of northwestern Connecticut, and a personal security apparatus that at one time was rumored to cost him upward of $250,000 a year. But at the very least the visibility afforded him by the Council helped to fasten the attention of influential people upon him and won him access to circles that a generation earlier would almost surely have been closed to someone of his background.

I do not wish to put excessive weight on Kissinger as a symbolic figure. Certainly his present exalted status does reflect a major evolution in the nature of the self-perpetuating elite that manages the least accountable of the major power complexes in this country. But one career alone cannot provide the answers to some questions inevitably raised by the change in the ethnic composition of that elite—such as when and how did that change occur and what if any difference has it made in the functioning of the institutions involved. To find those answers requires a closer look at each of the component sectors of the not-for-profit universe.

NO ONE can honestly claim that the remarkable readiness of Americans to underwrite private institutions designed to meet public needs is a trait that has chiefly been confined to wealthy WASPs. Hospitals supported by funds largely raised among Jewish and Catholic Americans have a long history, and the tide of Eastern European Jews that flowed into this country in the late nineteenth century inspired the members of the already established German-Jewish community to create an extensive network of philanthropic bodies and service agencies to assist the newcomers. In the twentieth century, non-WASPs as well as WASPs have contributed to the proliferation of small to medium-sized family foundations, and they have also played a prominent role in the creation and financing of cultural and educational institutions.

Partly because of their importance as donors and partly for other reasons with which I shall deal later on, non-WASPs have long found some sectors of the not-for-profit world available to them as vehicles of upward social mobility. But traditionally that was emphatically not the case with the most highly endowed, publicly visible, and eagerly courted of American philanthropic institutions. In his book *The Big Foundations*, which was published in 1972, Waldemar Nielsen, an astute observer of the foundation scene as well as a prominent participant in it, bluntly declared: "Those seldom included on the boards of the big foundations include young people, females, nonwhites, Catholics, Jews, Democrats, and persons whose forebears came from such places as Ireland, Italy, Greece, or Poland."

As I have already suggested, it would be a great mistake to conclude from the state of affairs Nielsen was describing that even at that time the big foundations served essentially as associations for the advancement of WASPdom. On the contrary, it is doubtful that any major nonprofit organization in America has ever pursued programs more subversive of narrowly conceived WASP interests than the Ford Foundation did under the leadership of McGeorge Bundy. To all appearances, Bundy himself is an exemplar of the WASP aristocracy in its most intimidating form, a man whose undeniable brilliance is reinforced by an inbred sense of social and moral assurance. Yet it was under the aegis of this cool Yankee patrician that executives of the Ford Foundation in a 1975 memo to the trustees described its purpose as "the redress of inequity" and the achievement of "a juster distribution of the material and nonmaterial things that society prizes most."

But in all of this—even in such antiestablishment activities as the Ford Foundation's successful drive to win racial minorities a greater voice in the management of New York City's public school system—there were unmistakable overtones of benevolence from the big house on the hill. For in the innermost citadels of philanthropic power—at the Rockefeller, Ford, Carnegie, Sloan, and Russell Sage foundations —the authority to decide what programs would best serve the common good remained in the last analysis in the hands of male WASPs. And this, in turn, meant that as a general rule women and ethnics did not get the benefit of the influence and status conferred by the exercise of that power.

Yet unshakable as the grip of the male WASP on the great foundations long appeared to be, it was already beginning to slip at the time Nielsen drew public attention to it. In fact, if he had written his book as little as a decade later, Nielsen would have been obliged to offer a radically different description of the ethnic and sexual composition of foundation boards.

The most conspicuous example of the changes that swept the foundation world during the course of the 1970s was one to which I have already alluded: the election of black lawyer Franklin Thomas to succeed Bundy as operating head of the Ford Foundation. But in reality that was no more than a straw in the wind. For as of 1985, Ford's board of trustees numbered among its sixteen members people of Hispanic and Italian ancestry (Rodrigo Botero and A. Bartlett Giamatti), a black (former U.S. ambassador to the U.N. Donald McHenry), a Jewish industrialist (Irving Shapiro), and two women (Nina Garsoian and lawyer-educator Harriet Rabb).

By that time, moreover, Ford was no longer a bell-wether so far as the diversity of its trustees was concerned. At the Carnegie Corporation of New York the board was chaired by Manhattan lawyer Helene Kaplan (who was simultaneously chairman of the trustees of Barnard College) and included two other women as well as males bearing such "ethnic" surnames as Arcienaga, deLeon, Hechinger, and Lederburg. As of 1985, too, self-made tycoon Mortimer Zuckerman and educator Carl Kaysen sat on the board of the Russell Sage Foundation. At Chicago's MacArthur Foundation, which although established only in 1970 had captured public imagination with its "genius grants," the ten board members included no fewer than four Jewish Americans: physicist Murray Gell-mann, Dr. Jonas Salk, former University of Chicago president Edward Levi, and former presidential science adviser Jerome Wiesner.

In the eyes of many foundation-watchers, though, the most conclusive evidence of the new order was to be found at the Rockefeller Foundation. Old as foundations go (it was launched in 1913) and lavishly endowed (its assets at last report totaled $1.8 billion), Rockefeller was for the first half-century and more of its existence the quintessential symbol of WASP philanthropy. Yet by 1985 its board was chaired by a black—Clifton Wharton—and among its other active or recently active trustees were Father Theodore Hesburgh, former Urban League leader Vernon Jordan, industrialists Victor Palmieri and W. Michael Blumenthal, and Austrian-born cancer researcher Mathilde Krim. And in mid-1987 when Wharton retired from the board and four new trustees were named, those elected were author Frances Fitzgerald, educator Alice Stone Ilchman, Jewish-American businessman Arthur Levitt, Jr., and Canadian public health specialist John R. Evans (who succeeded Wharton as chairman).

What occurred between roughly 1970 and 1985, in short, amounted to a major transformation of the nation's philanthropic general staff—and a development of that magnitude clearly had to have profound causes. Carnegie's Helene Kaplan, for one, is persuaded that in this instance the basic explanation is to be found in the powerful new social currents that swept America in the 1960s: the civil rights movement, the beginning of the women's movement, and the general assault on traditional authority fueled by the Vietnam War. All these forces, she believes, conspired to open up American society in an unprecedented manner and to an unprecedented degree—and what happened in the nonprofit sector was "a kind of dribble-down effect."

That there was such a dribble-down effect on the foundation world will strike most Americans as only natural; unconsciously, we tend to assume that changes in the general society inevitably meet with more or less graceful accommodation by the elite. But to make that assumption is to ignore a characteristic of the American elite that is not invariably displayed by ruling groups. In their book *The American Establishment* Leonard and Mark Silk stated the matter this way: "The Establishment . . . knows that in a liberal society the best means to exclusivity is the maximum possible inclusivity. If other sects and sectarian tendencies can be co-opted, then you become the only game in town."

A somewhat more charitable way to express essentially the same point is that the traditional elites of the foundation world chose to put the vitality of the institutions they cherished ahead of their own narrow self-interest. And it was nothing less than the continued effectiveness of those institutions that was at stake. For in recent times, as Helene Kaplan points out, philanthropic activity in the United States has been heavily affected by three interacting developments. One of these has been a magnification of U.S. social problems, particularly those reflected in the emergence of a seemingly permanent underclass. Another has been a shrinkage in some of the resources traditionally available to the nongovernmental institutions that seek to ameliorate our social problems. And the third of these interrelated developments has been the exponential growth in the number of non-WASPs who command positions of economic power.

Occurring as they did more or less in concert, these three factors confronted the major foundations—and all other nonprofit organizations for that matter—with a situation in which the circles from which they traditionally recruited their leadership had from a purely pragmatic point of view become excessively restricted. And in purely pragmatic response, as Kaplan observed to me in mid-1986, the great philanthropic institutions began to display "greater receptivity to people who might have wealth but not old school ties or the 'right' ethnic background . . . Between cutbacks in government support and increased needs, such people became more acceptable because of their ability to bring to these boards various kinds of resources—and also connections in the business world."

On the face of things, it would seem logical to think that, in addition to money and useful connections, the new species of trustee might also bring to foundation boards social concerns and concepts of what constitutes effective philanthropic action somewhat different from those of the traditional elite. And here the potential effect on the nation's intellectual climate as well as on its approach to specific societal problems would be hard to exaggerate. For in addition to helping set the public agenda by means of the action programs that they choose to underwrite or manage, the foundations also do so through their choice of the scholars, writers, and researchers to whom they choose to give grants.*

In practice, however, it is extremely hard to determine how much effect the new diversity of their boards has actually had on the institu-

---

* Anyone who questions the impact of foundation predilections upon intellectual activity in the United States could profitably visit the college library in which I am writing these words. Here, on four different occasions in the space of ten days, I have spotted scholarly-looking individuals intently poring over *The Directory of American Foundations* and a variety of instruction manuals on the preparation of successful grant requests.

---

tional behavior of the big foundations. Quite clearly, it has helped to produce a similar diversity among the people who actually administer foundation activities; women and minority group members are notably more numerous on foundation staffs now than they were in the early 1970s. But insofar as the kind of program undertaken by the foundations has changed, few people seem prepared to argue that the credit —or blame—can be primarily ascribed to the changes in the leadership group. "I don't really know if you can make that kind of generalization," says Helene Kaplan. "I think that as one deals with problems such as those which focus on the underclass, the ghettos, and new immigrants, many prejudices and stereotypical views break down— and I would think that this in itself has led to an opening up on every level including the staff level. But it's sort of a chicken-and-egg phenomenon."

With less of a bow to judiciousness, at least one veteran of the foundation world—who understandably insists on anonymity—bluntly argues that in some cases ethnic diversification has actually diminished the innovativeness of major foundations. "Look at Ford," he says. "Mac Bundy could gamble because in the ultimate sense he was personally secure; if he got turfed out, he could always go up to Maine and sail. But Frank Thomas, lacking that kind of security, is far more cautious and careful to protect his flanks than Bundy was."

Somewhat sadly since he was an early proponent of it, this same observer asserts that on occasion ethnic diversification has had another negative consequence. "Too often," he says, "ethnic trustees have proved to be single-issue folks who weren't interested in much beside logrolling for their own groups. Certainly WASP trustees have always done their fair share of logrolling, too—John McCloy for Amherst, for example, and Cy Vance for Yale. But they didn't do so obstructively, whereas under the new dispensation logrolling has sometimes reached such proportions that it has greatly reduced the efficiency of particular boards."

To this man's way of thinking, in fact, Helene Kaplan's Carnegie "is the only big foundation where the board's operations have actually been improved by diversification." And along with that judgment he offers another: "In general, the ethnic factor has been less meaningful than the sexual one; the work of women who have achieved real status in the foundation world *has* made a difference."

BECAUSE THE American Establishment essentially consists of a self-perpetuating set of interlocking directorates, it is virtually certain that anyone who serves on the board of a major foundation will also turn out to be a luminary of another key sector of the not-for-profit universe: the one made up of what are sometimes referred to as policy discussion groups.

In reality, the phrase "discussion group" considerably understates the role of these bodies: a number of them conduct ambitious research and study programs, publish or sponsor the publication of periodicals and books, engage in a variety of educational activities, and provide public figures with platforms from which to launch trial balloons. And all of them, in greater or lesser degree, help to shape whatever social, political, and economic consensus prevails in the Establishment at any given time.

At least in theory, however, the central function of these organizations is to furnish a neutral ground for informed discussion of policy alternatives by their members. And whatever special interest anyone may have, there is bound to be at least one policy discussion group that focuses on it. If you are particularly concerned with Japanese-American relations, the Japan Society is clearly the place for you, but if your concern is with the Far East in general, the Asia Society is the ticket —and for the Eurocentric there's the Atlantic Council. To cover the full range of international affairs, of course, one can turn to the Council on Foreign Relations or the Foreign Policy Association. Economic policy and other issues of special concern to the corporate community are the particular province of the Conference Board and the Committee for Economic Development. And so it goes down a list that is so long and composed of organizations so varied in the networking opportunities they afford that those who enjoy elite status or are in the process of acquiring it frequently feel compelled to participate in several of them.

For a considerable period the splashiest of all these organizations and the one that made the least bones about serving the networking function was the Aspen Institute for Humanistic Studies. Originally—

and somewhat improbably—launched in the fashionable resort town of Aspen, Colorado, by a group of Goethe enthusiasts, this unique body in its glory days resembled nothing so much as an elitist Chautauqua —a kind of international six-ring circus for grown-ups.

In the late 1970s when I was briefly involved in its activities,* the board chairman of the Aspen Institute was Robert O. Anderson, the soft-spoken but notably self-assured oil industry tycoon who founded Arco. And the fact that a central location at the Institute's Colorado "campus" was graced by a life-sized bust of Anderson was scarcely surprising. For in addition to lending Aspen his considerable prestige in the business world, Anderson funneled substantial amounts of money into the organization through Arco and even provided the Institute's headquarters staff with Arco-controlled office space in New York.

Important as Anderson's role was, however, the Institute's real moving spirit at that time was its president, an ebullient, fast-talking economist named Joseph Slater. Probably the most ingenious intellectual impresario the not-for-profit community in the United States has yet produced, Joe Slater bounced from one ambitious project to another with startling rapidity, indefatigable enterprise and the cool nerve of a highwire artist. Starting off as an aide to John McCloy during McCloy's years as U.S. proconsul in occupied Germany, Slater had developed an extraordinary range of interests and information—and even more important, an extraordinary range of acquaintances in the American Establishment. Under his restless, driving leadership, the Aspen Institute became the most ubiquitous of the nation's policy discussion groups. With permanent installations in Washington, D.C.,

---

* By long-standing tradition, members of Britain's House of Commons are expected to "declare an interest" when dealing with issues in which they have a personal stake. In keeping with that useful principle, I feel obliged to note here that for something over a year I was employed by the Aspen Institute to run a Mideast program underwritten by California's Fluor Corporation. In that capacity I organized a series of seminars on Islamic history and Middle Eastern affairs, perhaps the most memorable of which was held on the island of Hawaii. At first blush Hawaii may seem an odd vantage point from which to survey the Islamic world, but as experienced seminar planners pointed out to me at the time, even the most eminent invitees are likely to find that a midwinter meeting in Hawaii fits more conveniently into their schedules than one held, say, in Manhattan.

Maryland, Hawaii, and West Berlin as well as in New York and Colorado, it sponsored a bewildering array of programs dealing with everything from monotheism to arms control and periodically sent task
forces out to pursue enlightenment all the way from Teheran to Tokyo.

For a number of years all of this activity climaxed each summer in
a kind of Rocky Mountain high at Aspen where the Institute not only
possessed an elaborate conference center but operated its own hotel as
well. There, under the management of the Institute staff, which moved
to Colorado from New York virtually en masse for the summer months,
a curious sort of status-based camaraderie was cultivated.

By far the largest number of participants in these gatherings were
business executives whose companies deemed it worthwhile to treat
them to one of a series of pricey two-week "refresher courses" in which
Mortimer Adler and other certified intellectuals conducted Socratic
dialogues on the great ideas of Western civilization. But also on hand
at any given moment were members of a large and constantly changing
cast of prominent Americans and foreigners drawn from the ranks of
almost every conceivable sphere of human activity.

My own memories of the summer I spent at Aspen, in fact, consist
essentially of a kaleidoscopic blur of encounters with notables: Henry
Kissinger, Robert McNamara, Itzhak Perlman, John Gardner, Danny
Kaye, TV correspondents Marvin Kalb and Daniel Schorr, Sen. Jacob
Javits, former SEC chief Harold Williams, Chicago banker Gaylord
Freeman, columnist Joseph Kraft, pollster Daniel Yankelovitch, then
treasury secretary W. Michael Blumenthal, Urban League leader Victor Jordan, former Pan American Airways chairman (and father-in-law
to the King of Jordan) Najeeb Halaby, former ambassador to Japan
Robert Ingersoll, former British cabinet member Shirley Williams—
and, most unforgettable of all, a portly onetime Egyptian foreign minister whom I shall always admire for the aplomb he displayed when his
trousers fell down around his ankles as a result of his overvigorous
participation in the staging of an excerpt from one of the plays of
Aristophanes.

As this last incident suggests, life at Aspen's summer camp for
the successful had its lighter moments—and by no means all of them
were inadvertent. It was, in fact, difficult to avoid the unworthy suspicion that some of the more eminent campers—who generally attended

at the Institute's expense—had been attracted less by a taste for high thinking than by the opportunity to rub shoulders with their peers on the tennis courts and river rafting trips or at the cocktail parties, musical performances, mountaintop picnics, and other diversions for which the Rockies provided a glorious physical backdrop. Nonetheless, all of them dutifully sang for their supper, sometimes by delivering one of the nightly lectures that all Aspenites were expected to attend, but more often by gracing with their presence one of the numerous Institute seminars that might deal with anything from the Japanese economy to a somewhat amorphous concept that Joe Slater liked to describe as "governance." And a considerable number of the superstars, including Henry Kissinger, had a permanent advisory affiliation with the Institute that involved them in some of the manifold programs it conducted in less glamorous surroundings during the rest of the year.

Like most such organizations, Aspen used the ideas generated at its countless brainstorming sessions as the raw material for a continuing stream of papers and policy proposals on matters of undeniable importance. Yet at least in part because the Institute has never had any clear central focus, it is questionable how much impact its deliberations have actually had upon either public opinion or governmental behavior. Even in Aspen's heyday one disillusioned alumnus declared that it reminded him of the classic description of the Powder River— "a mile wide and an inch deep." And in recent years the Institute's operations have become considerably less ambitious: Joe Slater has departed, the real focus of Institute activities has shifted from Colorado and New York to Wye Plantation in Maryland, its international ventures have diminished, and a number of its programs have been abandoned for lack of adequate financing.

Still, to argue that the Aspen Institute was never anything more than a collective ego trip would be to misread the way in which the upper echelon of American society functions. However minimal its direct impact on national policy may have been, Aspen has clearly had an indirect impact of some significance by promoting interaction among the members of the nation's various occupational and professional elites. Even more important, the premium that it placed upon personal achievement and power rather than upon ethnicity in its recruitment of members made it an early harbinger of the progressive de-WASPification of the American Establishment.

DESPITE ALL THE CACHET Joe Slater succeeded in winning for the Aspen Institute, it is nonetheless doubtful that that organization would ever have been the first choice of a shrewd elitist who found himself obliged by some malign fate to settle for membership in just one policy discussion group. For, as Leonard Silk proclaimed in *The American Establishment*, if one wishes to hobnob with that potent confraternity "in its purest form," then "the Council on Foreign Relations is the place."

Simply in physical terms, in fact, the CFR bears the unmistakable stamp of the Establishment. Housed in a stately old mansion at the corner of Park Avenue and East 68th Street in Manhattan, the Council boasts huge, high-ceilinged public rooms decorated in the solidly opulent style of a good men's club and hung with portraits of past leaders bearing names such as Hamilton Fish Armstrong, Bayless Manning, and Winston Lord. From the ground floor a broad, semicircular marble staircase leads impressively to what was once obviously a ballroom and now serves as a meeting room in which statesmen from all over the world make their pitch to blue ribbon audiences.

That the audience will on any occasion be an impressive and challenging one is assured by the makeup of the Council's 1,800 members. In a study he made of the CFR membership list for 1978–79, sociologist G. William Domhoff found that 70 percent of the one hundred biggest U.S. industrial enterprises had at least one officer or director who was a Council member, as did twenty-one of the nation's twenty-five biggest banks and sixteen of its twenty-five largest insurance companies. And to reinforce the potent delegation from the business and financial communities, the Council's roster abounds with leading figures from journalism, academia, the law, and government.

To the Council's credit, its general membership, although restricted to American citizens, includes a substantial number of women and has long been thoroughly diverse ethnically. Until the early 1970s, however, its leadership was in fact though not in theory essentially chosen by a controlling oligarchy composed almost exclusively of male WASPs. And when a committee (on which I served) was charged with democratizing the institution's electoral process, the changes that it managed to agree upon were so modest that I concluded they would have little real effect. But that proved an excessively pessimistic forecast. By early 1986, in fact, people of "minority" background—three women, five Jews, two blacks, two Greek Americans, and one Italian American—made up half of the Council's Board of Directors.

Even more notable has been a development to which I referred at the very beginning of this book—the ethnic change that occurred in 1985 in what might be called the CFR's public face. To be sure, the election of Greek-American Peter Peterson to the chairmanship of the Council and of Jewish-American Peter Tarnoff to its presidency in no way marked any departure from the traditional elitism of the CFR. Peterson, after all, had been successively the CEO of a major corporation (Bell & Howell), a cabinet member in a Republican administration, and chairman of one of the country's most prestigious investment banking houses. As for Tarnoff, he is a personable, incisive ex–Foreign Service officer whose choice to head the Council's sizable permanent staff was obviously at least partly inspired by the fact that he had served as special assistant to longtime CFR power Cyrus Vance when the latter was secretary of state.*

All that being conceded, however, the fact remains that two of the most conspicuous positions in what is sometimes rather grandly described as "the foreign policy community" are now occupied by men whom that community would have regarded as rank outsiders only a generation ago. And that marks a change that cannot be shrugged off as insignificant. For unlike the Aspen Institute, the Council on Foreign Relations does have real impact upon the conduct of the nation's affairs. Articles in its weighty periodical *Foreign Affairs* frequently help to establish the terms of debate in Washington, and the findings of the numerous CFR study groups have on more than one occasion contributed to the launching of major new initiatives in American foreign policy. But perhaps most important of all, the Council is less prone

---

* In this respect among others Tarnoff resembles his immediate predecessor as CFR president, Pillsbury heir Winston Lord. Lord, who left the Council to become U.S. ambassador to China, first made his mark in Washington as a protégé of Henry Kissinger.

---

than Aspen and a number of other policy discussion groups to concentrate primarily upon the recruitment of people already at the peak of their careers. Both in its selection of members and its staff appointments, the CFR also seeks out people who are still on the way up, and by so doing it influences the mindset of America's leadership of the future.

For all its preeminence, however, the CFR is by no means unique among policy discussion groups in having become markedly less WASP-dominated in the 1970s and 1980s. Where once they were content simply to be accepted as rank-and-file members, "ethnics" increasingly began to move into leadership roles in these institutions. Thus, over the years since 1970, Isaac Shapiro, a partner in the lofty New York law firm of Milbank Tweed & Hadley, has served as president of the Japan Society, Polish-born Zbigniew Brzezinski as director of the Trilateral Commission, and Greek-American Stephen Stamas as president of The American Assembly, a group established by Dwight Eisenhower while he was president of Columbia.

Quite obviously the widespread admission of non-WASPs to positions of influence in the major policy discussion groups coincided, broadly speaking, with a trend toward greater questioning of traditional assumptions on the part of such institutions. This, in turn, makes it tempting to conclude that the first of these developments was responsible for the second. But while it is possible that such a cause-and-effect pattern may actually emerge in the years ahead, it is difficult to establish that it has done so yet. Just as in the case of the big foundations, the transformations that have occurred in the policy discussion groups so far, both in terms of ethnic diversity and receptivity to new ideas, appear to be consequences rather than causes—the result of the changed social, economic, and intellectual circumstances that the turbulent events of the 1960s created in the United States.

OF ALL the various sectors of the not-for-profit community—which could less loftily but no less accurately be described as the tax-exempt community—the one that most clearly reflects the impact of the melting pot upon the American elite may well be the clutch of policy research organizations colloquially known as think tanks. And that impact, judging from the contemporary state of these organizations, has been curiously at variance with some of the assumptions of progressive mythology.

Generally speaking, the people who support and direct the nation's think tanks tend to be drawn from the same interlocking directorate that supplies the leadership of the big foundations and the policy discussion groups. But the think tanks with which an ambitious and influential American chooses to become involved offer an especially reliable indication of his political and economic predispositions. For unlike policy discussion groups that ostensibly exist for the enlightenment of their members, the typical think tank does not bother to recruit a general membership; instead, its operative arm consists of a relatively small number of scholars, analysts, and displaced bureaucrats who seek to achieve a direct and continuing voice in the shaping of governmental policies. And although the more traditional of them indignantly deny that they have any particular political or ideological coloration, nearly all think tanks in reality do.

Yet for all their political overtones, the most highly regarded think tanks do attach genuine importance to scholarship, and presumably for that reason they began to open leadership positions to non-WASPs well before the foundations or even the policy discussion groups generally did. By most people's reckoning, the most prestigious and establishmentarian of the think tanks is still Washington's Brookings Institution, which in its present form dates back to 1927 and whose board of trustees in decades past was graced by such figures as Dean Acheson, Edward Stettinius, Karl Compton, and Vannevar Bush. As early as the 1960s the presidency of Brookings had already been conferred upon the late Kermit Gordon, a handsome and unabashedly patrician economist who happened to be Jewish.* And while chairman of the Brookings board of trustees as of 1986 was a Boston Brahmin named Louis Wellington Cabot, a substantial number of the other members of the board were non-WASPs—among them, two eminent

---

* Those who believe that intelligence is primarily determined by genetics will no doubt be gratified to learn that some years after Gordon became the first Jewish president of Brookings his cousin, Kermit Lansner, became the first Jewish editor in chief of *Newsweek* magazine.

---

blacks: former secretary of transportation William T. Coleman, Jr., and the former U.N. ambassador Donald McHenry.

In all this, however, Brookings is by no means unique among think tanks; in a sense, in fact, "ethnics" have played an even more seminal role in the affairs of the American Enterprise Institute, for many years Brookings' most serious rival for influence. Founded in 1962 by a Lebanese American named William T. Baroody, AEI remained under Baroody management until 1986 when a combination of financial difficulties and loss of political clout prompted the founder's son, William Jr., to resign the presidency of the organization. And throughout its history AEI has been conspicuously indifferent to the ethnicity of its luminaries; though its board as of the end of 1986 was also headed by a pillar of WASPdom, Chase Manhattan Bank chairman Willard C. Butcher, two of the most influential opinion-makers based at the institute during the Reagan years were Jewish Americans: author and columnist Ben Wattenberg and the prolific Herbert Stein, a Brookings alumnus who, like Paul McCracken, served for a time during the Nixon years as chairman of the Council of Economic Advisers.

Along with their mutual indifference to ethnicity, AEI and Brookings have another important attribute in common: the insistence that their stock-in-trade is objective analysis rather than furnishing the rationalizations for preconceived political positions. In practice, that claim has frequently worn extremely thin: during the 1960s Brookings at times appeared to function very much like a planning arm of the Kennedy and Johnson administrations, while AEI, then and in the 1970s, performed essentially the same function for the Republican party. Both institutions, moreover, have made a habit of producing short, punchy publications clearly designed to win maximum media coverage and thereby promote their particular ideological stance. And under the leadership of former Reagan administration official Christopher DeMuth, who assumed its presidency shortly after the downfall of the younger Baroody, the AEI has become rather more unabashedly right-wing both in pronouncements and personnel than it used to be.

Even at their most political, though, both Brookings and AEI have maintained generally high standards of scholarship and intellectual honesty. In their genuflections to objectivity, they have seldom carried things as far as the smaller Carnegie Endowment for International

Peace, which in 1986 dispatched two staff members to testify at congressional hearings on Nicaragua—one to make the case for U.S. aid to the contras and the second to make the case against it. But only on very rare occasions has either Brookings or AEI gone to the other extreme and lapsed into anything resembling active lobbying.

This, for better or for worse, is a posture that became something of a liability to both institutions in the Reagan era. Increasingly they found themselves being upstaged by so-called advocacy think tanks—organizations that were not content simply to generate and disseminate policy ideas but that made determined and unabashed efforts to promote the adoption of their proposals by Congress and the bureaucracy.

In ideological terms, the advocacy tanks run the gamut of what is more or less generally accepted as tolerable political opinion in the United States. By all odds the farthest to the left is the relatively small (1986 budget: $1.8 million) but extremely vocal Institute for Policy Studies. Serving as a bridge between truly radical and merely liberal opinion, IPS was originally sparkplugged by two Jewish Americans, Richard Barnet and Marcus Raskin. But its board is ethnically ecumenical, having included at one time or another an Arab American (former senator James Abourezk), a leading Catholic progressive (author Garry Wills), and a black lawyer and ex-journalist who in 1987 served as chairman of the Pulitzer Prize Board (Roger Wilkins).

Far to the right of IPS but arguably within the great middle band of the political spectrum is Georgetown University's Center for Strategic and International Studies. Somewhere on the borderline between the traditional think tanks and the outright advocacy groups, CSIS began life in 1962 with a markedly conservative cast—so much so that in 1981 its then director, David Abshire, was tapped by incoming president Ronald Reagan to head the "transition team" charged with ensuring that the key levers of bureaucratic power were tranferred to suitable new hands. But in recent years CSIS's conservatism has become both less extreme and less predictable, in part no doubt because the organization became a roost for figures as hopelessly centrist in the eyes of true blue rightists as Henry Kissinger, Zbigniew Brzezinski, and James Schlesinger.

But moderation, at least where rhetoric was concerned, never sold well in the top circles in Ronald Reagan's Washington, and predictably the advocacy tanks that made the biggest splash in the early and mid-1980s were the ones that most religiously adhered to the conservative creed—the most notable of these being California's Hoover Institute on War, Revolution, and Peace and the Washington-based Heritage Foundation once approvingly described by The Great Communicator himself as "that feisty new kid on the conservative block."

An uneasy affiliate of Stanford University, whose predominantly liberal faculty are horridly affronted by the association, the Hoover Institute dates back to 1919 and is thus the granddaddy of all conservative research organizations in this country. During Reagan's quest for the presidency, Hoover in effect served as his brain trust—and it seems fair to say that a preponderance of the most impressive brains on tap there belonged to non-WASPs ranging from black economist Thomas Sowell to Jewish-American sociologist Seymour Martin Lipset. (Other outstanding non-WASPs who have adorned Hoover's seventy-man research roster include economist Milton Friedman, physicist Edward Teller, philosopher Sidney Hook, and historian Bertram Wolfe.)

When Reagan finally reached the White House, Hoover also served him initially as a prime recruiting ground, supplying the new administration with a small army of high-level appointees including its first national security adviser, the ill-fated Richard V. Allen. But as time wore on, Hoover's star declined somewhat in White House circles while that of the shriller and more amply financed Heritage Foundation rose.

Though a Johnny-come-lately to the think tank world—it was launched in 1973 by Colorado beer baron Joseph Coors—Heritage grew at a dazzling pace: by 1986 it boasted a spanking new $10-million headquarters in Washington and a staff of more than one hundred people. More important, it had achieved such clout in the capital that one Washington insider described it to a *Time* reporter as being "for all practical purposes . . . a closer, more integrated part of the Reagan adminstration than, say, the Department of Energy."

Inevitably, some of the older kids on the conservative block looked upon Heritage as a callow upstart, and there could be no denying that its policy analysts were as a group not only far younger but far less distinguished and intellectually impressive than those at the Hoover Institute. But in one respect Heritage did resemble Hoover: its personnel clearly reflected the large non-WASP component of the New Right. Its president during the Reagan years was a Roman Catholic (Edwin Feulner, Jr.), two of its other senior executives (vice president Burton Y. Pines and public relations director Herb Berkowitz) were of Jewish origin, and so were two of its most eminent trustees, Lewis Lehrman and Midge Decter.

In stressing the prominence of non-WASPs at Hoover and Heritage, I don't wish to be seen as implying that the shock troops of conservatism in the present-day United States consist exclusively or even predominantly of "ethnics"; on the contrary, WASPdom is also heavily represented in the movement and supplies probably the lion's share of its financial resources. But what the importance of ethnics in these two organizations does serve to highlight is the fact that the multiethnic character of the new American elite is visible in the leadership of public institutions located at every point along the political spectrum.

As late as the 1960s—perhaps even the early 1970s—it was still possible to argue without fear of concrete disproof that if the descendants of nineteenth and early twentieth century immigration were accorded a fair share of power in this country, the inevitable result would be a general liberalization of American institutions. But in practice the facile equations "WASP = reactionary" and "ethnic = progressive" simply have not been sustained by the developments of the last generation in the not-for-profit world. Rather, judging from such evidence as that world supplies, it seems impossible to establish any consistently reliable connection at all between the ethnicity of members of the American Establishment and their ideological inclinations.

IF THERE IS any single generalization that *can* safely be applied to the contemporary leadership of the not-for-profit world, it is to be found, I think, in a confession made to me by one of the luminaries of the new establishment: "In large measure it's the same old boys club it always was. Except now it involves a different set of boys—and some of the boys are girls."

To say that the new multiethnic elite operates very much like the traditional WASP one is not, however, another way of stating Norman Podhoretz's proposition that its non-WASP members have all transformed themselves into facsimile WASPs. "I don't agree with that at all," says the Carnegie Corporation's Helene Kaplan. "And I could name names—which wouldn't be an attractive thing to do—of people who have certainly maintained their deep [ethnic] qualities." To put the matter even more strongly, the fact that they are unmistakably non-WASP has significantly enhanced demand for the services of some members of the new establishment and is rightly regarded by them as an asset to be capitalized upon rather than something to be concealed or downplayed.

But even when they differ conspicuously from the members of the old elite in manner, the new boys and girls follow the traditional modus operandi of the successful WASP in one central respect: like a John McCloy or a Cyrus Vance, the standouts among them are indefatigable in playing multiple roles in the great American interlocking directorate.

Perhaps the most notable example of this is to be found in the career of the recently retired president of Notre Dame, Father Theodore Hesburgh. The *Who's Who* entry on "Father Ted" for 1986–87 shows that in addition to having served on a clutch of high-powered governmental and private commissions, he has at various times been a member (and generally a trustee) of a round dozen not-for-profit organizations ranging from the Council on Foreign Relations and the Rockefeller Foundation to the United Negro College Fund and the Nutrition Foundation. And almost incredibly, to this mind-boggling list of memberships and affiliations is appended the laconic word "others."

In Father Hesburgh's case, such ubiquitousness might seem a more or less inevitable consequence of the high degree of national visibility he enjoyed as head of an educational institution that enjoys special prestige among a large segment of the population. But résumés very nearly as impressive as his are not uncommon even among members of the new elite who are considerably less well-known to the general public. To cite just two of many examples:

> An economist by training, Greek-American Stephen Stamas is a former Rhodes Scholar who spent twenty-six years with the Exxon Corporation where he wound up as vice president in charge of public affairs. By 1986, when he left Exxon to head The American As-

sembly, the list of nonprofit organizations that Stamas
had served either as an officer or a trustee ran to well
over a dozen and included the Board of Overseers of
Harvard, the New York Philharmonic, the Council on
Foreign Relations, the Atlantic Council of the United
States, the William H. Donner Foundation, and
Rockefeller University.

A native of Washington, D.C., Eleanor Holmes Norton attended the only public high school in the nation's capital that as of the early 1950s offered black
youngsters a college preparatory curriculum. After
graduating from Antioch University and Yale Law
School, she became successively assistant legal director of the American Civil Liberties Union, Commissioner of Human Rights for New York City, and a
professor at Georgetown Law School.* By 1986, Mrs.
Norton was a trustee of both the Rockefeller Foundation and Yale University as well as a director or member of the advisory boards of numerous other
organizations including the National Women's Political Caucus, the National Urban Coalition, and the
Center for National Policy, a Democratic advocacy
tank established in 1981 under the chairmanship of
Cyrus Vance.

That the broadening of the leadership of the nonprofit community
to include people such as this has been a healthy and overdue development in our national life cannot be denied except by bigots and
reactionaries. Yet it also seems clear that, like their predecessors, the
new members of the old-boys net plunge so enthusiastically into the
interlocking directorate game not only out of a dedication to public
service but on the strength of career and status considerations as well.
And while there is nothing ignoble about that fact, it has surely served

---

* In a private capacity she also helped bring about a kind of sexual revolution at *Newsweek* during my years there by helping to negotiate an agreement with management that
opened up meaningful editorial jobs to women employees.

---

to diminish somewhat the impact that the infusion of so much new blood might otherwise have had upon Establishment behavior patterns.

But if, as I am convinced, it is difficult to make a strong case that America's not-for-profit sector operates with significantly more effectiveness under its new management than it did in decades past, that is by no means to say that no progress at all has been made. Whatever the deficiencies of our public service organizations may be, today those deficiencies at least derive from our general national ethic rather than from the myopia of a single segment of the population whose claims to leadership rested in substantial part on ethnic background.

7
MATTERS OF OPINION

In the course of a forty-year involvement with journalism, I have been struck over and over again by the strong resemblance between members of the press* and clergymen. Both professions in my observation seem to attract people with uncommon confidence in their own rectitude as well as in their qualifications to instruct the rest of society on how to conduct its affairs.

One reason for this surely is that the rest of society shows itself so ready to pay special attention to the clergy and the press—and in these

---

* Here as in the rest of this chapter the word "press" is used to refer collectively to all the institutions that gather and disseminate news and opinion: daily newspapers, magazines, the wire services, and radio and TV news operations. Eccentric as it may seem, I find the now ubiquitous word "media" unsatisfactory on two counts. It is essentially an advertising construct that by implication reduces all forms of journalism to selling vehicles for slickly packaged goods and slickly packaged information alike. And because it is intrinsically a plural word, "media" is awkward to apply to what is at bottom a single form of activity; to say "the media is powerful" grates on the ear, but to say "the media are powerful" sounds pedantic.

---

degenerate latter days most especially to the press. To be sure, criticizing the press remains one of the most popular indoor sports in America. But even the charges most frequently leveled against the press—that it suffers from rampant inaccuracy and lack of objectivity—are tributes of a kind. What its critics complain about, in short, is not so much that the American press exercises excessive power as that it exercises its power wrongly.

Upon closer examination, moreover, the charge that the press uses its power irresponsibly generally turns out in practice to mean that whoever is bringing the charge believes that control of the press is in the wrong hands. The difficulty is that there is no consensus as to which set of wrong hands are on the wheel.

In recent years the loudest complaints concerning press bias have come from conservatives—people such as direct mail impresario Richard Viguerie, who believes that "the major media in this country are dominated by people who have a left-of-center bias" and who some years ago asserted that in order to present the public with the truth it was necessary "to bypass the monopoly that Walter Cronkite and Katharine Graham have on the information that is fed to the American people."

Although perhaps less widely held now than it once was, a school of thought diametrically opposed to Viguerie's also stubbornly survives. As people such as Ben Bagdikian, a onetime *Washington Post* editor who subsequently became dean of journalism at the University of California at Berkeley, see matters, the real trouble with the press is not left-wing bias but conservative bias stemming from the fact that ownership of the nation's newspapers, magazines, and broadcasting licenses is increasingly concentrated in the hands of great conglomerates whose interests interlock with those of the general business establishment. "The news media," Bagdikian declared in 1983 in his book *The Media Monopoly*, "suffer from built-in biases that protect corporate power and consequently weaken the public's ability to understand forces that shape the American scene. These biases in favor of the status quo . . . do not seem to change materially over time."

The Viguerie and Bagdikian positions—to use shorthand—have one thing in common: both ascribe the alleged deficiencies of the press to ideological or economic interests that cut across ethnic lines. But that, of course, is not the case with all press critics. With ever increasing vehemence, a substantial number of black Americans insist that the mainstream press is dominated by "white racism." And complaints of an excessive concern for Jewish causes on the part of the American press long predate the creation of Israel and have been by no means confined to Arabs and their sympathizers in this country; a long line of prominent Americans extending from Henry Adams to Jesse Jackson have railed against "Jewish control" of the press.

If one accepts the adage "Where there's smoke, there's fire," all this discontent can be taken to indicate that the performance of the American press does indeed offer grounds for worry. But if so, none of the standard complaints that I have described really explains why; every one of them simply shows, to paraphrase H. L. Mencken, that for any problem there is an explanation that is neat, simple, and wrong.

Diverse as they seem, in fact, all of these criticisms suffer from the same flaw: in greater or lesser degree they rest on the assumption that it is possible for a single group of like-minded individuals united by ideology, class interest, or ethnicity to determine what Americans will read in the printed press, hear on the radio, and see on their television screens. That assumption, however, flies in the face of observable fact. In reality, the most influential arms of the U.S. press operate, like those of the U.S. government, on a system of checks and balances—a perennial tension between two forces sometimes referred to by journalists as "church and state."*

Properly speaking, the second half of that antithesis—the word "state"—refers to the entire business staff of a publication or broadcasting operation. But the business staff of such an organization mirrors the interests of the ownership—and those interests, so antiestablishment mythology has it, consist simply of maximizing profits and advancing whatever political, economic, and social causes that the owners happen to favor. Along with this excessively cynical belief, moreover, goes another assumption: that financial control of a news-

---

* This is a phrase that in a journalistic context, I first heard applied at Time Inc. in the 1950s. Today, perhaps in part because of the extraordinary diffusion of Time Inc. alumni throughout the U.S. press, it seems to have become accepted jargon at a number of other publishing and broadcasting enterprises as well.

---

paper, magazine, or network automatically carries with it the power to set its editorial tone.

In a fair number of cases—the great majority of which involve essentially local or regional enterprises owned by a single person or family—the American press does, sadly, function very much in the way its more liberal critics charge. But in the nation's largest and most influential organs of communication, the power of the owner or owners is significantly circumscribed by that of the "church"—which is to say the editorial and news-gathering staff. Operating as they do in glass houses, even the most strong-willed press lords have to exercise caution in throwing their weight around editorially at a major newspaper or broadcasting enterprise.

Some press lords, in fact, make little or no attempt to do so; at two of the larger newspaper chains—Newhouse and Thomson—the owners deliberately refrain from tampering with the traditional political slant of the papers they have acquired. Even more often, owners find it either necessary or expedient to muffle considerably their basic intolerance for views differing from their own. To my personal knowledge, Katharine Graham, though possessed of a very highly developed sense of the prerogatives of ownership, has more than once been confronted with articles in *Newsweek* that ran counter to her personal opinions. During the years that he owned New York's *Village Voice*, Rupert Murdoch, authoritarian as he is, nonetheless recognized that he had no practical alternative to permitting that publication to express economic and political views that were clearly abhorrent to him. And just as William Paley even in his heyday did not lightly cross swords with Edward R. Murrow, so the present titan at CBS, Laurence Tisch, has to reckon with the storm of adverse publicity he could incur by issuing to Dan Rather or *60 Minutes* producer Don Hewitt the kind of summary directives he freely might to a senior executive in one of his tobacco or insurance enterprises.

Clearly, though, the authority of the church is far from being untrammeled, too. Even at journalistic establishments keenly sensitive to their public image and reputation, the most prestigious editors, reporters, anchormen, and producers can only resist the owner's desires up to a point. The top editors at the *New York Times*, for instance, make no bones about the fact that it was not any enthusiasm on their part for the talents of former Nixon speechwriter William Safire that originally won him a regular slot on that paper's Op Ed page; it was the uneasiness of publisher Punch Sulzberger over what had become the unrelievedly "liberal line" of *Times* columnists. More significant yet, the dogged and historic pursuit of the Watergate affair by the *Washington Post* would not have been possible had it not been for editor Ben Bradlee's ability to persuade owner Katharine Graham to countenance what were for that time significant departures from conventional journalistic practice. (One eminent former *Post* staffer, in fact, insists that, in addition to being the secret of his long survival in the top echelon of an organization famed for rapid executive turnover, Bradlee's tireless attention to the state of Mrs. Graham's psyche has constituted perhaps his single most important contribution to the effective editorial functioning of the *Post* over the years.)

Though it may not accord with a purist's concept of editorial independence, Bradlee's approach has the supreme virtue that it has, in fact, served to preserve and maximize his editorial influence. For, as I have sought to demonstrate, the editorial tone of even the most esteemed publications and broadcast news operations in this country is generally the product of a complex, often inexplicit, and usually semiconcealed interaction between whoever exercises economic control of the organization in question and the journalists that it employs. And this, in turn, necessarily means that the only way to arrive at any valid judgments about the biases of the American press is to examine the characteristics both of those who own it and those who staff it.

ONE OF THE FIRST things that becomes apparent from a look at the ownership of the mainstream U.S. press is that it is no longer overwhelmingly vested in the members of any single ethnic group.

That fact in itself marks a significant change from the situation that existed in this country more or less until World War II. To be sure, press ownership in this country has been in a sense ethnically diverse ever since the emergence beginning in the nineteenth century of newspapers aimed at one or another of the major immigrant groups —publications such as the *Staats-Zeitung*, *Il Progresso*, the *Irish Echo*, and *Vorwärts*. And with the advent of radio, Jewish entrepreneurs

David Sarnoff and William Paley joined the ranks of major communications moguls. But with some notable exceptions control of newspapers and magazines, the most influential purveyors of news and opinion in the pretelevision era, was predominantly in WASP hands.*

Today, however, no such tidy generalization concerning the ownership of the daily press is possible. The two individual papers generally regarded as the nation's most influential—the *New York Times* and the *Washington Post*—are controlled by Jewish or partly Jewish families,† and the third-largest American newspaper chain is owned by the Newhouse clan, whose forebears were part of the turn-of-the-century Jewish immigration from Eastern Europe. But WASP families hold either outright control or the largest single interest in the Times Mirror Co. (the *Los Angeles Times, Newsday*, the *Baltimore Sun*, the *Hartford Courant*), Dow Jones (the *Wall Street Journal, Barron's*, etc.), Affiliated Publications (the *Boston Globe*), and Knight-Ridder, which, with holdings including the *Miami Herald* and the *Philadelphia Inquirer*, is now the country's second-largest newspaper chain.

To complicate the picture still further, at least three major players in the contemporary American newspaper world really stand outside conventional ethnic classification. The undistinguished but lucrative Thomson chain is Canadian-owned,‡ while that aggressive new boy among American press lords, Rupert Murdoch, did not renounce his

---

* The first Henry Ford's angry assertion that "Jews absolutely control the circulation of publications throughout the country" was among the most ill-grounded of his many ill-grounded pronouncements on public affairs. In a 1936 survey entitled *Jews in America*, the editors of *Fortune* noted that "it still remains true that the Jewish interest in journalism is extraordinarily small."

† Washington Post Co. chairman Katharine Graham, who, aided by her siblings and children, keeps a firm grip on the Washington Post Company's voting stock, is the daughter of Col. Eugene Meyer, one of the most prominent Jewish entrepreneurs of the pre–World War II period. Mrs. Graham's mother, however, was of German Lutheran ancestry, and her late husband, Philip Graham, was a cousin of evangelist Billy Graham.

‡ Though his late father forfeited Canadian citizenship by accepting the title Baron Thomson of Fleet from Britain's Queen Elizabeth II, the present head of the Thomson empire is so devoted to his native land that he has moved his corporate headquarters from London back to Toronto and styles himself simply Kenneth Thomson.

Australian citizenship until well into middle age. And ownership of the biggest and most voracious of all U.S. newspaper chains, Gannett, is too diffuse for the ethnicity of its individual stockholders to have any conceivable significance.

Difficult as it is to come up with any tidy analysis of the ethnicity of American newspaper proprietors, it is even harder to do so when it comes to magazine ownership. There is, to be sure, a solid WASP presence in this field. The *Reader's Digest*, still the most widely circulated of the nation's subscription magazines, was for most of its history owned outright by DeWitt and Lila Wallace, who were WASP traditionalists to the core, and it is still essentially WASP-directed.* And the same holds true for the *National Geographic*, which although legally owned by a nonprofit body has actually been dominated since its inception by members of the Grosvenor family.

Over the last generation or so, however, an increasing number of major magazines have been founded or acquired by non-WASPs. Along with its less prestigious (but considerably more profitable) newspaper empire, the Newhouse family now owns a stable of eleven big-name American periodicals including *The New Yorker*, the revived *Vanity Fair*, *Vogue*, *Mademoiselle*, *House & Garden*, and *Parade*.† Like the Newhouses, Canadian-born Mortimer Zuckerman, who owns both *The Atlantic* monthly and *U.S. News & World Report*, is Jewish, as are the members of the Sulzberger family whose non-newspaper holdings include *Family Circle*, *Golf Digest*, and *Tennis* magazine. Two other magazines that have to be accounted impressive at least in circulation terms—Robert Guccione's *Penthouse* and the *National Enquirer* of the late Generoso Pope, Jr.—were built by Italian Americans. And in 1987 the string of special interest magazines (*Field & Stream*, *Road & Track*, *Woman's Day*, etc.) that had been so expen-

---

* One of the major voices in the junta that now exercises the controlling power in *Digest* affairs is Laurance Rockefeller.

† Though its enterprises do not rank No. 1 in any single field of communications, the Newhouse family may well be able to lay claim to one awesome superlative. In August 1987, *Fortune* estimated that between their newspaper, magazine, book publishing, and cable television interests, the Newhouses owned enterprises worth $7.5 billion—which put them in a nip-and-tuck race with the Waltons of Wal-Mart Stores for the title of the richest family in America.

sively put together by CBS was sold to a group headed by Peter Diamandis, a Greek American whose combination of uncommon good looks and sartorial elegance conjure up deceptive images of a latter-day Beau Brummell.

The fact that Diamandis is of Greek ancestry, however, proved completely irrelevant to the operations of the new company that emerged from what had been CBS Publications. Indeed, how small a role ethnic concerns played in Diamandis's approach to publishing became apparent in the spring of 1988 when he and his partners sold their fledgling company at a whopping profit to France's Hachette. And the utter absence of ethnic coloration that characterized Diamandis Communications is equally visible in a number of other and more prestigious magazine operations. As with Gannett in the newspaper field, the ownership of Time Inc., for instance, has become so depersonalized since the death of founder Henry Luce that the company's lingering image as outstandingly WASP and preppy is thoroughly out of date. In fact, there is little to choose these days in that respect between *Time* and *Newsweek* despite the mixed ethnicity of the latter's proprietorial family.

Time Inc. and the Washington Post Co., moreover, have another important attribute in common: it would be misleading to treat either of them simply as an exemplar of ownership patterns in print journalism. Time, of course, has long since become a major factor in the cable television industry, the Post Co. derives its highest profit margins not from its newspapers and magazines but from its television stations, and a similar mix of print and electronic operations is now the rule in the majority of press empires. For better or for worse, the job of satisfying "the people's right to know" is today in large degree discharged by so-called communications conglomerates.

Inevitable as it now seems, though, the emergence of the modern communications conglomerate represents a shotgun marriage (the shotgun being profit hunger) between industries that were once not only separate but widely thought to be inexorably in competition with each other. And among the significant differences between those industries was the fact that in broadcasting, unlike the newspaper and magazine businesses, the original empire-builders were predominantly non-WASP.

Why this should have been so is debatable. To me, the likeliest explanation appears to be that, important as its journalistic aspect has become, broadcasting is above all a branch of the mass entertainment industry—and that is a field in which, for reasons I shall explore later, WASP entrepreneurs were notably slow to take an interest. But whatever the reason, it is undeniably the case that the three companies that ultimately became the titans of radio and television broadcasting were all effectively controlled in their formative stages by Jewish Americans —RCA by David Sarnoff, CBS by William Paley, and ABC by Leonard Goldenson.

Given that very different starting point, it is, I believe, a revealing manifestation of the general social processes at work in the United States that today the ownership picture in enterprises devoted exclusively or primarily to broadcasting is essentially the same as it is in the newspaper and magazine fields. At CBS a Jewish American in the person of Laurence Tisch is still conspicuously in the catbird seat, but both of the other major networks are now owned by ethnically indefinable conglomerates—NBC by General Electric and ABC by Capital Cities. And although it now appears he may have somewhat overreached himself, CNN's Ted Turner has even introduced a brash brand of WASP entrepreneurship into the newest and least predictable major sector of the broadcast industry.

In short, what is apparent not only in broadcasting but in every major arm of the nation's press is an evolution of ownership patterns that broadly parallels the one that has occurred in American industry in general in the last twenty years. To argue that the U.S. press is economically dominated by members of any particular ethnic group has become patently unrealistic, and insofar as the operations of the press may actually be affected by the ethnicity of its owners, the influences at work are obviously highly diverse ones.

BECAUSE OF THE DIVISION of authority between church and state that prevails in the most highly respected journalistic enterprises, the tone of the American press is in large degree determined by the standards its owners apply in appointing publishers, editors, columnists, and the presidents, producers, and stars of network news operations. And historically ethnicity undeniably was one of the factors—conscious or unconscious—that influenced such appointments.

Often enough, this fact manifested itself in straightforward adherence to the code of ethnic solidarity. Despite Boston's early emergence as the most Irish of major American cities, the top editorial position at the WASP-owned *Boston Globe* remained almost exclusively in WASP hands until 1986; then, after a relatively brief tour by a Jewish American, the job was finally conferred upon Irish-American John S. Driscoll. And what remained true for so long at the *Globe* was at one time a common pattern; until after World War II, in fact, the top editorial management at most WASP-owned newspapers was also WASP.

In a sadly ironic variant on this theme, WASP editorial management was at one time also the rule on a number of papers owned by non-WASPs. In an article he published in *The New Republic* in 1974, author-columnist Stanley Karnow charged that the chain of newspapers assembled by Jewish tycoon Sam Newhouse deliberately avoided the appointment of Jewish publishers and editors. To some extent the situation Karnow perceived at Newhouse in those days may have stemmed from causes other than ethnic sensitivity, but not so at the *New York Times* where the Sulzberger family for many years leaned over backward to avoid any appearance of favoritism toward Jews or Jewish causes. Indeed, not only were the top editorial slots at the *Times* reserved for non-Jews* but reporters with what were considered to be excessively Jewish-sounding names felt obliged to use initials in their bylines. (It was because of this practice that Abe Rosenthal, later to be the paper's editorial czar, became professionally styled "A. M. Rosenthal.") As late as the 1950s, in fact, the late Joseph Kraft, who was then working on the *Times* Sunday edition, privately told me that he had been denied a correspondent's post in Israel on the avowed ground that he was disqualified for it by being half-Jewish.

Today these instances of reverse discrimination are half-forgotten

---

* In 1937 when the late Arthur Krock, certainly one of the most distinguished journalists ever to work at the *Times*, aspired to the editorship of the paper's editorial page, then publisher Arthur Hays Sulzberger flatly informed him: "We have never put a Jew in the showcase."

---

history. At the Newhouse chain there is now no dearth of Jewish publishers and editors, a number of whom are, in fact, drawn from the proprietorial clan.* As for the *New York Times*, its correspondent in Israel as of late 1986 was Jewish-American Thomas Friedman (who had previously won a Pulitzer prize for his coverage of the Israeli invasion of Lebanon from the Lebanese side), and at that same point all six of the top editors listed on the paper's masthead were Jewish. Indeed, so far had the pendulum swung that in an interview with Leonard and Mark Silk reported in *The American Establishment*, *Times* publisher Punch Sulzberger declared that one of his goals was to achieve "a better balance" among his major editors in years ahead. "You look at the next generation," he told the Silks, "and some are [Jewish] and some aren't. And that's exactly the hell the way it ought to be."

That is also, as it happens, exactly the hell the way it has actually come to be in the U.S. press in general—and not just in terms of gentiles and Jews but in terms of "white ethnics" of every description. Even the most cursory glance across the spectrum of editorial managers in the contemporary United States, in fact, makes it abundantly plain that since World War II the role that ethnicity plays in the hiring and promotion policies of nearly all major press enterprises has changed in important respects.

To begin with, even where the ownership of a publication or network still has a clearly definable ethnic cast, the owners no longer reserve the top editorial jobs for "their own kind" or confine them to people of any single ethnic background at all. The extent to which "deethnicization" has come to prevail in this respect can be seen from even an impressionistic and highly incomplete survey of three major arms of the nation's press as of early 1987.

---

* How far this particular trend has gone is suggested by an anecdote recounted in the August 1987 issue of *Fortune*. Back in the early 1980s, so this story goes, someone asked Sam Newhouse's son Si why the Newhouses had not tried to outbid Rupert Murdoch for control of the *Chicago Sun-Times*. Si Newhouse's jocular response—"No relative available to run it"—appears to have been a classic example of what is sometimes called "kidding on the square."

NEWSPAPERS

Item: Though trusts shared by the conspicuously WASPy descendants of Bostonian Clarence Barron hold the lion's share of the stock in the Dow Jones communications empire, Warren Phillips, who was the company's chief executive officer as of 1987, is Jewish. So, too, were Phillips's heir apparent at that time, Peter Kann, and Norman Pearlstine, the top editor of the Dow Jones flagship publication, the *Wall Street Journal*. But Robert Bartley, who took charge of the *Journal*'s influential editorial page in the 1970s, is a Midwestern WASP, while Jude Wanniski, perhaps the most highly visible alumnus of the paper's editorial page, is a Slavic American.

Item: The situation at the top of the editorial heap at the *Wall Street Journal* was exactly reversed at the *Washington Post* where the Meyer-Graham clan rules. There, the overall editor of the paper, Benjamin Crowninshield Bradlee, was a Boston blue blood, while the editor of the editorial page, Meg Greenfield, was Jewish. And though the president of the Washington Post Co. in 1987 was a WASP, his predecessors had included a Jewish American and an Irish American.

Item: At the sprawling Times Mirror chain, effectively controlled by the social arbiters of southern California WASPdom, the Chandler family, ethnic catholicity has also become the rule. As I noted earlier, Robert Erburu, the company's chairman as of 1987, was of Basque ancestry, while its president, David Laventhol, was a Jewish American. To round out the picture, the top editors at the chain's flagship newspaper, the *Los Angeles Times*, and its eastern anchor, *Newsday*, were respectively WASP William Thomas (later succeeded by fellow WASP Shelby Coffee) and Italian-American Anthony Marro.

Item: Despite their notably different functions, both the Associated Press and the Pulitzer Prize Board in a sense mirror the values of the entire daily press. As of mid-1987 the top man at the Associated Press was Italian-American Louis Boccardi, and one of the fastest rising stars in the A.P. firmament was Claude Erbsen, a Jewish immigrant from Trieste. At that same point, the voting members of the Pulitzer Prize Board consisted of seven WASPs, six Jewish Americans, two blacks, and one Polish American.

MAGAZINES

Item: At Time Inc. the editors of major publications in 1987 included Swiss-born Henry Muller (*Time*), two Irish Americans (Patricia Ryan at *Life* and Mark Mulvey at *Sports Illustrated*), and a Jewish American (Marshall Loeb at *Fortune*). And in the office of the editor in chief, the command post for all Time Inc. publications, Henry Grunwald, a Jewish immigrant from Vienna, was succeeded in the spring of 1987 by Jason McManus, a Presbyterian WASP.

Item: Given the revolving-door character of the top editorial post at *Newsweek*, it is difficult to determine exactly what criteria have been applied in filling it, but ethnicity has clearly not been among them. Of the six men who reached the editorial summit at *Newsweek* in the 1970s and 1980s, three were WASPs and three Jewish. More striking yet, *Newsweek*'s foreign editors since the early 1960s have included an Englishman, a Belgian immigrant, a Jewish American, and two WASPs.*

Item: To reinvigorate the two somewhat beleaguered magazines he had acquired, Jewish real estate tycoon Mortimer Zuckerman began by settling upon top editors who were WASPs—William Whitworth at *The Atlantic*, and in rapid-fire succession, ex–*Washington Post* star Shelby Coffee and former Reagan aide David Gergen at *U.S. News & World Report*. But like Mrs. Graham, Zuckerman clearly did not make his choices with ethnic considerations primarily in mind. In his original search for someone to fill the *U.S. News* slot, he extended serious feelers not only to former *Newsweek* editor Osborn Elliott, one of the surviving band of influential Manhattan WASPs, but also to Jewish-American Edward Kosner, the editor of Rupert Murdoch's *New York* magazine. And in 1988 when David Gergen stepped aside to become a columnist, the top job at *U.S. News* passed to Roger Rosenblatt, previously one of the most stylish editors and writers in the *Time* magazine stable.

Item: In early 1987, Si Newhouse, who runs his family's magazine properties, created a small tempest in the magazine world by replacing longtime *New Yorker* editor William Shawn with another Jewish Amer-

---

* Of whom, by general perception at least, I was one.

---

ican, former Random House boss Robert Gottlieb. But at that same period the Newhouses' revived version of *Vanity Fair* was under the editorship of an imported British journalist, Tina Brown, while at *Vogue* the long reign of Italian-American Grace Mirabella still continued. And when, in early 1988, Mirabella was summarily ousted, her replacement proved to be another English import, Anna Wintour.

TELEVISION NEWS

Item: Because the senior positions in network news operations change hands so frequently, any listing of individual names would be both ephemeral and tedious. It would also, rather curiously, reveal somewhat less ethnic diversity than prevails in the printed press. With relatively few exceptions—one of the more notable ones being Irish-American Gordon Manning, an uncommonly durable NBC News vice president—the top executives and "gatekeepers" in television news are still predominantly WASP or Jewish.

Item: WASPs and Jewish Americans, of course, also still make up the majority of the on-screen stars of television news.* But as the emergence of people such as Connie Chung, Bryant Gumbel, Charlayne Hunter-Gault, and CNN senior anchor Bernard Shaw makes plain, there is a trend toward greater ethnic diversity among TV newscasters—and that trend seems sure to grow stronger as more of the numerous "minority" anchors and reporters employed by CNN and local news operations graduate into the big time.

WHILE IT IS CLEARLY trending in the right direction, however, TV news still lags well behind print journalism in terms of the ethnic diversity of its practitioners. Before starting work on this book, I had never paid

---

* My reason for treating television anchors and correspondents as a category separate from news executives and gatekeepers is simple enough: although anchormen and correspondents usually do function at least in some degree as journalists, journalistic skills are not always the most essential ingredient in their success. Under sodium pentothal, I suspect, most anchormen in particular would echo a rueful statement that I heard Walter Cronkite make at the end of the 1960s: "I'm not really a newsman anymore; I'm a personality."

---

any special attention to the ethnicity of my colleagues in the magazine and newspaper worlds, but when I began to review them from that perspective, I realized that although many were WASP, Jewish, or Irish Americans, a very high percentage fell into the category "none of the above." The following lists of print journalists classified by ethnic background are obviously impressionistic and woefully incomplete, as they are exclusively composed of former colleagues or others whose work for one reason or another has been of personal interest to me.* But they are also, I believe, representative and revealing.

Italian Americans: Bonnie Angelo (London bureau chief, *Time*); Ken Auletta (writer, the New York *Daily News* and *The New Yorker*); Peter Bonventre (writer and editor, *Newsweek* and *Inside Sports*); Elaine Sciolino (correspondent, *Newsweek* and the *New York Times*); John Tagliabue (correspondent, the *New York Times*); Gay Talese (reporter and editor, the *New York Times*); Loretta Toffani (reporter, the *Washington Post* and *Philadelphia Inquirer*).

Greek Americans: Dean Brelis (correspondent, *Life* and *Time*); Nicholas Gage (reporter, the *New York Times*); Peter Osnos (reporter and editor, the *Washington Post*).

Slavic Americans: Tony Collings (correspondent, *Newsweek* and CNN—and despite his name, of Russian parentage); Nicholas Daniloff (correspondent, UPI and *U.S. News*); Dusko Doder (correspondent and editor, the *Washington Post*); Andrew Nagorski (correspondent, *Newsweek*); Jude Wanniski (editorial writer, the *Wall Street Journal*).

Chinese Americans: Paula Chin (writer, *Newsweek*); Melinda Liu (correspondent, *Newsweek*); Daniel Chu (writer, *Newsweek* and *People*).

Japanese Americans: Michiko Kakutani (book reviewer, the *New York Times*); Takeshi Oka (correspondent, the *New York Times* and the *Christian Science Monitor*); Fred Nakayama (correspondent, *Fortune*).

Armenian Americans: Michael Arlen (writer, *The New Yorker*);

---

* Some of the people listed have now moved on from newspaper or magazine work to other fields, and a few are still in the process of making their reputations, but most are both prominent and practicing journalists as of this writing. The affiliations given are not necessarily current but rather those that obtained when the person involved most strongly impinged on my consciousness. And inevitably, some of those mentioned could legitimately be listed under more than one ethnic category: Ken Auletta, for example, is of half-Italian and half-Jewish ancestry.

the late Vartanig Vartan (financial writer, the *New York Times*); Ben Bagdikian (editor, the *Washington Post*).*

As I glance back over these lists, more and more names keep occurring to me. But the point really does not require further reinforcement: even in its highest and most elite reaches, the American press today is an ethnic potpourri.

AS WAS TRUE originally in my own case, none of the distinguished journalists with whom I discussed the deethnicization of the American press had previously given the matter much thought. Upon reflection, they all conceded that there had been notable and steadily accelerating change in this respect since World War II. But none of them was prepared to assert with assurance that this had made a significant difference in the way the press covers and presents the news. "I have not noticed any change in editorial content that I would attribute to greater incidence of white ethnics in journalism," Dean Ben Bagdikian of the Graduate School of Journalism at Berkeley wrote me. "There has been a radical decrease since the 1930s in blatantly racist and prejudicial ethnic references in the mainstream media, but I think this comes from the general discrediting of these things in society as a whole."

With similar caution, Lou Boccardi of the Associated Press told me: "Maybe it's made a difference in the sense that you have a more diverse set of minds working on this thing called journalism." But Boccardi clearly wasn't totally sure even about that. "In my own case," he added, "I don't have a heavy sense of [ethnicity] about myself. It's just not part of what I have focused on." And he dismissed out of hand any notion that the changed composition of the press corps helped to account for the most dramatic development in American journalism in the last generation: the emergence of unconcealed and almost universal skepticism toward authority and a hair-trigger readiness to chal-

---

* Although it certainly does not constitute an ethnic classification, I cannot forbear from noting that there are also a number of eminent American journalists of Canadian birth. Among them: Elie Abel (correspondent, the *New York Times* and NBC); Peter Jennings (anchorman, ABC News); Robert MacNeil (*The MacNeil/Lehrer Newshour*); Abe Rosenthal (executive editor, the *New York Times*); Morley Safer (CBS News); Gavin Scott (correspondent, *Time*).

lenge official pronouncements and behavior. "Certainly the relationship between the press and government has changed fundamentally," Boccardi admitted. "But I don't think you can trace that to the ethnic thing at all. That change was brought about by Watergate."

On the face of things, it is difficult to find fault with Lou Boccardi's analysis; the lessons that emerged (or seemed to emerge) from coverage of the Watergate trauma have undeniably left a permanent mark on the American journalistic psyche. But on a deeper level it seems to me that the manner in which the press covered Watergate was in itself the consequence of an earlier development—one shrewdly summed up in 1971 by Daniel Patrick Moynihan. "One's impression," Moynihan wrote then, "is that twenty years and more ago, the preponderance of the 'working press' (as it likes to call itself)* was surprisingly close in origins and attitudes to working class people generally. They were not Ivy Leaguers. They now are or soon will be. Journalism has become, if not an elite profession, a profession attractive to elites."

Moynihan's sweeping attribution of Ivy League background to the entire press corps was, of course, gross hyperbole, but the point that his exaggeration was meant to dramatize is a thoroughly valid one. There are many fewer American journalists of working class origin today than there were in the 1940s and fewer still, regardless of social origin, who retain much trace of a working class ethos. Unlike a considerable number of their prewar predecessors, the journalists of the 1980s are not for the most part people who by education and upbringing might equally well have wound up as bookkeepers or bank tellers. Generally of middle class background, they are almost invariably the possessors of college degrees—and increasingly often, of graduate degrees as well—and whatever their political or ideological beliefs their basic mindset tends to be that of the intellectual elitist rather than that of the man in the street.

By conventional social standards, in short, journalism today attracts "a better class of people" than it formerly did. There are proba-

---

* The phrase "the working press" is one that has always bemused me as much as it apparently does Senator Moynihan. It would clearly seem to imply the existence of a parallel institution known as "the nonworking press," but try as I might, I have never been able to identify anyone lucky enough to hold membership in the latter body.

bly a number of reasons for that, but the most important one, I believe, lies in the vastly increased prestige the journalistic profession has acquired in the last few decades—a phenomenon aptly summed up by the late Joseph Kraft in *The Imperial Media*. "We [journalists] have been among the principal beneficiaries of American life," Kraft wrote. "We have enjoyed a huge rise in income, in status and in power . . . We have advanced almost overnight from the bottom to the top; from the scum of the earth . . . to the seats of the high and mighty."

To those who recall the exalted position that Walter Lippmann, for one, occupied in this country as far back as the 1930s, Joe Kraft's assertion, like Pat Moynihan's, may seem to smack of hyperbole. But it is actually a simple statement of fact. Until well after World War II only a handful of the most eminent journalists could truly be counted members of the American Establishment; today, on the other hand, any successful journalist who aspires to it can command that status. Where once they were routinely relegated to places well below the salt, journalists are now admitted to Establishment clubs, sit on the boards of such elite institutions as the Council on Foreign Relations and the Rockefeller Foundation, and find a ready welcome, whether as distinguished visitors or eminences in residence, at the most prestigious universities and think tanks. For those who do not feel it incompatible with their journalistic principles, there is even the possibility of moving in and out of government at suitably high levels. (Just among the men with whom I worked at Time Inc. in the 1950s and 1960s, two subsequently served in advisory roles in the White House, two others as assistant secretaries of state, one as ambassador to South Africa, and two more as senior appointive officials in the administration of New York City. As of this writing, moreover, still another is the United States ambassador to Kurt Waldheim's Austria.)

Along with these advances in influence and social status, as Kraft noted, has come vastly increased income—both material and psychic. To be sure, as a general rule only television journalists can aspire to anything approaching the kind of salary now commanded by a really hot baseball player, but even in print journalism a significant number of people at the top now enjoy six-figure incomes. And in the ultimate accolade accorded by our society, not only TV's morning and evening stars but some print journalists as well have become celebrities in their own right.* It is, for example, a fair assumption that millions of Americans who could not with any assurance identify the current secretary of labor could unhesitatingly tell you who Robert Woodward and Carl Bernstein are.

The fact that the period during which the rewards of journalism so notably improved was also one that saw a sharp and continuing increase in the ethnic diversity of the members of the press cannot, I think, be dismissed as mere happenstance. In his book *A Certain People*, Charles E. Silberman quotes several distinguished journalists of my own generation as recalling that to their parents or grandparents journalism seemed entirely too scruffy and disreputable an occupation to be suitable for "a nice Jewish boy." And essentially the same attitude was expressed in my youth by the parents of Japanese- and Greek-American acquaintances of mine. As the decades wore on, however, it became less common for parents to take that position or, if they did, much harder for them to offer convincing arguments in support of it. For anyone primarily concerned with making a great deal of money, an MD or MBA was clearly still the safest ticket. But for those who craved public influence and prestige, journalism became a serious option.

To my way of thinking, though, what was most significant about this development was not so much its impact on the ethnic composition of the press as the change it produced in the type of person, regardless of ethnicity, who tended to be drawn into journalism. Not only are the journalists of the 1980s considerably better educated on average than those of forty years ago, they are also far less modest in their professional goals. Unwilling to be simply observers and recorders of events, they are much more apt to regard themselves, avowedly or una-

---

* For the print journalist who manages this feat, the payoff in terms of book, lecture, movie and/or television contracts can be startlingly large. Indeed, in 1987, according to a survey published by *The Washingtonian*, the one hundred most highly paid individuals in the nation's capital included at least four newspapermen and columnists. The four, with their incomes for that year:

Bob Woodward .... $1.7 million
Jack Anderson.. $1.25 million
Art Buchwald .... $1 million
George Will $988,000

---

vowedly, as the keepers of society's conscience ánd hence at least indirectly as social and political engineeers.

Though they do not always recognize it, it is this view of the journalist's role that basically disturbs those who insist that it is the primary responsibility of the nation's press to present the news as objectively as possible—and that far too often it conspicuously fails to fulfill this responsibility. But self-evident as it is widely assumed to be, the notion that journalists have an obligation to report the news objectively is not, in fact, inherent in the concept of a free press; when they adopted the First Amendment, the last thing that the Founding Fathers anticipated was evenhanded coverage of events by individual publications; their assumption was that the way the truth would out and reasonable balance might be achieved in the information available to the public would be through the clash of contending journalistic polemicists.

But even if one accepts this disenchanted eighteenth-century view of the limitations of journalism, it is still possible to argue, as a great number of Americans now do, that in practice things haven't worked out that way—that the nation's press has actually come to be overwhelmingly dominated by people of one broad political and social tendency. And that, as I noted at the beginning of this chapter, is not infrequently perceived, both by bigots and people who profess to despise bigotry, as a consequence of an exclusive concentration of journalistic power in the hands of one particular ethnic or racial group.

To deal thoroughly with the charge of ideological uniformity would carry me well outside the scope of this book, so I shall merely note that anyone who can seriously assert that the *Wall Street Journal*, the *Washington Post*, the *Reader's Digest* and the New York *Daily News* are all run by ideological soulmates would appear to have a rather shaky grip on reality. And the second charge—that there is some clear and consistent correlation between the ideology and the ethnicity of the members of the journalistic establishment—is even more impossible to sustain.

The strongest proof of that, I believe, is to be found in those areas of American journalism in which open expression of bias is universally conceded to be legitimate. Consider, for example, a reasonably representative sampling of the nation's better-known columnists. Patrick Buchanan and Mary McGrory, both Irish Americans, stand at opposite ends of the political spectrum—while Jimmy Breslin, who supplies one of the few authentic working class voices in the big-time commentary business, defies conventional ideological classification. On the Op Ed page of the *New York Times*, the most consistently conservative views are expressed by one Jewish American, William Safire, and the most predictably liberal by another, Anthony Lewis. And a similarly wide divergence exists between the political preconceptions of two leading WASP pundits—*Newsweek*'s George Will and the *New York Times*'s Tom Wicker.

This same pattern—or more accurately, lack of pattern—also characterizes the manifold journals of opinion that, though often small and struggling, exert significant influence because of the close attention they receive from the nation's movers and shakers and the trickle down of their views into the mainstream press. Among publications of this ilk in the conservative camp, two of the most notable, *The National Review* and *The American Spectator*, are edited by Irish Americans William Buckley and R. Emmett Tyrrell, while two others, *The Public Interest* and *Commentary*, are masterminded by Jewish Americans Irving Kristol and Norman Podhoretz. At the opposite political pole, two influential liberal-left publications are also run by Jewish Americans— *The New York Review of Books* by pipe-puffing Robert Silvers and *The Nation* by Victor Navasky. But the publisher of *The Nation* throughout the first half of the 1980s was Hamilton Fish III, a scion of one of New York's oldest aristocratic WASP clans and a grandson of FDR's ancient foe.* And among the presiding gurus at less easily classifiable magazines of opinion, three of the more outstanding have included a WASP (Charles Peters at *The Washington Monthly*), a Jewish American (Martin Peretz at *The New Republic*), and until he fell afoul of Mortimer Zuckerman a few years ago, an Irish American from upstate New York (Robert Manning at *The Atlantic*).

Supplying the members of the public with commentary and news analysis, to be sure, is only one of journalism's functions, and in most

---

* Who became so outraged by his grandson's "radical" politics that he once threatened legal action to bar the younger man from using his baptismal name.

---

eyes a less important one than supplying them with the information necessary to arrive at their own judgments of events. For that reason, today's conventional wisdom holds that it is the responsibility of the press, in the words of a once ubiquitous *Newsweek* advertisement, to "separate fact and opinion." That, of course, is a less simple task than it sounds, and whether the contemporary American press tries hard enough to achieve it in what is commonly called "straight news reporting" can legitimately be debated. If that debate is to be a useful one, however, it must take into account two realities clearly observable in our columnists and openly polemical periodicals. One of these is that by no means all of those journalists who seek, openly or covertly, to engage in social engineering are working from the same set of blueprints. The other indispensable reality is that the particular blueprint that a journalist of this kind chooses to follow has no predictable correlation with his or her ethnicity.

IT MIGHT AT FIRST blush seem odd that comparatively little attention has been paid even by journalists themselves to the greatly increased extent to which the American press has become multiethnic in ownership and staffing. Yet the reasons for that are, I think, easy to see. One of them is that what has occurred in the press has simply mirrored what has been occurring in the general society, and as a result, it is not likely in itself to appear particularly remarkable to the casual observer. At the same time, the emergence of white ethnics as a major factor in the journalistic elite has tended to be obscured in everyone's mind by the undeniable and well-publicized fact that the number of blacks and Hispanics who have achieved significant success in the press is still disproportionately small.

The degree to which this holds true, to be sure, varies notably from one branch of the press to another. As of 1985, according to the *Columbia Journalism Review*, some 14.5 percent of the professional jobs in television were occupied by Hispanics and nonwhites. But a 1986 survey of daily newspapers conducted by the American Society of Newspaper Editors revealed that the comparable figure in their newsrooms was only 6.3 percent—and 57 percent of the nation's nearly 1,700 dailies confessed to having no Hispanics or nonwhites at all on their editorial staffs.

To lump all of these minority groups together, though, is obviously deceptive. Given the fact that so large a percentage of today's Hispanic and Asian-American populations reflects relatively recent immigration, the rate at which members of these groups have begun to achieve responsible positions in the press is reasonably gratifying. But that emphatically does not yet hold true for blacks.

That the underlying cause for the relative dearth of successful blacks in the mainstream press is white racism cannot be questioned. But despite such clamorous incidents as the controversial 1987 court decision in which a jury held that the New York *Daily News* had discriminated against several of its black editorial employees, I believe the problem does not stem so much from present-day manifestations of racism as from the consequences of racist practices pursued in the past. Inevitably, the discrimination so long characteristic of American society in general served to restrict artificially the pool of blacks who possessed advanced education, and even though that pool has greatly expanded in the last few decades, it is nonetheless true that in today's civil-rights conscious environment young blacks who have such qualifications find themselves in demand in a number of fields that tend to offer larger and quicker financial rewards than journalism. And as an additional disincentive, young blacks attracted to journalism have historically found so few role models in senior positions in the field that they often felt uncomfortably isolated and foredoomed to very limited advancement.

To its credit, the contemporary journalistic establishment in the United States as a whole makes no attempt to defend this state of affairs. It would be naïve in the extreme to think that racism has utterly vanished from the newsroom any more than it has from other American institutions. Still, it is demonstrably true that for some time now the leaders of the American press as a group have been engaged in a conscious effort to ensure greater participation by blacks at every level of journalism.

Thus, whether realistically or not, the American Society of Newspaper Editors has formally set for its members the goal of achieving racial "parity" by the year 2000—parity in this case being interpreted to mean that the percentage of blacks on the staff of any newspaper should be at least equivalent to the percentage of blacks in the overall population of the region the paper serves. Even to approach that target will obviously require a greatly increased flow of young blacks into journalism, and there are more and more efforts to promote that— efforts ranging from the establishment of minority internships by individual publications to an active search for black students on the part of journalistic educational institutions. And to combat the dead-end syndrome, the 1986 Associated Press managing editors' convention featured a panel devoted to considering ways of improving career paths for young blacks already in journalism.

These and other similar developments had already begun to bear fruit by the early 1980s. Though still too scarce, black students had become significantly more numerous than before at such places as Columbia University's prestigious Graduate School of Journalism, and while no major newspaper with which I am familiar had yet attained parity, both the *Detroit Free Press* and the *Philadelphia Daily News* had boosted the number of blacks in their newsrooms to roughly 17 percent of total staff by 1987.

Perhaps most important of all, however, there had emerged by the 1980s a number of black journalists senior enough and influential enough to serve as role models and/or mentors for younger colleagues. Some of these were people who enjoyed considerable public visibility —columnists such as Carl Rowan and the *Washington Post*'s William Raspberry or TV personalities such as Ed Bradley, Bernard Shaw, Bryant Gumbel, and Charlayne Hunter-Gault. But there were also some top journalistic managers—people such as Robert Maynard, the editor-publisher of the *Oakland Tribune*, my erstwhile *Newsweek* colleague Jonathan Rodgers, who in 1986 was appointed general manager of Chicago's WBBM-TV, and Jay Harris, the executive editor of the *Philadelphia Daily News*. And these latter, in my view, were especially key figures for a reason that a white staffer of the *Philadelphia Daily News* spelled out to a *Columbia Journalism Review* author. "Clearly," this man said, "Jay Harris is the boss here—and the boss is a black man. That changes people's perceptions."

But at best, of course, all this marked only limited progress, and to some it seemed far too limited to offer great cause for optimism. Berkeley's Dean Ben Bagdikian clearly spoke for many white journalists and the majority of blacks in a letter he sent me in the summer of

1986. "Whether there will be a dramatic change for blacks and Hispanics in journalism remains to be seen," he wrote. "There is no global trauma like World War II or massive opening of society like the G.I. Bill to effect deep change in hiring of blacks and browns. And the record in the media so far is not good. So I think it is not necessarily automatic that what happened to white ethnics will happen to people of color, or at least not happen in the same way."

Bagdikian's final point is, I think, his strongest one. As Lou Boccardi of the Associated Press pointed out to me, the managing editors of the A.P.'s member papers never organized panels on how to improve career prospects for Jewish, Italian, or Greek-American journalists. The process by which blacks achieve free access to the journalistic establishment, in other words, seems destined to involve conscious and organized effort at reform to a far greater degree than was the case with white ethnics. But that this process will in fact occur and that the presence of blacks at every level and in every branch of journalism will ultimately become commonplace is, in my view, a certainty.

What is less certain is the precise impact that this will have upon the performance of the American press. In purely ideological terms, I suspect, that impact is likely to be less than some might expect. It seems reasonable to assume that the same kind of political diversity that has come to characterize journalists of white ethnic background will also manifest itself among black journalists—as, indeed, it has already begun to do among black social scientists.

But that is not to say that there will be no significant impact at all. Inevitably, I think, a major increase in the black presence in journalism will serve to enhance the accuracy of the picture the press presents of American society as a whole. For as David Lawrence, Jr., the publisher of the *Detroit Free Press*, told an interviewer in early 1987: "I can be the most thoughtful white progressive you've ever met, but I've got no idea what it is like to be black. What I need to do is make sure that this newspaper is peopled and managed by people who look at the world differently than I do."

Yet valid as Lawrence's point is, it may well prove to be one of decreasing importance as time goes by. As black journalists come to take equal access to positions of influence and authority more and more for granted, it is probable that the degree to which they see the world differently from their white professional peers will diminish—provided, of course, that the enhanced black role in journalism is matched in other fields of endeavor.

One of the clear lessons of the American past has been that there is a direct relationship between the degree of acceptance the general society accords to any particular ethnic group and the professional behavior patterns of the members of that group. In general, as discrimination against them declines, the ablest members of a given minority tend to focus more heavily upon the achievement of purely individual aspirations. As it happens, personal ambition is already a notable characteristic of black journalists; studies conducted by the Institute for Journalism Education, in fact, indicate that the percentage of nonwhite journalists who aspire to management positions is greater than that among their white colleagues. And that strongly suggests a somewhat ironic conclusion: the faster those ambitions are gratified, the sooner the day will come when it will be as difficult to generalize about a distinctive black influence upon the American press as it now is about a distinctive Irish, Italian, or Jewish one.

8

PROGRESS BY DEGREES

As the child of schoolteachers I have always been acutely conscious of the fact that while Americans in general profess to attach great importance to education, their attitude toward those who impart it is distinctly ambivalent. In so saying, I am not only referring to the modest social status and even more modest financial rewards accorded the great majority of American educators. I have in mind, too, the common tendency among blue collar citizens to regard teachers as underworked, and the equally widespread tendency among men of affairs to perceive "pointy-headed professors" as being at best impractical theorists and at worst downright subversives. So strong, in fact, are these strains in American thought that it was my own father, a dedicated and outstandingly able high school language teacher, who first cited to me with wry acceptance the old adage: "Those who can, do; those who can't, teach—and those who can't teach, teach teachers."

Yet, somewhat paradoxically, a successful career as an academic or educational administrator—at least at the university level—is also one of the recognized springboards to elite status in the United States. In no other country with which I am familiar, in fact, have so many people parlayed reputations won in academia into political power. From Woodrow Wilson on, a surprising number of American educators have transformed themselves into effective vote-getters. The first governor of Connecticut of whom I have any memory was a tweedy Yale English professor named Wilbur Cross, and at the other end of the continent the redoubtable marine biologist Dixy Lee Ray was unquestionably the most colorful if not necessarily the most effective governor the state of Washington has had in recent decades. Among national political figures, the only two with whom I can claim any direct acquaintance also happen to be ex-professors: Mike Mansfield, surely the most generally beloved Senate majority leader in modern times, was teaching history at the University of Montana when he first ran for office, and New York's Sen. Daniel Patrick Moynihan, despite the high degree of political savvy he has acquired, still betrays the mindset of the Harvard social scientist he once was.

Understandably, though, the majority of American academics who have succumbed to the temptation of playing philosopher-king have chosen to eschew the messy process of actually running for office and instead have vaulted into the upper ranks of the federal establishment through presidential appointment. To grasp the profound effect such people have had on our national life, it is only necessary to recite the litany of Ivy League educators—McGeorge Bundy, Henry Kissinger, Zbigniew Brzezinski—who served as national security adviser in the Vietnam and immediate post-Vietnam years, or to recall the degree of power over the American economy exercised by former University of Chicago professor Arthur Burns during his years as Federal Reserve Board chairman.

Such relatively long-term players on the Washington stage, moreover, do not reflect the full extent of the professorial infiltration of the nation's governing elite. Even more numerous are the in-and-outers— men and women who, while ready and eager to serve temporarily in government, carefully keep their bolt-holes back to academia open. To what extent some of the more highly publicized in-and-outers actually are successful in shaping government policy can legitimately be debated; if, for example, John Kenneth Galbraith's advice to the Kennedy administration was as indispensable as he clearly assumed it to be, it seems odd that President Kennedy did not find a post for the professor somewhat closer to the center of power than the United States embassy in New Delhi. On the other hand, both the strengths and vulnerabilities of the American economy in the late 1980s obviously stemmed to a significant degree from policy assumptions epitomized in Arthur Laffer's famous—or infamous—curve.

If the precise importance of the role that academics play in our political life is hard to pin down, it is even more difficult to assess the exact consequences of their participation in the nation's business life. Nonetheless, it is clear that the role they play in private industry is one of considerable and growing significance. Since World War II, as the contribution of MIT and Harvard scientists to the development of the information industry in Massachusetts classically attests, the professor as entrepreneur has become an increasingly familiar figure on the American scene. And much more commonplace yet is the professor who augments his academic income by selling advice to businessmen; a survey taken by the Carnegie Commission on Higher Education in 1969 showed that in the preceding two years some 17 percent of the professors at major American universities had served as consultants to national corporations.

Almost certainly that figure would be even higher if a similar survey were taken today. However deplorable its long-term impact on the corporate world may have been, the extraordinary increase in the size and influence of graduate schools of business over the last few decades has spawned a host of academics assumed to possess special expertise in the alleged science of management. At the same time, the corporate establishment has displayed ever growing readiness to employ the services of specialists in disciplines only tangentially related to business; among my own acquaintances are a New York University Arabist who has developed a lucrative sideline as a consultant to firms doing business in the Middle East, and a Columbia professor whose particular field of expertise is Japanese politics but who has been enlisted by a major newsmagazine to serve as senior editorial adviser to its Japanese language edition. Such activities, moreover, have served to propel a fair number of scholars into decidedly nonacademic tax brackets: between 1975 and 1979, for example, AT&T reportedly paid Eugene

Rostow, a longtime professor at Yale Law School and former dean of that institution, more than $450,000 for his advice on how to deal with the company's antitrust problems.

To be sure, the great majority of college professors do not enjoy anything approaching the degree of direct power and influence I have been describing—and the number of educators at the primary and secondary school level who do so is, relatively speaking, minuscule. Yet it is, I believe, an incontestable fact that even the great mass of teachers and school administrators who labor in modestly paid obscurity have had critical indirect impact upon the way in which our society manages its affairs. Taken as a whole, they have almost certainly done more than the members of any other single profession to bring about changes in the composition of America's elite. And in that process they have radically changed the face of their own profession.

THOUGH HE RETIRED back in the 1960s, my father still recalls with pride some of the students who attended Hillhouse High School in New Haven, Connecticut, during the thirty-five years that he taught there. Two who occupy special places on his list are Eugene Rostow, who went on to become not only dean at Yale Law but deputy secretary of state, and Gene's younger brother, Walt, who played an important role in LBJ's White House. But there are others as well: Barry Zorthian, the son of uneducated Armenian immigrants, who was elected to Skull & Bones at Yale and after serving as the top U.S. public affairs officer in Saigon became a senior executive of Time Inc.; Levi Jackson, the brilliant broken-field runner who was the first black to captain a Yale football team as well as the first to be elected to Skull & Bones;* Edward Migdalski, who parlayed a youthful passion for fishing into the curatorship of ichthyology at Yale's Peabody Museum; and—perhaps closest of all to Dad's heart—Tom Viglione, who never achieved national renown but who became a highly prosperous inventor and industrial consultant.

Much as it may sound so, I have not rigged this list to prove a point—but the point is there. Hillhouse was never an elite public high

---

* And who once dryly observed that in his time at Yale he could not possibly have been elected to Bones if his given name and surname had come in reverse order.

---

school in the mold of Boston Latin (which produced among other distinguished alumni, the late Theodore White) or the Bronx High School of Science (which at last count numbered six Nobel laureates, all Jewish, among its alumni). Nonetheless, my father's school performed admirably two traditional functions of public education in this country: it "Americanized" the children of immigrants, and for those non-WASP youngsters bright and ambitious enough to get onto its fast track, it opened the way to higher education and thus to enhanced earning power, professional achievement, and social status.

Today, partly because of middle class flight to the suburbs (and/or private schools) and partly because of a long period of disdain among educational theorists for any hint of "elitism," there are far fewer Hillhouses in the United States than there used to be.* Indeed, in purely academic terms, the quality of education now available to youngsters in most big city school systems is almost certainly inferior to what it was forty years ago, and the degree to which such systems are failing the children of the black and Hispanic underclass has become a national disgrace.

To compound the problem, even as their academic standards have declined, the function of the public schools as instruments of "Americanization" has come under increasing challenge. "When I went to school in Brooklyn," Norman Podhoretz recalled to me, "we had our fingernails inspected and were asked if we had brushed our teeth—and we were punished in some fashion if we were deficient in such respects . . . Our parents didn't object because nobody had any doubts that this was Americanizing immigrants and that that was what schools were for." But in the America of the 1980s, of course, any public school—or at least, any urban public school—that tried to enforce the sort of standards imposed upon Podhoretz and his classmates in the 1930s would run serious risk of being accused of violating the civil liberties of its students.

Obviously there are arguments to be made on both sides of this

---

* Symbolically enough, in fact, the Hillhouse School in which my father taught no longer exists physically. The property where it used to stand was sold some years ago to Yale University, and the school that now bears the name Hillhouse is, at least in educational terms, no match for the original.

---

issue. *Washington Post* columnist William Raspberry is only one of a number of commentators with impeccably liberal credentials who have suggested that part of the reason for the high unemployment rate among black youths in the United States is that far too many of them have never been instructed in the kind of social behavior that would render them acceptable to potential employers. On the other hand, it is undeniable that the power to enforce their own standards of dress, hygiene, and deportment can bring out the petty tyrant in educators and be needlessly humiliating to children exposed to it.

Paradoxically, however, many of the same people who would rise in outrage at the notion of compulsory fingernail inspection have enthusiastically endorsed the use of compulsion in bringing about a significant erosion of the Americanization function of our public schools. By effectively restricting the use of certain federal funds to bilingual education programs, the Congress has since the 1970s imposed a proliferation of such programs upon frequently reluctant local school systems. And while bilingual education is most often presented as a means of easing the transition of non-English-speaking children into the educational mainstream, many of its supporters rather inconsistently hail it on the grounds that it also enables such children to maintain a sense of separate cultural identity.

To say that these trends in the character of primary and secondary education have sparked widespread public concern is to belabor the obvious. With the exception of self-defensive members of the educational establishment, relatively few informed Americans today would be prepared to argue that our public schools as a whole are adequate to the nation's needs in purely academic terms. Somewhat more surprisingly, a number of people who cannot simply be dismissed as WASP bigots worry about decreased emphasis in the schools upon a common national culture. Noting that bilingual education is often prolonged far beyond what might reasonably be considered a transitional period, Harvard's Nathan Glazer dryly told a New York audience in 1986: "It has been my impression that you could get a wonderful education in Spanish in the American school system." And Norman Podhoretz, who sees what he regards as "a kind of Balkanization" of the school system as a symptom of the collapse of WASP self-confidence, believes that the consequences of that collapse are visible even in the

elite private institutions that used to be more or less exclusive preserves of the children of the privileged. "Exeter, Yale—those places
aren't what they were," he says dismissively.

In that final observation, Podhoretz is unquestionably accurate.
Though they scarcely qualify as egalitarian institutions even yet and
still exist above all to give their graduates a head start in the race for
social and economic status, the nation's most prestigious private secondary schools have indeed become very different places from what
they used to be in at least one important respect. At Los Angeles's
swank Harvard School, which a generation ago was populated almost
exclusively by the scions of WASP families, more than 40 percent of
the student body was Jewish as of 1986 and more than 10 percent
Asian-American. And at the New England paradigm of preppiedom
specifically cited by Podhoretz, there have been even more dramatic
changes. Traditionally an all-male bastion, Exeter vastly distressed
some of its alumni by going coed in 1970. By 1987 well over 40 percent
of its students were girls, and that same year the school acquired its
first female principal, a personable, athletic Harvard graduate (with a
Columbia Ph.D.) named Kendra Stearns O'Donnell. By that time, too,
nearly a quarter of Exeter's student body was Asian, black, or Hispanic
—which represented a doubling of the school's nonwhite population in
just ten years.*

Even if they are interpreted as an abdication of leadership on the
part of the traditional WASP elite—a proposition that seems to me to
confuse altruism with failure of nerve—the developments of the last
twenty years at places such as Exeter and the Harvard School will
surely strike most Americans as positive. And their importance is not
to be minimized, for precisely because the private preparatory schools
do tend to give their students a head start in life they have an impact
on our society disproportionate to the number of people who actually
attend them. Nonetheless, their role remains a limited one; it is clearly
the management of the public educational system that will most pro-

---

* In this respect Exeter apparently was right on the norm. According to the National
Association of Independent Schools, the number of minority students in nondenominational
private schools as a whole doubled in the ten years beginning in 1977.

---

foundly affect the nation's future. And there, too, despite the existence of a long and legitimate list of grave complaints, particularly where inner-city schools are involved, I believe the dire warnings of the pessimists to be somewhat exaggerated.

To begin with, the public education system in America has always served as a vehicle of social and cultural mobility not just for children of immigrant parentage but for adult members of minority groups as well. Historically, schoolteaching has been a path to middle class status for strivers from each successive wave of immigration—first the Irish, later Jews, and then Italians. And that process continues unabated; today schoolteaching and educational administration are serving the same function for Hispanics and blacks. (Since the 1970s, in a classic example of this progression, the public school system of New York City has successively been headed by Frank Macchiarola, Luis Alvarez, Nathan Quinones, and its first black chancellor, Dr. Richard Green.)

Though its clearest result has been to improve the social status of the minority group individuals involved, this process presumably has also had some effect upon the character of the educational system itself. In 1963, commenting upon the New York City public schools of that era, Nathan Glazer and Daniel Patrick Moynihan wrote in *Beyond the Melting Pot:* "It is not easy to figure out what the impact of a largely Jewish teaching force is on students compared with, for example, the largely Irish and German and white Protestant teaching force of thirty or forty years ago. Yet the groups are so different in their intellectual attitudes, cultural outlook, and orientation toward education and college that some influence, one must be sure, can be felt."

In my own view, the convergence in cultural outlook between various ethnic groups has now gone far enough that the point made by Glazer and Moynihan probably does not apply as strongly to the changes in the teaching force that occurred in the 1970s and 1980s as to those that occurred earlier. But most people, I think, would accept that it applies in some degree—and not a few find the implications of that disturbing. In the context of the 1980s, for example, the most obvious consequence of change in the ethnic composition of the people who staff the public school system is clearly the prevalence of bilingual education, pressure for which is relentlessly maintained by the considerable number of teachers and educational bureaucrats whose career prospects depend heavily upon its perpetuation.

Yet there is one potentially decisive counterweight to that pressure—which is that in most areas of the United States whenever they are given free choice, minority group parents who are ambitious for their children generally reject bilingual education. Within this generation, Roman Catholic parochial schools that used to teach in French have switched to English in even the most heavily French-Canadian areas of New England. Similarly, classes conducted in Spanish have virtually disappeared from Catholic parochial schools with sizable Hispanic enrollments. And in the Budlong school district in Chicago's Greektown, according to sociologist Charles Moskos, the majority of Greek-American parents vehemently opposed having their children taught in Greek in public school.

All this in my view raises the distinct possibility that in the end vested interest groups in the educational and political bureaucracies will be unable to carry the day and that our public schools for the most part will eventually beat the same kind of quiet retreat from bilingual education that they long since have from the "new math" fad of the late 1960s. But even if that fails to happen, sweeping charges that the nation's public schools have universally ceased to perform their traditional assimilative mission will still be unjustified. In urban areas all the way from Los Angeles to those drab eastern reaches of New York City stigmatized by TV's Norman Lear as Archie Bunker country, the children of Chinese, Korean, and Indian immigrants are today finding their way into the American mainstream through the schools. The same holds true in large degree for the children of Israeli, Soviet-Jewish, and many Caribbean immigrants. And in the late spring of 1986 my casual reading of two local weeklies revealed that in three small communities along the eastern Connecticut shoreline either the valedictorian or the salutatorian of the graduating high school class was of Indochinese birth.

To be sure, the fact that a lot of youngsters from immigrant families are doing well in school doesn't in itself disprove the assertion that they are not being inculcated with a common national culture. But it seems to me that on close examination that assertion falls of its own weight. All schools, whether they mean to or not, induce conformity of one kind or another in their students.* And while it is distressingly true that in some big-city schools the conformity effectively enforced is to the values and behavior patterns of the underclass, in most instances our public schools are still imparting upwardly mobile and assimilative standards. The reason this is not recognizable as Americanization to many people in their fifties and sixties lies, I believe, in the failure of such people to perceive that Americanization no longer implies the same things that it used to. When Norman Podhoretz and I were in grade school, Americanization meant the imposition of something known in the arcane jargon of sociologists as "Anglo-conformity." But today what it means is something quite different: the imposition of a common culture that is truly unique to this nation and that, although reflective of the values of the overall white majority, can no longer be accurately described as dominated by the sensibility of any single ancestry group.

THE FACT THAT so many people unthinkingly equate Americanization with Anglo-conformity is, I believe, essentially the result of a cultural lag: until quite recently in our national history the two were, in fact, treated as synonymous in the U.S. educational system. As late as 1941 when I entered college, higher education in this country not only imposed WASP values but was still essentially confined to a privileged minority predominantly composed of WASPs.

Apart from WASPs, the only other group disproportionately represented in the undergraduate bodies of American colleges and universities in those days was the nation's Jewish population. And even in that case the WASPs rigged the game: at elite private universities such as Harvard, Yale, Dartmouth, and Columbia the number of Jewish students admitted was rigidly controlled by quota systems. In 1930, for example, Harvard had by various devices frozen the number of Jews in its student body at 10 percent and at Yale the ceiling was slightly more

---

* This is a reality that was strongly driven home to me when my oldest son finally rebelled against my decree that he must wear a jacket and tie to a school largely populated by the offspring of determinedly progressive exurbanites. "Don't you see, Dad," he protested, "that makes me the only conformist in my class."

---

than 8 percent. Perhaps most shameful of all, Columbia in the years between 1914 and 1920 actually cut back on the number of Jews it admitted so drastically that they fell from 40 percent of the undergraduate body to only about 15 percent.

So far as I can determine, none of the colleges that had Jewish quotas ever imposed similar arbitrary restrictions on students of Italian, Polish, Asian, or other patently non-WASP ancestry; it wasn't considered necessary because relatively few such people applied for college admission in the U.S. before World War II. A WASP born before 1930, for instance, was four times as likely to attend college as an Italian American of corresponding age. Indeed, the percentage of Roman Catholics of any ethnic background who earned college degrees was substantially lower than Catholic representation in the population at large, and the number of Catholics who got their degrees at secular colleges was far smaller still.

At the end of 1942 when I cut short my sophomore year at Yale to join the army, there was no particular reason to think that this time-honored state of affairs would not endure indefinitely. Yet by the time I returned to college four years later, it had already begun to change rapidly. What made the difference, of course, was the G.I. Bill—a measure that, according to Notre Dame scholar David C. Leege, "may have had more of an impact on the Catholic Church [in the United States] than the Second Vatican Council." Be that as it may, the G.I. Bill undeniably set in motion the deethnicization of American higher education. And over the last three decades that process has been mightily reinforced through the adoption of "need blind" admissions policies by an increasing number of private universities, the availability of government-guaranteed student loans, and the emergence of a public climate unreceptive to ethnic discrimination of any kind.

The upshot of all this has been steady and remarkable progress toward greater uniformity in the educational attainments of the various ethnic and religious groups that make up the American nation. In the twenty years between 1967 and 1987, for example, the relative number of American Catholics with college educations more than doubled, reaching some 17 percent of the total Catholic population. And among Catholics drawn from the older waves of immigration, the increase has been even more notable: since the beginning of the 1970s, college attendance among Irish Catholics has consistently exceeded the average for the general population, and among males of wholly or partly Italian ancestry born since World War II, the college graduation rate now stands at roughly 25 percent—a figure virtually indistinguishable from that prevailing among male WASPs.

Yet while many of the disparities in the college attendance rate of different ethnic groups had disappeared by the late 1980s, some still persisted, and some new or intensified ones had appeared. For a complex set of social, economic, and cultural reasons there were striking variations in the degree to which particular groups took advantage of the greater openness in the national system of higher education. In relation to their percentage of the overall population, blacks and Hispanics remained generally underrepresented in university student bodies while members of two of the country's smaller minorities—Jews and Asian Americans—had outstripped all other ancestry groups.

In a development that clearly had important implications for the composition of America's future elites, this last phenomenon had become particularly notable at the most prestigious colleges and universities. In 1986, for example, roughly a fifth of the students at Harvard were Jewish—and at Yale it was estimated that perhaps one undergraduate in three was Jewish. What this clearly reflected was the elimination of Jewish quotas by these institutions—a process, incidentally, that was not completely accomplished at Yale until as late as the 1960s. But that explanation certainly did not account for the parallel surge in Asian-American attendance at topflight universities.

Though it is sometimes alleged that a number of major universities have quietly adopted fixed quotas on Asian-American students in recent years, that has never to my knowledge been conclusively demonstrated and in a strict sense is very probably wrong. At the same time, it seems clear that some universities have deliberately loaded the dice against Asian-American applicants, the preferred bureaucratic dodge being to reduce the weight given to a candidate's test scores and academic record and increase that given to extracurricular activities or such indefinable attributes as "leadership." In any case, despite all the loud protestations of innocence on the part of college admissions offices, an indisputable pattern has emerged: as college applications from Asian Americans have soared—at some institutions they multiplied tenfold between the mid-1970s and the mid-1980s—the percentage of successful Asian-American applicants at prestige colleges has steadily declined. At Yale, to cite just one case, 39 percent of all Asian-American applicants were accepted in 1977; by 1987, the figure had fallen to 17 percent.

Even more to the point, perhaps, is the fact that at a number of top American colleges—among them Harvard, Princeton, and Brown—the percentage of Asian-American applicants accepted was consistently smaller as of the mid-1980s than the comparable figure for the overall pool of applicants. At Stanford, in fact, the admission rate for Asian Americans was a full third lower than that for Caucasians.

Remarkably, however, all this hanky-panky has not yet succeeded in preventing an almost meteoric rise in Asian-American college attendance. And this has been true not just in terms of absolute numbers but in terms of the relative size of the Asian-American contingent at leading universities. In the fall of 1987, Asian Americans accounted for nearly 14 percent of the entering freshman class at Harvard, 20 percent of that at MIT, and 21 percent of that at the California Institute of Technology. And at the University of California at Berkeley the figure reached a full 25 percent.

Asian Americans, in short, have in a sense turned the concept of ethnic-blind college admissions upside down by the simple expedient of outperforming every other ancestry group in the United States in terms of academic achievement. And that fact has caused undisguised concern even among educators who as a matter of principle implacably oppose systematic discrimination against the members of any ethnic or religious group. In its most disinterested form, the question that troubles university administrators is one posed to me by Nathan Glazer in the summer of 1987: "If we are producing leadership for a nation that is two to three percent Asian, can we afford to run up to forty percent Asian in our student body?" And in an interview with *Time* that same year, another famed Harvard sociologist, David Riesman, put the matter in more pragmatic terms. The way things were going, he asserted, a university such as Stanford "could become forty percent Jewish, forty percent Asian-American, and ten percent requisite black. Then you'd have a pure meritocracy and that would create problems for diversity and alumni."

The potential problems foreseen by Glazer and Riesman cannot, I think, simply be brushed aside as immaterial. But those raised by Riesman seem to me to be of two very different orders of importance. No one can reasonably deny that it is crucial for a private university to retain the loyalty and financial support of its alumni, but past experience strongly suggests that any reduction in alumni support caused by changing ethnic admissions patterns would at worst be transitory. The universities that abandoned Jewish quotas a generation ago have certainly found their increasingly numerous Jewish alumni no less generous than WASP alumni, and there is no reason to think the story will be different with Asian-American alumni. On the contrary, it seems probable that anyone engaged in raising money for Harvard would regard a proliferation of An Wangs as cause for unalloyed delight.

It is less easy, however, to wave away the possibility of decreasing ethnic diversity in university student bodies and the potential implications of such a development for the national leadership of the future. Clearly, both individuals and society as a whole benefit when the college students who will supply the bulk of tomorrow's elites are exposed during their formative years to other Americans from the widest possible range of backgrounds. And it is not necessarily self-evident that the national interest would be best served by the replacement of a leadership that has traditionally been disproportionately WASP by one that was disproportionately Jewish and Asian.

Yet, assuming that that is a realistic possibility, it is difficult to devise any just way of forestalling it and even harder to conceive of one that would be politically feasible. Controversial though they are, affirmative action programs for the most disadvantaged groups in our society enjoy sufficient public support that they seem likely to remain a fixture of the American scene for the foreseeable future. But there are obviously finite, if still undefined, limits beyond which affirmative actions cannot be carried without making a complete mockery of the principle that all Americans are equal under the law. To pursue the affirmative goal of ethnic diversity in university student bodies by restricting admission of Jews or Asian Americans would patently exceed those limits. And so far as I am aware, no educator of any substance has even by implication proposed such measures—if only because in the contemporary United States it is impossible to advocate systematic discrimination against the members of any ethnic or religious group without incurring an intolerable degree of public obloquy.

At bottom, then, those who worry about "the Asian problem" in higher education can offer no remedy for it that is either equitable or politically feasible—and in my judgment, that is fortunate. For, in reality, no intervention is desirable; any objective look at the way in which American society is now evolving indicates that the problem, insofar as it may really be one, will essentially solve itself over the course of time. And it will do so in the same way that many other such problems have been resolved in the United States in the past: Americans descended from earlier immigrant groups who today think of Asian Americans as "them" will increasingly come to see them as part of "us."

The chief reason for anticipating this change in perception is that it will, in fact, reflect reality. With each successive generation in this country, the difference in values and behavior patterns between Asian Americans and the rest of the population diminishes. Though it is frequently alleged that Asian-American college students tend to "keep to themselves," that is visibly untrue of many of those I see daily on the campus at Columbia—youngsters who mingle freely with Caucasian classmates, are indistinguishable from them in speech and dress, and appear to have very similar career aspirations. And while those who were actually born in China, Japan, and Korea or are only one generation removed from those countries do as a rule display greater industry and more commitment to academic excellence than most of their non-Asian contemporaries, it seems a safe bet that *their* children will succumb even more completely to the general American ethos. Indeed, according to the *New York Times*, a Chicago study of third-generation Asian Americans indicated that as a group they were less interested in school and did less well academically than first- or second-generation Asian Americans—a dubious blessing surely in terms of our national productivity, but at the same time an impediment to ethnic stereotyping and the survival of overriding ethnic loyalties.

To a significant degree, too, the cultural absorption of Asian Americans into the mainstream of our society will be reinforced by a process of purely physical absorption stemming from the increasing prevalence of ethnic intermarriage. As I noted earlier, this process has already served to blur ethnic lines in the United States considerably and is certain to do so in snowballing fashion in the years ahead. What's more, it will complicate not merely subjective perceptions of ethnicity but the statistical classifications upon which any attempt to achieve ethnic diversity of student bodies by artificial means would have to be based. How, for example, is a university admissions officer supposed to classify the offspring of a WASP father and Chinese-American mother or of a Japanese-American father and a Jewish-American mother?

In short, the widely held belief that our leading institutions of higher education are in long-term danger of being overwhelmed by a huge, indigestible body of Asian Americans seems to me exaggerated and simplistic. I see no way that I or anyone else can confidently predict what the ethnic composition of this country's college population will be thirty or forty years from now. Certainly any such prediction based upon extrapolation from today's college admission figures cannot be taken seriously—unless you are prepared to ignore the fact that there is no way the current influx of Asian Americans into the nation's universities could have been extrapolated from the admissions figures of the late 1950s.

More important yet, the whole thrust of our society strongly suggests that the ethnicity of Asian Americans will seem considerably less relevant to other Americans a generation or two hence than it does today. And as perception of them as somehow intrinsically alien dwindles, so presumably will concern over their numbers in the college population, whatever those may ultimately prove to be.

MY FATHER USED TO cite to me a bit of folk wisdom which says that hardheaded men of affairs sometimes regard teaching teachers as a rather airy-fairy occupation, but it is one to which academics attach supreme importance. To a lamentable number of university professors, in fact, the instruction of undergraduates appears a boring but unfortunately indispensable step in the all-important process of producing still more professors. For this reason, if no other, it was inevitable that the ethnic diversity that came to characterize American undergraduate bodies after World War II would in due course be reflected in what in academic circles is somewhat gradiloquently referred to as "the professoriate."

Logically enough, the order in which the various minority groups won significant representation on college and university faculties mirrored the order in which members of each group had begun to attend college in large numbers. Thus, the first non-WASPs to join the professoriate in force were Jews—who had largely been excluded from it before World War II.* Then, in the late 1950s and early 1960s, Catholics penetrated the academic establishment in sufficient quantity to begin to constitute a meaningful factor. By 1969, in fact, a Carnegie Commission survey showed that 9 percent of all college faculty members nationwide were Jewish and 20 percent were Catholic. (At the country's seventeen most prestigious universities, however, those figures were almost exactly reversed with Jews outnumbering Catholics two to one.)

By 1974, this process of ethnic diversification had reached the point that Stephen Steinberg could write in *The Academic Melting Pot*: "It is apparent that Protestant domination of higher education is becoming a thing of the past." A dozen years later that fact had become even more apparent—and the end was by no means in sight. "The rate of diversification is bound to accelerate still further as today's incumbents retire," Columbia's Prof. James Shenton told me in the summer of 1987. "The change in this respect between now and the end of the century will, I believe, be staggering."

One fact that seems to reinforce Shenton's prophecy is that members of some of the nation's newer and/or particularly disadvantaged minorities have increasingly begun to follow the academic trail blazed a generation ago by the better-established white ethnics. In 1983, just over 4 percent of all U.S. college professors were black, 3.5 percent Asian-American, and only 1.5 percent Hispanic. But an ethnic breakdown of the nearly 32,000 Ph.D.'s awarded in the U.S. in 1986–87—a figure that mirrors the talent pool from which the professors of tomorrow will be drawn—produces a significantly different picture. Here,

---

* Between 1914 and 1939, for example, only a single Jew—Felix Frankfurter—managed to win an appointment to the faculty of the Harvard Law School.

---

although blacks still account for only 4 percent of the total, Hispanics have risen to 3.5 percent—and Asian Americans, who make up only 2.5 percent of the overall national population, have soared to nearly 12 percent of all successful doctoral candidates. And since Asian-American academics typically produce more articles, monographs, and books than their white, black, or Hispanic colleagues it seems reasonable to assume that in the years ahead they will enjoy disproportionate success in a profession whose watchword is "publish or perish."

Whatever the changes in the ethnic composition of the professoriate in the decades immediately ahead, they are sure to be reflected —if at a few years' remove—on the highest rungs of the educational establishment. Or such at least seems to be the lesson of the past. In 1966, Morris B. Abram, then president of the American Jewish Committee, unhappily reported that of the one thousand presidents elected by publicly supported colleges and universities during the previous seventeen years, not one had been Jewish. Yet within little more than twenty years thereafter that barrier had not just been breached but obliterated: by 1987 many of the country's most highly regarded colleges, including MIT, Columbia, Dartmouth, Pennsylvania, and Chicago all had—or had had—Jewish presidents. And that same year Dr. Harold T. Shapiro, the son of the proprietor of Montreal's fanciest Chinese restaurant, resigned the presidency of the University of Michigan to become the eighteenth president of Princeton.

Here, too, Jewish Americans in a sense broke ground for the members of other minority groups. At the beginning of the 1980s, New York University acquired a Greek-American president, former Indiana congressman John Brademas, and from 1978 to 1986 the State University of New York was headed by black economist Clifton Wharton. In neighboring Connecticut during the same period, Italian surnames became a commonplace in the educational firmament: at various times during the eighties, A. Bartlett Giamatti served as president of Yale, John DiBiaggio held the same job at the University of Connecticut, a scholar of Italian-Jewish ancestry named Guido Calabresi was dean of the Yale Law school, and Claire Gaudiani became at one stroke the first Italian American, the first woman, and the first of its own alumni to head New London's Connecticut College. And as the decade drew to a close, two of the nation's most prestigious academic institutions turned for leadership to educators of Middle Eastern background: in 1987, Donna Shalala, a diminutive Lebanese American, left the presidency of New York's Hunter College to take command at the sprawling University of Wisconsin, and the following year, Brown University, perhaps the trendiest but also the least well endowed of the Ivy League colleges, chose as its president Dr. Vartan Gregorian, an Armenian of Iranian birth and a proven virtuoso in the art of fund raising.

For me, this broad process was cast into bold relief by the experience of the three universities with which, for personal or family reasons, I feel the closest ties: Chicago, Yale, and Columbia. When I was a teenager, all three of these institutions were headed by members of the WASP ascendancy: the ineffably self-assured Robert Hutchins at Chicago, the redoubtable Nicholas Murray Butler at Columbia, and benign "Uncle Charlie" Seymour at Yale.

Today, the president of the University of Chicago, Hanna Gray, is a naturalized American of German birth, while the presidency of Columbia is held by the prodigiously energetic Michael Sovern—who, as a result, has become ex officio the first Jewish member of the ruling body of New York's Cathedral Church of St. John the Divine. Perhaps most revealing of all, however, is what has transpired at Yale—a place that in the 1940s one of my more cynical and perceptive classmates there used to describe as "the West Point of Wall Street."

By the late 1970s, the prevailing ethos at this traditionally WASP preserve had sufficiently altered so that the Corporation, as Yale's trustees are collectively known, felt emboldened to offer the presidency of the university to Henry Rosovsky, a Jewish American of German birth who had won distinction as dean of Harvard. But although his Israeli-born wife stongly urged him to take the job, Rosovsky in the end refused it—partly because he believed he had important unfinished business at Harvard, but also, as he later confessed, because for all the courtesy and respect accorded him by the members of the Yale Corporation, he could not conquer the feeling that at bottom "I wasn't their kind of guy."

Rosovsky would surely have made an outstanding president of Yale—but so, too, in my judgment, would Hanna Gray, a distinguished scholar and highly effective administrator who as provost of the university had become acting president upon the resignation of the previous incumbent, Kingman Brewster. Perhaps because there were limits to how many traditions they were prepared to scrap at one blow, however, the members of the Corporation disappointed feminists by turning instead to A. Bartlett Giamatti, an English professor with no significant previous experience as an administrator.

On the surface of things, the election of a president with an Italian surname appeared to mark as much of a new departure for Yale as the installation of a Jewish president would have, but in reality it represented a less radical break with the past than casual observers assumed: unlike Rosovsky, Giamatti was a product of Yale himself, and while his father was of Italian ancestry, his mother was a member of a prominent Yankee family—an aspect of his heritage emphasized by the fact that his given names are invariably rendered as "A. Bartlett" rather than "Angelo B."

Indeed, in all essential respects, "Bart" Giamatti was the very model of the modern Yale establishmentarian, a symbol of continuity more than radical change. And when, after eight years in office, he decided to seek new challenges,* a search committee led by—who else?—Cyrus Vance turned to another figure of similar stripe, Columbia Law School dean Benno Schmidt, Jr.

Though his name scarcely qualifies as Anglo-Saxon—like a surprisingly large number of Texans his family was of German origin—Schmidt is the son of a prominent financier and was educated at Exeter and Yale, where he played hockey, joined a fraternity, and in the ultimate social accolade, was "tapped" for a senior society. He has, in short, all the caste marks of what was known in my time at Yale as a "white shoe boy." Yet as a lawyer and a teacher he has been in the forefront of liberal opinion on such issues as race relations, freedom of the press, and government secrecy. In this respect, in fact, there is scant difference between him and his predecessor as dean at Columbia Law, Michael Sovern—or between him and "Bart" Giamatti.

---

* It may say something about changing American priorities that where his predecessor, Kingman Brewster, had moved on to become ambassador to Great Britain, Giamatti opted for the presidency of the National Baseball League.

THE FACT THAT there is so much similarity between people of such different heritage as Giamatti, Sovern, and Schmidt—and for that matter, between all of them and Greek-American John Brademas or Lebanese-American Donna Shalala—seems to me to bear directly upon a thorny but unavoidable question: what if any effect has the increasing ethnic diversity of the academic establishment had upon the intellectual and ideological tone of higher education in the United States?

No one, I think, can convincingly deny that as American colleges and universities have become less WASPish in personnel, they have become, broadly speaking, notably more "liberal" in social and political terms. For those addicted to *post hoc, propter hoc* logic, this makes it tempting to jump to the conclusion that it is the rise of the ethnic academic that primarily accounts for the strongly liberal and even radical climate on so many contemporary campuses. And it is easy enough to produce anecdotal evidence—and even some statistics—that would seem to support that conclusion.

In his book *The Academic Melting Pot*, for example, sociologist Stephen Steinberg notes that surveys conducted in 1969 among faculty members at hundreds of American colleges and universities indicated that Jewish academics as a group held markedly more liberal sociopolitical views than their Protestant and Catholic colleagues.* And on the surface of things, this finding might appear to lend plausibility to all sorts of ethnic generalizations such as an eminent Harvard professor's offhand—and totally uncensorious—comment to me that the high proportion of Jewish faculty members at leading U.S. law schools nowadays might help to account for the increased political activism among their students and recent graduates.

But self-evident as some of them may seem at first blush, judg-

---

* Two of the numerous specific benchmarks in the surveys cited by Steinberg were these:

1) In the 1968 presidential election, 30 percent of the Protestant professors and 23 percent of the Catholic ones at prestigious universities voted for Richard Nixon. Among Jewish faculty members at the same institutions, the comparable figure was only 5 percent.

2) As of 1969, 63 percent of the Jewish faculty members at prestigious universities believed that marijuana should be legalized, but among both Protestant and Catholic professors only 45 percent held that view.

ments about today's academic scene that are based primarily on the ethnic and religious backgrounds of its inhabitants do not stand up well to close scrutiny. In fact, on the strength of the 1969 surveys he used, Stephen Steinberg concluded that the most important determinant of an academic's political attitudes was not the particular religious faith he professed but the strength with which he espoused it. For Protestants, Catholics, and Jews alike, the general rule was that the more devout a professor the more conservative he tended to be politically.

Unpalatable as true believers may find the fact, moreover, it would seem to be this correlation rather than any link between political beliefs and particular brands of religion that explains the growing ascendency of liberalism in academia over recent decades. For Steinberg's surveys also indicated that when their work is measured by such conventional standards of scholarly productivity as research activity and number of books published, deeply religious (and hence more conservative) academics tend as a group to be outperformed by their less devout (and more liberal) colleagues. Strong religious convictions, in other words, appear to be an impediment to scholarly achievement* and thus to advancement in the academic hierarchy.

Inevitably, the fact that religiosity constitutes something of a professional handicap has rendered it increasingly uncommon among academics, particularly at the elite universities that attract the most productive and highly regarded scholars. This is not to say that successful academics universally spurn religion entirely, but rather that in most cases it at best plays second fiddle to other considerations in their intellectual scheme of things. Indeed, in James Shenton's view, "the role of religion has come to be more in the context of what I would call ancestor worship. It's a kind of statement about where you have come from." And more often than not the same holds true in contemporary academia for religion's frequent companion, the strong assertion of a particular ethnic identity.

---

* One possible reason for this has been suggested by Columbia University's Prof. James Shenton. "At its best," he notes, "academic life involves a commitment to what you might call disciplined analysis; it means being committed to remaining open to a variety of intellectual hypotheses." And that, of course, is less feasible for anyone who insists that a large body of dogma must be taken as given.

Obviously, though, a profession of faith or ethnicity that is in substantial degree symbolic and/or nostalgic is not as confining in terms of day-to-day behavior as the original article. And as a result, statistics on the religious and ethnic composition of an academic community no longer necessarily offer a simple, surefire indication of its political and intellectual inclinations. Historically, for example, American Catholics have often been perceived as an essentially conservative force. Yet, as Shenton points out, "here at Columbia, where the student body has a reputation for being left of center, substantially more than half our undergraduates are now Catholic." By the same token, the most outspokenly conservative Columbia faculty member I have encountered during my own years there is a philosophy professor who happens to be Jewish.

So far as I can see, then, it is impossible to establish any clear connection between the political orientation of the American educational establishment and the ethnic diversity that has come to characterize it since World War II. In so saying, however, I do not mean to imply that the steady increase in the diversity of faculty and student bodies has not had significant consequences. It has, in fact, been of critical importance in creating an ever growing body of Americans whose origins would once have confined them to the lower rungs of the national ladder but who now possess skills, credentials, and caste marks that have carried them to the top.

Beyond that, by embracing ethnic diversity, our educational establishment has somewhat ironically helped to diminish the importance that members of America's various elites attach to ethnicity, whether in themselves or in their colleagues. In practical terms the fact that Secretary of Defense Frank Carlucci and the chief of staff of the U.S. Army, Gen. Carl Vuono, are both Italian Americans is of considerably less significance than the fact that one of them graduated from Princeton and the other from West Point. For quite clearly Carlucci has more in common with his fellow Princetonian George Shultz and Vuono with Gen. Roscoe Robinson, Jr., a black graduate of West Point, than either of them is likely to have with an Italian-American bricklayer.

To belabor a point, then, education in America still promotes conformity all right, but what it promotes can no longer accurately be described as Anglo-conformity. In an implicit comparison of the behavior patterns of university students in his own undergraduate days and those of the students he now teaches at Columbia, James Shenton mused: "There are emerging some important modifications . . . I get a rather striking sense that we are going forward step by step into a world in which, without even thinking about it, we are absorbing all kinds of value nuances that once would have seemed unacceptable."

9

NO BUSINESS
LIKE SHOW BUSINESS

One night in the 1970s as I was walking through Manhattan's East Forties with a group of fellow journalists, I spotted drawn up at the curb a spanking new Rolls-Royce of a type that had only recently come on the market. Recalling that one of the few such models so far shipped to the United States had been purchased by Reggie Jackson, then at the height of his prowess as a home-run hitter, I remarked to my companions in mild excitement that this might well be Reggie's car. But at that moment a man in a chauffeur's cap stepped out of the shadows and said with evident amusement: " 'Fraid you're wrong about that, friend. *My* boss is a quiet millionaire."

The kind of condescension toward an uncommonly talented and intelligent man that was implicit in that comment helps to explain why Americans of liberal persuasion so often wax indignant over the role played in our pop culture by the members of ethnic and religious minorities. At best, the high visibility of minority athletes and entertainers is perceived by many dedicated progressives as fostering ethnic stereotyping of the "blacks are born with a sense of rhythm" variety. At worst, the relatively favorable reception that performers from minority backgrounds encounter in sports and our other forms of mass diversion are seen as a form of exploitation, a device through which mainstream America relegates ambitious and gifted "outsiders" to positions of no real power or prestige.

That there is some substance to these charges seems to me impossible to deny. But like many partial truths, this one only serves to obscure a central reality—which is that the various forms of popular culture, at least since they became national rather than regional in their means of diffusion, have played a vital part in diminishing the importance that Americans attach to ethnicity. And ironically, what made this possible was the historic tendency of Americans from the longer-established ethnic groups to shun careers in sports and show business.

Given the childlike enthusiasm with which even the WASPiest and most prestigious members of the American Establishment often embrace the jock culture and court the acquaintance of golf champions, football quarterbacks, and tennis stars, it might seem odd that in the past relatively few Americans with the opportunity to do anything else have chosen to play games for a living. Yet that is a pattern which was visible almost from the time that professional and semiprofessional sports first emerged in this country. Because the life of a professional athlete is often dangerous and until recent times generally offered very limited economic rewards, Americans whose backgrounds gave them ready access to other fields have traditionally found it expedient to leave athletic careers to the members of ethnic groups somewhat lower on the national totem pole. In the 1890s, in fact, there were so many Irish-American ballplayers in the big leagues that, in an eerie foretaste of the inanities sometimes voiced today about black sprinters and basketball players, it was seriously suggested in some quarters that the Irish had a special genetic talent for the game.

For a paradigmatic example of ethnic patterns in U.S. sports, however, there is perhaps nothing to match the history of professional boxing. In his 1976 book *Sports in America,* James Michener reports the findings of a sociologist who made a study of prize fights in Boston over a hundred-year period: at first, the combatants were heavily of

English working class origin, but as the decades rolled on, the predominant group became successively Irish, Jewish, "French," * and finally black.

As anyone with even a passing interest in boxing is aware, this sequence has been duplicated with certain local variations throughout the U.S. In the fights that I followed as a boy in the 1930s, the up-and-coming boxers were mostly Jewish and Italian-American—though some of them, curiously enough, fought under Irish names in the belief that this would somehow enhance their crowd appeal.† But by the time my own sons began to take an interest in boxing, Jewish and Italian fighters had been almost entirely supplanted by black ones—who, in turn, are now being crowded, at least in the lighter weight classes, by Hispanics.

On the face of it, then, the history of boxing clearly belies any notion of unique ethnic adaptation to particular forms of athletic activity; it seems highly implausible, to put it mildly, that over the last couple of generations Americans of Irish or Jewish heritage have undergone genetic mutations that have somehow diminished their natural talent for fisticuffs. Instead, the obvious conclusion is that the changing ethnic patterns in professional sports have essentially reflected changing patterns of economic and social opportunity—in other words, that as the members of any particular ethnic group have become more completely integrated into middle class American society, they have tended to leave the harsh existence of the hired gladiator to the hungry members of more recently arrived or less thoroughly integrated groups.

Whether this process will prevail as strongly in the future as it has in the past, though, appears uncertain. There are, in fact, indications that the attractiveness of an athletic career to Americans of middle class background and aspirations has markedly increased in recent years. And the reason that this is so relates directly to the way in which mass entertainment has developed in twentieth century America.

---

* Presumably in this case shorthand for French-Canadian.

† One such pseudo-Irishman was Frank Sinatra's fireman father, Marty Sinatra, who fought out of Hoboken, New Jersey, under the *nom de ring* of O'Brien.

IT WAS, as I suggested earlier in this book, a fact of considerable historic significance that Americans of "the old stock," WASP or otherwise, played very little part in the creation of the first quintessentially American source of mass entertainment: the motion picture industry. By-blows of the kind of carnival-style attractions offered at places such as Coney Island, "store shows" first began to appear in number around the turn of the century in Manhattan's Lower East Side, then the citadel of recent Jewish immigrants. To respectable businessmen and investors, it seemed abundantly clear that this kind of cheap amusement, explicitly tailored to the tastes of the poor, the unlettered, and the foreign-born, would never achieve real economic importance. And no one in the Eastern financial establishment saw it as any loss when, shortly before World War II, the center of the infant film industry migrated from New York City to southern California.

The result of this WASP shortsightedness was that in its crucial formative years the movie business came to be dominated by men who had started out in vaudeville, nickelodeon parlors, amusement parks, and assorted other forms of petty enterprise. The Warner brothers, for example, were the sons of a butcher, Samuel Goldwyn's original occupation was that of glove salesman, William Fox was a onetime clothing merchant, and Louis B. Mayer as a youth drove a junk wagon for his father in St. John, New Brunswick. And all of these nascent tycoons, like the majority of other first-generation movie moguls, were Jewish.

It does not, I think, speak well for either the vision or entrepreneurial initiative of this country's traditional economic elite that what occurred in the movie industry was in considerable degree duplicated in later decades in what were obviously destined to be even more pervasive and readily accessible forms of entertainment than the movies. As the electronic era dawned, it was once again entrepreneurs of minority origin who were quickest to recognize and capitalize upon the potential of the new technology. First in radio and then in television the pioneering empire builders were not scions of WASPdom but Jewish Americans such as David Sarnoff, William Paley, and Leonard Goldenson.

To be sure, in all of the major fields of mass entertainment, the traditional economic establishment was quick to offer its services once it had become unmistakable that there were enormous profits to be garnered. But by the time the respectable money got into the act, outsiders had become insiders in the popular entertainment business to such an extent that it was no longer possible to impose there the kind of ethnic discrimination that so long prevailed in fields such as banking and heavy industry. Both in their management and in their operating practices, the mass entertainment industries were from the start irretrievably de-WASPified.

Purely in terms of its economic impact, this has been a phenomenon of extraordinary importance. For mass entertainment has not only defied the expectations of yesteryear's conventional wisdom by becoming big business, it has come to play a role in our national economic life even greater than the astronomical movie and television salaries familiar to every *People* magazine reader might suggest. It is one of the few businesses in which the United States still retains unquestioned worldwide preeminence and manages to export substantially more than it imports. According to *Forbes* magazine, in fact, entertainment exports—television programming, movies, videocassettes, and musical recordings—earned a bigger net profit for the U.S. in 1986 than the exports of any other industry except the defense-aerospace complex.*

Even that rather remarkable statistic, however, understates the role that the entertainment industry now plays in American economic life. Specifically, it fails to reflect the fact that since the 1960s the boundaries of the entertainment business have effectively expanded to include a vast new province. In his book *Spoiled Sport*, John Underwood accurately observes that with the emergence of TV as the prime force in American popular culture, it became apparent to alert entrepreneurs that "sport was not sport at all but a tool for extracting incalculable riches from a sports-hungry population." The result, in Underwood's words, was that sports became "the shill of television"— or as Howard Cosell more gently phrased it, that in contemporary America, "sports aren't life and death; they're just entertainment."

---

* Disquieting though drumbeaters for high technology may find the fact, the nearly $5-billion trade surplus rung up by the U.S. entertainment industry in 1986 was more than three times as large as the one achieved by American computer manufacturers the same year.

As part of the entertainment industry, American sports—including not only once "gentlemanly" pastimes such as golf and tennis but in many instances, avowedly amateur college sports as well—have inevitably been transformed into profit-driven enterprises. This, of course, is a development that those who cling to a kind of classic Greek concept of the ennobling function of athletic endeavor find unrelievedly distressing. But it also has its positive aspect: like the rest of the entertainment industry sports have become not just a dubious haven for the disadvantaged but, for those athletes who are exceptionally talented, lucky, and shrewd, a potential highway to wealth and status.

ALTHOUGH THE FACT is often overlooked by envious workaday folks, there is solid economic logic behind the seemingly hyperinflated sums paid big-name entertainers and athletes. The cost of producing a movie or putting on a big league baseball game for a very large audience is not inherently much greater than the cost of doing so for a small audience. This means that every extra ticket sold or TV advertising dollar attracted by a performer who pulls in big crowds adds a disproportionately large amount to the profits of the enterprise—which, of course, gives such performers a high degree of bargaining leverage. And over the more than three-quarters of a century since popular entertainment began to become big business, shrewd performers and their agents have made ever more effective use of that leverage. Where movie stars of the Francis X. Bushman and Mary Pickford eras were for the most part only richly rewarded hired hands, today's topflight performers routinely command a piece of the action through such devices as residuals, syndication rights, profit participation, and even by the assumption of entrepreneurial functions themselves.

One consequence of this process has been the creation of a state of affairs widely deplored by earnest souls concerned with the nation's value system: the most successful American entertainers nowadays command bigger incomes than the men who run the nation's largest industrial enterprises. In 1986, as I noted earlier, the most highly paid corporate executive in the United States was Lee Iacocca, whose total take from salary, bonuses, and stock options was just short of $21 million. But that same year, according to *Forbes* magazine, there were no fewer than eight show biz figures whose earnings surpassed Iacocca's.*

Professional athletes, of course, have not yet achieved such stratospheric heights since like the movie stars of old they remain essentially hired hands. But with the full flowering of the television age, they have become notably expensive hired hands, the most desirable of whom command salaries rivaling those paid to all but the most exalted figures in the corporate world. As far back as the early 1980s, in fact, there were already some seventy big league baseball players whose salaries were at least four times as large as that of the president of the United States. By the late eighties, million-dollar salary packages had also become old hat in professional basketball and football, and an average player in the National Football League was earning $100,000 a year.

Television, however, did more than merely inflate the salaries of professional athletes. It also endowed the more notable of them, people such as Joe Namath, O. J. Simpson, Walt Frazier, and Earl "the Pearl" Monroe, with that most cherished of attributes in contemporary U.S. society: celebrity. This, as Sen. Bill Bradley noted in his memoirs of his own basketball career, means that increasingly professional athletes have become "perfectly cast to tickle the consumer appetites of affluent America." As a result, even in sports with a less than universal following such as golf, skiing, and hockey, the standout performers can supplement their salaries handsomely through product endorsements and participation in radio and TV commercials.

To argue that all this has been an unalloyed blessing for those engaged in professional and big-time "amateur" sports would be patent nonsense. Athletes, both white and black, who emerge from college uneducated if not functionally illiterate, young men who in the headiness of sudden wealth and notoriety succumb to the lure of drugs and/or easy sex, onetime national idols who have squandered fortunes and wake up in their thirties to find themselves with neither financial se-

---

* The golden eight, together with the *Forbes* estimates of their 1986 earnings: Bill Cosby ($57 million), Michael Jackson ($30 million), Eddie Murphy and Bruce Springsteen ($27 million each), Madonna ($26 million), Whitney Houston ($24 million), Steven Spielberg ($23 million), Sylvester Stallone ($21 million).

---

curity nor marketable skills—all these are sadly commonplace spectacles. But what is important to bear in mind, too, is that they are considerably less than universal phenomena. And they do not, I think, loom large enough to outweigh another truth about sports as a career choice in today's America. That truth, to quote Bill Bradley once again, is that the professional athlete who makes it to the upper rungs "has become a financial success in a materialistic society which believes that money earned accurately measures accomplishment."

Partly for this reason it is likely, I believe, that in years ahead the social origins of professional athletes will increasingly come to resemble those of performers in the more undisguised forms of show biz. For many decades now the huge financial rewards potentially available to movie actors have helped induce people of relatively privileged upbringing and a strong theatrical bent to take a flyer on a film career in preference to a safer and "more serious" occupation. Along with the children of a dozen disadvantaged minorities, Hollywood in its glory days also attracted the likes of Princetonian Jimmie Stewart, imperious Yankee aristocrat Katharine Hepburn, that improbably preppy Humphrey Bogart, and even, at least for a time, John Davis Lodge of the Boston Lodges.* And in similar fashion the fame and fortune conferred by TV stardom have proved an irresistible lure to such as Johnny Carson, Dick Cavett, Chevy Chase, and Suzanne Pleshette—all eminently equipped by social and/or educational background to have pursued more conventional middle class callings.

Today there are at least some indications that this same pattern may be emerging in big-time sports. To be sure, some of the most visible symbols of increased middle class participation in professional sports—former Rhodes Scholar Bill Bradley in basketball, University of Southern California graduate Tom Seaver in baseball, ex–naval officer Roger Staubach and economics aficionado Jack Kemp in football—have already banked the big money and moved on. But in virtually every sport deemed worthy of prime-time exposure, the supply of

---

* The younger brother of the late Henry Cabot Lodge, John Lodge appeared in half a dozen 1930s Paramount films including *Little Women* and *The Little Colonel*. In his post-Hollywood incarnation his roles included governor of Connecticut and U.S. ambassador to Spain.

---

would-be superstars who bear unmistakably bourgeois earmarks now appears to be substantially larger than in the past;* in late 1987, for example, the *Yale Alumni Magazine* somewhat boastfully reported that there were five recent Yale graduates then playing in the National Hockey League—an institution that, much as some of us may cherish it, cannot be said to possess a truly classy image.

At first blush the prospect that the scions of the middle class will increasingly penetrate show biz in all its branches might seem to portend its increasing WASPification as well. But that, I believe, is not in the cards—or at least only marginally so. For one thing, the American middle class as a whole is now irretrievably multiethnic and that is bound to be reflected in those of its members who choose to pursue careers in entertainment and sports. Beyond that, the fact that prolonged and expensive education is not a prerequisite for success in these fields means that they will continue to offer uncommon opportunity to people from disadvantaged backgrounds and hence will presumably attract them in disproportionate numbers.

Ethnically, in other words, what appears to lie ahead for show business is more of the same—or to be more precise, an intensification of the present situation. And that is one of almost incredible complexity. Of the individual entertainers whom *Forbes* identified as the biggest money earners in 1986, four (Bill Cosby, Michael Jackson, Eddie Murphy, and Whitney Houston) were black, one (Steven Spielberg) was Jewish, and three (Madonna, Bruce Springsteen, and Sylvester Stallone) were of mixed ethnicity.†

When one moves beyond the ranks of these latter-day Croesuses, moreover, the ethnic diversity of successful entertainers and athletes almost defies description. There are, obviously, numerous representatives of each of what might be called the nation's major minorities— Italian Americans ranging from Perry Como and Martin Scorsese to Yogi Berra, Jewish Americans from Barbra Streisand and Mel Brooks

---

* The most notable exception to this rule is boxing, presumably because of its uniquely brutal nature and the understandable reluctance of most upscale citizens to risk having their brains pounded into guacamole.

† Though all of the last three share Italian ancestry, Madonna's mother was of French-Canadian origin, Stallone's mother was a showgirl of French heritage, and Springsteen is of Dutch background on his father's side.

---

to Sandy Koufax, Greek Americans from Telly Savalas to Alex Karras, Slavic Americans from Karl Malden* to Carl Yastrzemski and Bernie Kosar, Hispanics from José Feliciano to Lee Trevino. But there are also many members of less visible minorities—Lebanese (Danny Thomas, Jamie Farr), Lithuanian (Vitas Gerulaitis), Cajun (Ron Guidry, Bobby Hebert), and Albanians (the late John Belushi).

What is most striking, though, is that more and more often the ethnicity of individual show biz and sports celebrities is impossible to define in a single word. In inevitable reflection of what has been happening in the general population, a growing number of these people are of multiple ethnic heritage. Even a cursory, top-of-the-head roll call of such figures who for one reason or another have captured my particular attention results in a remarkable list: Alan Alda, Peter Bogdanovich, James Caan, Cher, Keith Hernandez, Liberace, Jim Plunkett, Burt Reynolds, Linda Ronstadt, Sissy Spacek, John Travolta, Raquel Welch. Every one of these dozen men and women represents a blend of anywhere from two to four different ethnic strains, and among them they boast at least twenty different heritages including Armenian, Bolivian, Cherokee, Czech, Dutch, English, German, Irish, Italian, Jewish, Lithuanian, Mexican, Polish, Scots, Serbian, and Turkish.

Inevitably, as is also the case with the general population, this blending process is gradually serving to blur and in some instances even effectively to obliterate ethnic distinctions. It seems a safe bet that even at the height of Dave DeBusschere's fame few basketball fans knew (or cared) that he was the grandson of Belgian immigrants. By the same token, it is doubtful that the majority of movie buffs who have enjoyed their performances could testify with any certainty to the ancestry of Henry Fonda (WASP, Dutch, and Italian), Paul Newman (German and Hungarian), or Charles Bronson (Russian and Lithuanian). And in the final ironic turn of the wheel, some of the most notable "ethnic" performances in successful television series have been out-and-out masquerades: both the late John Bonner, who played the bumbling, ineffably Germanic Wehrmacht sergeant in *Hogan's Heroes* and Henry Winkler, who portrayed the unmistakably Italian-American "Fonz" in *Happy Days*, were, in fact, Jewish. As for Detec-

---

* Né Malden Sekulovich.

---

tive Sergeant Wojohowicz, the earnest "Polish" cop in *Barney Miller*, the actor who created that role bears in real life the name Maxwell Trowbridge Gail, Jr.

None of this is to argue that show biz and sports have now entered into some nirvana in which ethnicity has no bearing whatever upon success. What is clear, however, is that the most egregious ethnic barriers to success in these fields have either already fallen or were as of the late 1980s in the process of doing so. Entertainers born with distinctively Italian or Jewish surnames are no longer automatically expected to change them—a fact that, as I shall shortly discuss, marks a significant departure from traditional practice—nor does the retention of such a name any longer constitute an impediment to winning "upscale" roles.

More impressive yet, in the 1970s and 1980s the oldest and most disadvantaged of American minorities (except, of course, for the continent's original inhabitants) began to win comparable acceptance on the top rungs of the show biz ladder. Suddenly Bill Cosby and Robert Guillaume could play leading roles in TV sitcoms—an art form exceeded by few others in its meticulous calibration to the least common denominator in popular taste. And even in the more regressive precincts of the National Football League, blacks by the end of the eighties were no longer just running backs, tight ends, and linemen; in 1988, Doug Williams of the Washington Redskins became the first black quarterback ever to lead an NFL team in the Super Bowl.

I belabor these familiar facts to underscore a reality that is often denied by understandably impatient minority spokesmen: the changes in ethnic practices that have occurred in entertainment and sports in the last few decades have not merely conferred fame and affluence upon a relative handful of exceptionally fortunate individuals of minority origin; those changes have also reflected in a significant way an altered status for entire groups in our society.

This is, in fact, so obvious a reality that some particularly sanguine souls have cited it as evidence that the people who shape popular culture in America have consciously and courageously led the way in battling ethnic discrimination. But that, for better or for worse, is a claim that a dispassionate consideration of the past behavior of the powers that be in sports and show biz renders highly suspect.

FOR MORE THAN half a century a remarkably diverse assortment of people have agreed that the U.S. movie industry consciously seeks to manipulate public attitudes in order to further political and social objectives that, depending upon one's point of view, are either inutterably sinister or incontestably admirable. As far back as 1940, Martin Dies of Texas, the paramount congressional know-nothing of his day, charged that Hollywood was infested with people who were sneakily serving the communist cause, a fact he sought to explain by observing that "most of the producers are Jews." At the other end of the spectrum, both politically and in time, liberal-minded folk in the 1980s have unhappily denounced the increased acceptability they feel people such as Clint Eastwood and Sylvester Stallone have given to right-wing vigilantism and mindless chauvinism.

But it has not by any means been brickbats all the way for the moviemakers. In Hollywood's defense, its partisans have pointed to what they see as landmarks in the struggle against bigotry in this country—films such as *Crossfire* and *Gentleman's Agreement*, which marked the first major assaults on anti-Semitism in popular entertainment, and a long list of productions ranging from *Home of the Brave* to *Beverly Hills Cop* that have implicitly condemned or openly satirized prejudice against blacks.

There is, however, an overriding difficulty with all of these allegations of cinematic brainwashing, whether malignant or beneficent: they ignore the fact that the last thing a mass entertainment medium is inclined to do is to alienate any significant element of its potential audience. And precisely for this reason, the presentation of highly controversial political themes even in disguised or heavily sugared form has traditionally been shunned by the movie industry. Admittedly, screenwriter John Howard Lawson, one of the "Hollywood Ten" pilloried by Congress in 1947, proudly asserted in a left-wing journal that in the scripts on which he had worked it had invariably been "my aim to present the Communist position." But in reality, the most politically charged script Lawson had actually written was for *Blockade*, a 1938 movie on the Spanish Civil War that, as Otto Friedrich sardonically notes in his history of Hollywood, "somehow unaccountably failed to say which side was which."

As Friedrich makes plain, however, the fact that *Blockade* was ideologically caponized was not unaccountable at all. In the eyes of the men who held the purse strings in Hollywood in those days, the size of the box office was not just a major concern but the sole concern of any real importance. Louis B. Mayer, for one, was so anxious to keep his films playing in German theaters that even after the Nazis had come to power in Berlin, he gave a German diplomat a special preview of *Three Comrades* in an effort to insure its acceptability to the Hitler regime. Indeed, among the movie tycoons of that era in general, overt hostility to Nazism and Fascism was remarkably slow to appear: in the 1930s Harry Cohn of Columbia Pictures kept an autographed portrait of Mussolini on his office wall, and as late as 1940 it was still a violation of the Hollywood Production Code to make a film urging U.S. intervention in World War II. And while this may at first blush seem merely ancient history of no contemporary relevance, anyone who takes that view should reflect on another point made by Otto Friedrich: none of the anti–Vietnam War films that became so ubiquitous in the 1980s appeared until safely after the U.S. withdrawal from Indochina.

Given this history of ideological timidity, it is scarcely surprising that upon close examination the movie industry's role in coming to grips with ethnic issues also proves to have been considerably less than a pioneering one. For several decades, indeed, it was precisely the contrary. In the era before World War II, naked anti-Semitism was still a powerful and pervasive force in the United States, and in response to that ugly reality Hollywood's heavily Jewish management adopted what were essentially diversionary tactics. In their *History of the Jews of Los Angeles*, Max Vorspan and Lloyd Gartner recall that in the prewar movie business "Hollywood's Jewish associations were regarded as not proper to acknowledge . . . As a group, the producers were extremely sensitive to public opinion and strongly desired to be known as 'American' and not 'Jewish' . . .''

In their efforts to achieve this goal, the men who ran Hollywood insisted that their films reflect what they regarded as traditional "American," i.e., WASP, values, an approach that perhaps reached its apogee in Mickey Rooney's vastly popular Andy Hardy films. Rather less defensibly, they also imposed pseudo-WASP identities on the stars who were the industry's most visible figures. Until well after

World War II, any actor who bore a "foreign" name and had not already voluntarily Anglicized it was virtually certain to be presented by studio bosses with a list of suitably WASP—or at least ethnically neutral—replacements to choose between, and the litany of actors and actresses who bowed to this requirement is a staggeringly long one.* And the process was by no means always confined to name changes: David Kaminsky, for example, not only became Danny Kaye, but because his appearance struck Sam Goldwyn as "too Jewish," he was also induced to have his reddish-brown hair dyed blond.

In the context of the 1980s when the retention of "ethnic" surnames by entertainers has become a commonplace, all this might seem so much water over the dam. And in any case, the notion that the movie industry has consistently displayed ethnic as well as political timidity would seem to be belied by the fact that since World War II, it has churned out a steadily increasing volume of films that directly or indirectly preach against ethnic bigotry and even in some instances glorify minority group members and lifestyles. Yet welcome as that state of affairs is, it is impossible in my view to find persuasive evidence that it reflects greatly increased courage on the part of the motion picture establishment or that it has been a primary force in producing new and more enlightened public attitudes on ethnicity.

To begin with, it is far from clear how and to what extent popular entertainment has any direct effect upon the convictions and behavior of those exposed to it; years of scholarly study of the impact of television violence upon children, for example, have not yet produced conclusive evidence as to whether that impact is good, bad, or nonexistent. What does seem certain is that a good deal of the time a show with a

---

* What a superannuated copy of the *World Almanac* that still reposes on my bookshelf calls a "selected" list of entertainers who changed their names runs to a page and a half of extremely small type and includes such notables as Lauren Bacall (Betty Joan Perske), Anne Bancroft (Anna Maria Italiano), Theda Bara (Theodosia Goodman), Tony Bennett (Anthony Benedetto), Jack Benny (Benjamin Kubelsky), George Burns (Nathan Birnbaum), Tony Curtis (Bernard Schwarz), Doris Day (Doris von Kappelhoff), Kirk Douglas (Issur Danielovich), Melvyn Douglas (Melvyn Hesselberg), June Havoc (June Hovic), Rita Hayworth (Margarita Cansino), Dean Martin (Dino Crocetti), Edward G. Robinson (Emanual Goldenberg), Raquel Welch (Raquel Tejada), and Ed Wynn (Isaiah Leopold). In what I regard as a lamentable oversight, however, the almanac's editors chose to omit from their list the first film cowboy, "Bronco Billy" Anderson, who was born Max Aronson.

---

message simply serves to intensify opinions already held by those exposed to it—even when those opinions run directly counter to the one the show is intended to promote.* Thus, a contemporary survey of people who had seen *Gentleman's Agreement* revealed that while 76 percent of them professed to have come away from the film with a more favorable attitude toward Jews, a startling 23 percent said that it had made them more anti-Semitic than they already were.

More important than this, though, is the fact that even assuming they do have the power to change audience preconceptions, the people who control the movie industry have not tested that power by getting out ahead of the crowd on questions of ethnic prejudice. Instead, the industry's "pioneering" films have either followed changes in the national consensus at a safe interval or at best, have paralleled such changes. The first film assaults on anti-Semitism did not appear until after World War II—by which time the horrors inflicted on Europe's Jewish inhabitants by the Nazis had stirred the public conscience in this country. Similarly, *Go for Broke*, Dore Schary's tribute to the gallant nisei troops of the 442nd U.S. Infantry Battalion and the first film to present Japanese Americans in a favorable light, did not appear until five years after World War II had ended—and even then Louis B. Mayer condemned the project, grumbling that there was no box office percentage in "making pictures about the Japs."†

In fairness it can perhaps be argued that the movie industry has been somewhat bolder in its treatment of the nation's black minority— but not outstandingly so. Since the early post–World War II years when blacks finally began to escape from Stepin Fetchit roles, the position they have occupied in our films has essentially mirrored the evolving attitudes of the majority of the nation's white population. The movies involving blacks that Hollywood made in the 1950s and 1960s were virtually all "problem" films in which blacks were accorded key roles only because they were black. Not until the 1970s did films begin

---

* This phenomenon, so I am told, is so common that it has come to be known in the social science trade as "the boomerang effect."

† As it turned out, Schary had read public opinion more accurately than Mayer; though not a major money-spinner *Go for Broke* was a solid commercial success.

to appear that showed blacks as a diversified and unremarkable element of the American population.

By that time, too, of course, television had long since supplanted the movies as the most pervasive force in American popular culture, and as an inevitable result of that fact, TV's ethnic content had also become a matter of lively concern to social scientists and special pleaders alike. And in television as in the movies, the 1970s saw a flood of successful shows featuring white ethnics and blacks in central and sympathetic roles—series such as *Chico and the Man, Kojak, Columbo, Barney Miller* and *The Jeffersons.* Indeed, the 1977 blockbuster *Roots,* which underscored the participation of blacks in the general American experience, pulled more viewers (an estimated total of 130 million people) than any other TV program up to that time. And by 1986 the *Cosby Show,* in which a prosperous black family coped with the same problems in the same fashion as a stereotypical white middle class family, was the season's top-rated program in terms of audience share.

To some, all this has suggested that, whatever its other shortcomings, TV must at least be credited with admirable leadership in combating ethnic prejudice. Perhaps above all, such leadership was attributed to Norman Lear, who was richly rewarded in cash as well as public esteem for what was perceived as his daring in ridiculing the blue collar bigotry of Archie Bunker in *All in the Family.*

Yet since TV moguls are at least as single-mindedly bent on maximizing their audiences as movie moguls, it would clearly be illogical to expect commercial television to be any more prepared to risk controversy than Hollywood—and in reality it has not been. In this respect, I believe, no one has put the accomplishments of Norman Lear and the television industry as a whole into clearer perspective than Ted Westover did in an article in *TV Guide.* "Norman Lear," Westover wrote, "toiled mightily in the 1970s to drag television situation comedy kicking and screaming into the 1960s."

Begrudging as it may sound, in fact, I am persuaded that insofar as television genuinely has helped to alter ethnic roles and perceptions in this country, it has chiefly done so as an inadvertent consequence of its co-option of professional sports and big-time amateur athletics. Certainly it is no mere accident of history that the period in which the number of black and Hispanic players began to soar coincided with the period in which television revenue, directly and indirectly, began to occupy a key role in big-time athletics.* As the profit potential ballooned, however, so did the number of teams in professional football, basketball, and even baseball, and this, in turn, created a competition for talent that left owners no rational choice but to tap sources they had previously neglected or scorned.

That is not to say that profit alone was the spur or that a concern for ethnic equity has been totally lacking in big-time athletics. It would, I think, be unduly cynical to argue that the late Branch Rickey was not at least partly motivated by his sense of justice when he decided to risk the most celebrated racial breakthrough in the history of American professional sports: the 1947 signing of Jackie Robinson to play for the Brooklyn Dodgers. And a deep hostility to racial injustice clearly helped to inspire broadcaster Howard Cosell's influential public support of the controversial Muhammad Ali and other black boxers.

Still, it would be naïve not to recognize that the overriding impetus for the acceptance of black and to a lesser extent Hispanic athletes in professional sports was supplied by the profit motive. Even Branch Rickey, as Jackie Robinson, who greatly admired him, once wrote, was "a shrewd businessman." And just how shrewd Rickey's blow for ethnic equity was in business terms became abundantly plain at the first game the Dodgers played in St. Louis after Robinson joined the team: so many black fans turned out that it was impossible to fit all them in the segregated area of the stadium to which they had previously been confined—whereupon segregated seating at baseball games was permanently abandoned in St. Louis.

In the great majority of cases, moreover, neither idealism nor even any rudimentary sense of civic obligation has had any visible role in the personnel decisions of big-time athletic institutions in the television

---

* This coincidence of events is clearly mirrored in the history of the professional basketball team with which I am most familiar, the Boston Celtics. Ex–Rhodes Scholar George Monroe, who as of this writing is chairman of the board of Phelps Dodge Corp., once recalled to me that when he played for the Celtics in the 1940s, there were no blacks at all on the team, and as of 1957 it still had only one black player, Bill Russell. By 1969, the Celtics squad included eight blacks and only four whites.

age. One classic demonstration of this reality was supplied by the University of Kentucky, which over the years has derived substantial income, directly and indirectly, from its status as a major power in collegiate basketball. In 1965, a highly touted Kentucky team was soundly beaten by a predominantly black team from Texas Western at El Paso; the very next year the previously lily-white Kentucky basketball program began actively to recruit black players.

A contemporary variation on this same theme—although more or less in reverse—can be found in professional hockey, a sport still essentially dominated by Canadian athletes. Since an extremely high percentage of the ticket and TV revenues of National Hockey League teams is earned in the United States, it would seem to make public relations sense for NHL franchise owners to lean over backward to insure sizable American representation on their squads. And it is clear that no blind Canadian chauvinism prevents them from doing so: they have eagerly bid for talented players from Sweden, Finland, and Czechoslovakia and are now apolitically endeavoring to raid Soviet teams as well. Nonetheless, the number of U.S.-born players in the NHL is still relatively small, and the reasons for that are strictly economic: the overall pool of professional-caliber American hockey players, while steadily increasing, remains rather limited, and when confronted with a choice between a team that panders to their national pride and one that wins games, U.S. hockey fans will back the latter every time.*

Like other show biz entrepreneurs, in short, those who own sports franchises are not in the business of changing public attitudes but rather confine themselves to capitalizing upon whatever attitudes currently prevail. And that fact makes it instructive to reflect upon how

---

* Considerations similar to those that restrict the American presence in the NHL in general also largely explain, I believe, the fact that hockey is still a "white sport." Those who suggest that this state of affairs stems from prejudice on the part of the hockey establishment and fans seem to me to overlook the reality that for both geographical and economic reasons blacks have not in the past played hockey to any great extent. It is clearly no accident that all three of the black players active in the NHL during the 1987–88 season were Canadians, and my own guess is that with the substantial increase in Canada's black population in recent years, it is only a matter of time until more black Canadians join Canadians of Italian, Polish, German, Czech, and other minority origins on NHL rosters.

radically the American sports scene has changed during the lifetime of people still in middle age. In 1939, in what was clearly intended to be a flattering *Life* article on Joe DiMaggio, journalist Noel Busch could write without fear of incurring universal obloquy that the Yankee Clipper "never reeks of garlic" and "instead of olive oil or smelly bear grease keeps his hair sleek with water." By 1988 not only was that kind of condescension toward any white ethnic group inconceivable, but Jimmy "the Greek" Snyder was instantly stripped of his lucrative CBS-TV contract when he incautiously opined to a reporter that "the black is a better athlete because he's been bred to be that way," and that if blacks were freely admitted to coaching jobs in professional sports "there won't be anything left for the white people."

As an alleged expert at calculating odds, Snyder should have known that such comments made his prospects for survival as a TV commentator a very bad bet: less than a year earlier one Al Campanis had been fired as a vice president of the Los Angeles Dodgers organization for publicly expressing the view that blacks lacked the "necessities" to perform front office jobs in baseball successfully. To be sure, the conspicuous dearth of blacks in managerial positions in baseball and football at that time indicated that a good many other members of the sports establishment privately shared the outlook of Snyder and Campanis. But such had the climate of public opinion in the United States become that in purely economic terms any open profession of bigotry had become potentially too costly to be tolerated.

SUPERFICIALLY the assertion that the purveyors of mass entertainment have consistently avoided taking truly controversial positions on ethnic questions might seem to belie my earlier claim that the various vehicles of popular culture have helped in a major way to diminish the significance that Americans attach to ethnicity. But in reality there is no conflict at all between those two propositions. It is just that the ways in which show biz and sports have influenced our national attitudes on ethnicity have been essentially indirect and more often than not unintentional.

One of the most notable ways in which this influence has been exerted lies in the image of our society that the entertainment industry presents to Americans. Looking at the United States through the eyes of show business is, in fact, a little like looking at oneself in a fun house mirror. In an essay on TV that he published in 1981, Michael Novak quite accurately charged that "in general, television [in the U.S.] is an organ of nationalization, of homogenization—and also, indeed, of a certain systematic inaccuracy about the actual concrete texture of American life."

In greater or lesser degree, I believe, Novak's charge holds true for all major forms of popular entertainment in this country. Despite the plethora of "problem" movies and the occasional, much-ballyhooed "hard-hitting" TV shows to which we are subjected, the America portrayed by show biz remains an unrealistically one-dimensional country. It is, broadly speaking, a place where, with the exception of obvious villains, everyone regardless of background or superficial differences in lifestyle is very similar and where serious ethnic conflict is either absent or plainly aberrant.

Admittedly, this kind of blinking at reality is not as a rule conducive to the creation of enduring art, and by the same token very little of what passes for searching social commentary in our popular culture genuinely deserves that description. But deplorable as these facts may be, they should not be allowed to obscure another important fact: inaccurate or not, the portrait of an essentially homogeneous America presented on our movie and TV screens has redeeming social value.

This is the case simply because, within limits, life *does* imitate art or is at least altered by it. For many, perhaps most, American children nowadays the fantasy world to which they are exposed while watching TV or the movies is as integral a part of their lives as the flesh-and-blood world they inhabit at school or on the streets. To an important degree, in other words, that fantasy world is actually an aspect of their "real" world.* As a result, even when they encounter ethnic prejudice or inequality in the flesh, they also continue to inhabit another, universally familiar environment in which the norm is ethnic equality.

---

* There is, in fact, some evidence to suggest that a considerable number of American youngsters perceive no inconsistency whatever between their experiences in everyday society and the world presented to them on the TV screen. A 1986 survey of 1,200 New York City high school students revealed that fully a quarter of those who watched four or more hours of television a day were convinced that TV programming reflected "what life is really like."

As I have indicated, this is a phenomenon that I believe operates particularly strongly upon children, and that, as a result, will have increasingly powerful effects upon our national behavior as successive waves of youngsters reach adulthood. But the same influence operates to some degree upon all Americans regardless of age and is perhaps most visibly fostered by our sports culture. Dr. Harry Edwards, the sociologist who made an abortive effort to organize a boycott of the 1967 Olympics by America's black athletes, argues that "if there is a universal popular religion in America, it is to be found within the institution of sport." It seems unquestionable that this assertion contains at least a kernel of truth, and that this lends uncommon importance to the multiethnic character of sports. For while a movie or a TV sitcom that carries a social message can be brushed aside as a biased distortion of reality, a sports event is generally assumed to represent a straightforward test of skills. When a Slavic tennis player, a black sprinter, or a Hispanic pitcher turns in a winning performance, even the most prejudiced spectator is unlikely to charge that the game has been rigged to make a propaganda point or that the victorious athlete has been the beneficiary of an artificially imposed equal opportunity program.

There is, moreover, another obvious respect in which both athletes and entertainers have an impact on public attitudes that is all the more powerful for being incidental rather than intended. It is a truism that Americans today live in a celebrity culture. To the dismay of those who see it as a manifestation of trivial values, successful athletes and show biz personalities are courted even in traditional bastions of power and dignity. They are invited to White House dinners, enlisted as spokesmen by worthy causes, and even on occasion awarded honorary degrees by famous universities.

Just how potent a tool celebrity status has become in America is, of course, strikingly demonstrated by the fact that a number of top culture figures, of whom Ronald Reagan is merely the most notable, have used it as a springboard to political power. But in general it seems safe to say that athletes and entertainers per se have relatively little direct political impact. There is, so far as I can determine, scant evidence that the ideological pronouncements of Jane Fonda, Ed Asner, or Charlton Heston have significantly affected the judgment of the electorate.* There is, however, overwhelming evidence that celebrities do have another form of influence. Mulititudes who clearly don't share Jane Fonda's politics have embraced her diet and exercise programs. And the Hertz Corporation would scarcely feature O. J. Simpson in its commercials unless its executives were convinced that potential customers, white as well as black, were secretly yearning to share O. J.'s seemingly insouciant mode of existence.

Above all, then, it is the lifestyles of celebrities that are admired and imitated by less lucky Americans. And the fact that those lifestyles and the people who lead them have increasingly come to reflect a multiplicity of backgrounds has perceptibly helped to undermine ethnic barriers in America—and will, I am convinced, continue to do so increasingly in the future.

This, of course, constitutes at best only a long-term antidote to prejudice, and for that reason it is understandable that in their impatience high-minded citizens periodically reproach the merchants of mass culture for lagging rather than leading on ethnic issues. Yet, coldly viewed, that seems to me very like reproaching a cat for killing birds; in both cases, the criticism ignores the inherent nature of the beast. At bottom, indeed, there would even seem to be grounds for reassurance in the cautiously reactive behavior of our entertainment and sports establishments. For what it suggests is that instead of being artificially induced by a self-appointed elite, the changes that have occurred and are still occurring in our national view of ethnicity are the expression of a fundamental thrust in American society.

---

* Norman Lear, whose People for the American Way contributed mightily to the successful drive to keep Judge Robert Bork off the Supreme Court in 1987, might conceivably be cited as an exception to this rule. That feat, however, rested primarily upon the financial and organizational resources Lear's lobbying group commanded rather than on the celebrity of its founding father.

10

THE REMAKING
OF THE
AMERICAN MIND

$\mathbf{A}$t the very end of the 1960s when one of the hottest items in the nation's bookstores was *Portnoy's Complaint*, Philip Roth's scabrously comic tale of a Jewish-American libertine, an editor at a New York publishing house is said to have returned an unwanted manuscript with the curt comment "No one is interested in reading novels about WASPs."

This editorial dictum, reported by journalist Peter Schrag in *The Decline of the WASP*, surely represented exaggeration for effect; Louis Auchincloss, to note only the most obvious example, has consistently won reasonably wide readership with novels about WASPs—and to my taste, rather dull WASPs at that.

Still, exaggerated or not, the statement Schrag quotes does serve as a reminder of a historic transformation of American intellectual life. While popular culture by definition constitutes a revealing gauge of the tastes and outlook of the general population at any given moment, the leading indicators in such matters are generally provided by high culture—the output of those creative artists and thinkers who are regarded as "serious" enough to command special attention from a significant number of the country's most successful and/or best-educated citizens. Gauche as they would find it to say so aloud, high culture is, in fact, regarded by many elite Americans as being in some sense their special preserve. And if only for that reason it has become an important means of access to higher status for the members of groups once largely or totally excluded from the American mainstream.

For most of U.S. history, that was by no means the case. The titans of nineteenth and early twentieth century American literature (Hawthorne, Emerson, Melville, Twain, James) were all WASPs or perceived as WASPs as were most of the great visual artists (Copley, Sargent, Whistler, Winslow Homer, Eakins, Hopper). And the same held true for the seminal thinkers: as late as 1950 Henry Steele Commager could publish a book called *The Making of the American Mind* in which not one of the major figures discussed was Catholic, Jewish, or black. Until sometime after World War II, in short, it was tacitly assumed by devotees of high culture that, as Peter Schrag put it, "the American mind was the WASP mind."

In considerable degree, this assumption rested on the fact that for at least a century and a half after the Revolution WASPs actually did provide most of the creative impetus in the development of high culture in this country. But it also reflected in part the fact that WASPs set the nation's cultural tone in a managerial sense as well. They were the leading patrons of the arts, they ruled all the major cultural institutions from museums to opera houses, and they selected the books and articles that intellectually inclined Americans read. In its 1936 survey of the economic activities of American Jews, in fact, *Fortune* magazine declared that relatively few of them were to be found in magazine or book publishing. And a search of those fields at that time for representatives of other major nineteenth century immigrant groups such as Italians, Slavs, and Greeks would surely have proved even less rewarding.

AS FAR AS financing and administration of the high culture is concerned, WASPdom is by no means a spent force. In recent decades it has continued to produce not only some of the most notable patrons of the arts—people ranging from Nelson Rockefeller to ballet enthusiast Lucia Chase—but highly influential cultural bureaucrats as well. As the 1980s drew to a close, there was probably no other major museum director in the nation who possessed quite the same combination of seniority and clout as the National Gallery's J. Carter Brown, a man who in addition to being a scion of the aristocratic Rhode Island family that gave its name to Brown University was for a time a member by marriage of Pennsylvania's only marginally less aristocratic Mellon clan. And for all Brown's personal charm and unquestioned ability, his social credentials could scarcely be dismissed as irrelevant to his success: even yet, there are far more WASPs on the governing bodies of many of the most prestigious institutions, advisory groups, and fund-raising committees that sustain the high culture than any form of ethnic proportional representation would justify.

What emphatically *is* a thing of the past, however, is the quasi-monopoly of such positions that WASPs once enjoyed. In a sense, the first meaningful challenge to that monopoly appeared in the early decades of this century with the emergence of an extraordinary succession of openhanded Jewish art collectors and patrons—retailing magnates Benjamin Altman and Michael Friedsam, investment bankers George Blumenthal, Jules Bache, and Robert Lehman, and most notable of all in terms of impact on contemporary art and architecture, Solomon Guggenheim of the great metals fortune.

Yet large as they loom in the history of cultural patronage in America, these men proved to constitute merely an entering wedge. They in their day were essentially oddities in a predominantly WASP landscape. But among the patrons who have come to prominence since World War II, an "ethnic" background is at least as common as a WASP one. Like their predecessors in the first half of the century, many of these latter-day Maecenases have been Jewish; even the most cursory listing of major collectors and cultural donors in the postwar decades would have to include the late Joseph Hirshorn, Walter Annenberg, Norton Simon, Armand Hammer, the late Joseph Meyerhoff (who personally underwrote half the $20-million cost of Baltimore's symphony hall), and arguably Robert and Ethel Scull.* But there are

---

* Unlike the other art patrons I have mentioned, the Sculls profited heavily from the resale of many of the works they collected. Still, it can scarcely be denied that the Sculls' activities gave added visibility and cachet to the abstract artists whom they favored.

---

new patrons of other ethnic backgrounds as well: two of the most important new art museums to open in the United States in the 1980s were underwritten respectively by Chicagoan Daniel Terra, the son of an Italian-born stone lithographer, and Houston's DeMenil family, which is of recent French origin.

Predictably, the munificence of such non-WASP donors has over time increasingly resulted in the creation of important cultural institutions that from the start were not subject to predominantly WASP governance. Of these, one of the most venerated—and certainly the most cherished by architectural mavens—is New York's Guggenheim Museum, which, although underwritten by mining magnate Solomon R. Guggenheim,* in large part reflects the taste of his artistic mentor, an Alsatian-born German baroness named Hilla Rebay.

But even before Guggenheim's massive collection of modern art went on display in Frank Lloyd Wright's fanciful structure on Fifth Avenue in 1959, a development that offered perhaps even more striking testimony to changing ethnic roles in the high culture was occurring at the other end of the continent: in the mid-1950s when she decided that the Los Angeles area ought to have a world-class music center, Dorothy ("Buffie") Chandler, the longtime czarina of cultural activities in the region, turned for most of the money required not to her fellow WASPs but to the members of southern California's wealthy Jewish community. And in recognition of their enthusiastic support, Mrs. Chandler saw to it that her Jewish allies were solidly represented on the new center's board.

What made Buffie Chandler's behavior particularly revealing was that at bottom it merely represented a logical extension of a process that had begun to transform the governing boards of many long-established cultural institutions that had traditionally been bastions of high WASPdom. In capsulized form, this process is strikingly illustrated by the modern history of two notably establishmentarian organizations, the New York Philharmonic-Symphony Society and the Metropolitan

---

* By a kind of economic *droit du seigneur*, the presidency of the Guggenheim as of 1988 was still held by Solomon Guggenheim's grandson. And in a kind of implicit statement about ethnic interactions in America, the gentleman in question was named Peter Lawson-Johnston.

Opera. When these two groups joined forces in the early 1950s to become the founding partners in what is now New York's Lincoln Center for the Performing Arts, the original prime movers nearly all had WASP names—Spofford, Bliss, Blair, Houghton, Rockefeller. But when Lincoln Center was finally incorporated in 1956, the positions of treasurer and chairman of the finance committee were both conferred upon prominent Jewish New Yorkers—Robert Blum and Frank Weil. And by the early 1980s, Lincoln Center's chairman of the board was yet another Jewish businessman, Russian-born Martin E. Segal.

Probably the most illuminating case study of how such sea changes have occurred is provided by the most prestigious of New York City's *pro bono* mafias, the board of trustees of the Metropolitan Museum of Art. Among old-line cultural institutions, the Met is unusual in that it acquired its first Jewish trustee, financier George Blumenthal, as far back as 1909 and from 1934 until his death in 1941 actually entrusted its presidency to him. Yet for all the deference paid him by his WASP colleagues, Blumenthal remained keenly aware that his position was a somewhat anomalous one—so much so, in fact, that in 1939 he vetoed the selection of a world-renowned Jewish art expert as the Met's director, saying that the appointment would be "unwise" in view of the fact that the Met already had two Jewish curators on its staff. And the attitudes that prompted Blumenthal's sensitivity had by no means entirely dissipated even a generation later: in 1954 noted art collector Robert Lehman, who by then had been on the Met's board for eighteen years, confided to an acquaintance that while he felt the directorship of the museum should properly be given to James J. Rorimer, a longtime Met curator of Jewish background, he did not feel free to urge Rorimer's appointment upon his fellow trustees. "I can't say these things," Lehman explained, "because I'm a Jew."

Given his age and background, it is easy to understand why Lehman might feel that way—though less than twenty years later he was to be named by his fellow trustees to the newly created post of chairman of the Met's board. It is, however, inconceivable that any Jewish trustee of the Met today should feel similarly isolated and vulnerable. For throughout the 1970s and 1980s the number of Jews on the museum's board steadily expanded—and even more significant, by no means all of the newcomers have been drawn from such aristocratic New York JASP families as the Lehmans and Sulzbergers. Indeed, as of the mid-1980s, by which time roughly one-fifth of the Met's board was Jewish, its members included such relatively recent recruits to the American Establishment as Henry Kissinger, CBS chairman Laurence Tisch, New York real estate developer Frederick P. Rose, and Mrs. Walter Annenberg.

Given the fact that the Met's board as of that time still abounded in socially prominent WASPs and included only one member with a Hispanic surname, such changes as had occurred in its composition were clearly less indicative of any devotion to ethnic egalitarianism than of a cold-eyed obeisance to economic realities. And to be fair, little effort has been made to disguise that fact: soon after he joined the Met's board in 1980, Frederick Rose succeeded in winning the museum a $10-million gift from his fellow real estate tycoon Harold Uris; thus inspired, the Met promptly launched what the *New York Times* characterized as a concerted campaign "to tap the real estate industry"—a bit of phraseology that, as Charles Silberman dryly notes in his book *A Certain People,* marked the coinage of "a new euphemism for 'wealthy Jews.' "

Inevitably, the economic and social forces that produced this sort of development at the august Metropolitan Museum have, in greater or lesser degree, operated upon other cultural institutions around the country. Having opened the board of her fledgling music center to Jews, Buffie Chandler proceeded to do the same in the late 1950s with the board of the more venerable Los Angeles Symphony. At roughly the same time the presidency of the Memphis Academy of Fine Arts was conferred upon a prominent local art patron named Benjamin Goodman. By the 1970s Stanley Marcus of the famed Texas retailing family was a director of the Dallas Symphony Society, while his kinswoman by marriage, Mrs. Edward Marcus, was president of that city's Museum of Fine Arts. Similarly, in Chicago the dynamic Ben Heineman became a trustee of both the Orchestral Association and the Lyric Opera (which as of the late 1980s also included among its trustees Italian-American Daniel Terra and Lester Crown, son of the legendary real estate operator Col. Henry Crown).

The scope and timing of the process I have been describing has

differed from city to city depending upon a variety of local circumstances including population mix, the depth of ethnic antagonisms, and
sheer historical accident. Perhaps because its major cultural institutions are of such relatively recent vintage—the earliest of them date
only from the 1930s—Kansas City was an early convert to cultural
power-sharing: local *prominenti* of Jewish and Italian background were
from the start active in the affairs of the city's ballet, symphony, and
art museum, and one of the cofounders of the Kansas City Lyric Opera
was a wealthy Italian-American liquor dealer, Mike Barbiglia. In Boston, on the other hand, the prestigious Museum of Fine Arts retained
an almost exclusively WASP board until the 1970s and to this day has
not fully capitalized upon the talents and resources of the city's Irish-
American community. But more often than not, once the transition
from WASP to multiethnic stewardship began, it proceeded with astonishing rapidity—a notable case in point being provided by the New
York Public Library, an institution that, despite its mass constituency,
has traditionally confined membership on its board to those enjoying
elite status in the Big Apple.

In the 1960s when she was first invited to become a trustee of the
New York Public Library, high-minded historian Barbara Tuchman
decided against doing so because, in her words, "I got the impression
that the board was somewhat stuffy—the old New York *Social Register*
kind of thing." What remedied that, oddly enough, was primarily the
adoption of the library as a pet cause by one of the chief adornments
of the *Social Register*—Brooke Astor, the brilliant, activist widow of
the late Vincent Astor. The awe-stricken New York journalist who once
described Brooke Astor as "the most powerful person in this city" was
perhaps laying it on a bit thick, but between her vast social prestige
and her selective personal management of the great financial resources
of the Vincent Astor Foundation, Mrs. Astor undeniably exercises
major influence over certain aspects of the city's life. And in the case
of the New York Public Library, she brought all her guns to bear.
Besides pumping millions of foundation dollars into the institution, she
gave it her personal imprimatur as well and thereby transformed it into
a particularly chic philanthropy—and favorite party site—for the arri-
viste members of what gossip columnist Aileen ("Suzy") Mehle likes to
call "the New Society." (Unlike most other products of the Old Society,

Mrs. Astor believes that "new blood is good; transfusions keep the thing going.")

It is clearly one measure of Brooke Astor's success that at the beginning of the 1980s Barbara Tuchman decided to join the New York Public Library Board after all. For in so doing, Mrs. Tuchman, a daughter of financier Maurice Wertheim and niece of the late treasury secretary Henry Morgenthau, Jr., was surely influenced in part by the fact that by then the chairman of the library's board was the notably public-spirited Richard Salomon, onetime chief executive officer of Charles of the Ritz and later chancellor of Brown University. And among the other non–*Social Register* trustees with whom Mrs. Tuchman served have been CBS chairman Laurence Tisch and Greek-American corporate philanthropist Stephen Stamas.

More conspicuously than in the case of the great foundations, such infusions of new blood into the governing bodies of some of our greatest cultural institutions have clearly had salutary effects—perhaps the most obvious being a broadening of the talent pool from which the professional administrators of such institutions are drawn. Not that directorial and curatorial jobs were historically reserved exclusively for WASPs; as I have already noted, James J. Rorimer, the director of New York's Metropolitan Museum of Art from 1955 to 1966, was Jewish. But Rorimer, whose father was born Louis Rohrheimer, regarded his background as something to be concealed—so much of a social and professional liability that in the mid-1960s he cautioned his protégé Henry Geldzahler, later New York City's Commissioner of Cultural Affairs, never to let the trustees of the Met know that he was Jewish, too.

Barely twenty years later, however, the professional staff of the Met included not only Jewish Americans who proudly proclaimed their heritage but people of a wide variety of other ethnic origins ranging from Hispanic to Chinese. Indeed, assuming that for some unfathomable reason he had wanted to do so, even the museum's conspicuously aristocratic director, Philippe de Montebello, could scarcely have hoped to pass for a true-blue WASP.* Nor was the Metropolitan in any

---

* This, of course, was not the case with Montebello's predecessor, Thomas Hoving, who is generally (and often hostilely) perceived as an archetypal high WASP and who indeed

way unique in this respect. From California's Roger Wong, the director of the Los Angeles Museum of Art, to John Szarkowski, curator of photography at Manhattan's Museum of Modern Art, America's cultural bureaucracy was by the mid-1980s thoroughly multiethnic.

Here again the New York Public Library supplies something of a paradigm. In 1981, after a search effort in which Richard Salomon played a major role, the library chose as its president the then provost of the University of Pennsylvania, Vartan Gregorian.* Born in Iran of Armenian parents, Gregorian is a charismatic and boundlessly enthusiastic man whose Middle Eastern volubility and penchant for lavishing bear hugs upon his acquaintances stand in sharp contrast to the reserved social behavior traditionally favored by WASPs and aspiring WASPs. Yet he proved an instant hit with the luminaries of the New Society, and his skill at extracting funds from the moneyed classes moved even Brooke Astor to awe. "It's quite extraordinary," Manhattan lawyer Helene Kaplan once mused, "to find an Armenian immigrant exercising a kind of coleadership with [Public Library board chairman] Andrew Heiskell, who really sort of epitomizes the Establishment." †

Besides winning favor with the Establishment, however, Gregorian's appointment also paid off in a way that his original sponsors almost certainly did not foresee. Within a few years after his arrival, the Public Library, although still heavily dependent upon private funding, was receiving more financial support from the city government of New York than ever before. And a major reason for this was clearly that Gregorian had developed uncommonly close personal ties with the equally voluble and uninhibited Mayor Edward Koch. Birds of a

---

clearly is one by upbringing, education, and outlook. The fact that he happens to be the son of an immigrant from Sweden is, in a social sense, irrelevant.

* Some years later when Gregorian moved on to the presidency of Brown University, the vice chairman of the Brown search committee that lured him away from the Public Library was none other than the ubiquitous Mr. Salomon.

† As it happens, Heiskell, a former board chairman of Time Inc. and Richard Salomon's successor as head of the Public Library's governing board, was born in Italy and educated in France. But while he has been known to claim that his overseas birth and upbringing give him a special bond with Gregorian, Heiskell is not only WASP by birth but, as Helene Kaplan implied, quintessentially so in appearance and manner.

---

feather, these two conspicuously non-U types had rapidly established a relationship that a mutual acquaintance described as "symbiotic."

Yet for all the credit Gregorian deserves on this score, the fact is that there has been a somewhat parallel evolution in Ed Koch's view of the Metropolitan Museum of Art. When he was elected mayor of New York, Koch automatically acquired an *ex officio* seat on the Met's board, but at first, as Ashton Hawkins, the museum's elegant vice president in charge of "donor relations," once pointed out, Koch was less than overwhelmed by this honor. "Six or seven years ago," Hawkins told the *New York Times* in early 1986, "the mayor thought culture was the province of the WASP elite." Yet by 1985 when *New York* magazine asked him what he thought was the single best thing about New York City, Koch named the Metropolitan Museum.

This, as Hawkins noted, marked "an important adjustment in attitude"—and one that surely was not unrelated to the election to the Met board of people such as Frederick Rose and Laurence Tisch. A man with a finely honed sense of power relationships, Ed Koch is obviously fully aware that at bottom the high culture is still largely supported and administered by an elite. What has apparently rendered him—and many other foes of inherited privilege—more tolerant of that reality is the fact that the elite in question is no longer so heavily composed of people of upper class WASP antecedents.

WELL BEFORE the management of the repositories of high culture began to pass into multiethnic hands, the management of its commercial aspects had already done so. At the time World War II began, WASP dominance of the enterprises that market serious music and drama, the graphic arts and books, had either been shattered or was under assault. By the beginning of the 1940s the name Sol Hurok had become virtually synonymous with the word "impresario" in the musical world, and in the theater the Shubert brothers wielded unequalled economic power. By then, too, the leading entrepreneurs in the art market represented an ethnic potpourri; a random survey of the galleries and dealers that consistently advertised in art magazines in the late 1930s and early 1940s turns up such names as Duveen, O'Toole, Knoedler, Wildenstein, Kraushaar, Pierre Matisse, and N. M. Acquavella. (Considering the importance of personal relationships in the art business and the enormous proliferation of art galleries in this country in the last forty years, it seems remarkable that the majority of these names could still be found in advertisements in *Art News* at the end of the 1980s.)

Of all the commercial activities serving the high culture, the last to become solidly multiethnic was book publishing. By the 1920s a certain number of Jews had already achieved prominence in that field, but they still remained essentially outsiders in what its leading figures chose to regard as an occupation for WASP gentlemen. Indeed, in 1927, Alfred Knopf was driven to establish something called The Book Table as an alternative to The Publishers Lunch Club, an organization that, according to publishing historian John Tebbel, "was not notable in those days for the number of its Jewish members." And even in the late 1930s, as Kenneth C. Davis notes in his book *Two-Bit Culture*, "many New York clubs—including those that catered to the publishing world—were still closed to Jews."

Here, as in so many other areas of American life, World War II proved to be the watershed. In the decades since then, classic WASP preppies such as Harper & Row's legendary Cass Canfield, who topped off an exclusive American education with attendance at Oxford, have played a steadily diminishing role in book publishing; though WASPs still abound in the trade, those in top positions by the late 1980s were more likely to be graduates of Ohio State or Michigan than of Harvard. And socially as well as professionally Jewish Americans had become firmly ensconced on the top rungs of the publishing ladder.

Arguably the most aristocratic of contemporary American publishers, in fact, is Roger Straus of Farrar, Straus & Giroux, a cultivated autocrat who is regarded by many—including, one suspects, himself —as "the conscience of the industry." And any roll call of the most respected and/or powerful figures in the publishing world, whether in editorial or executive positions, has to include a sizable number of Jews; among those whose names automatically come to mind are Robert Bernstein, Jason Epstein, and Joni Evans of Random House, Richard Snyder and Michael Korda at Simon and Schuster, Simon Michael Bessie at Harper & Row, Howard Kaminsky at Hearst, and Marc Jaffe at Houghton Mifflin.

So far as Jewish Americans are concerned, however, the present situation in publishing in a sense merely marks the logical culmination of a process that had begun to be visible well before World War II. Where change has been more notable in the industry in postwar decades has been in the rise to authority of a significant number of people who are neither WASP nor Jewish in background. Today both the editor in chief at Farrar, Straus & Giroux (Jonathan Galassi) and the chief executive officer of William Morrow (Allen Marchioni) are Italian Americans; William Jovanovich, who rules Harcourt Brace Jovanovich, is of Polish and Montenegrin ancestry; and several other well-known figures in trade book publishing and editing—Ted Akahishi at Harper, Beverly Lu at McGraw-Hill, Genevieve Young at Bantam Books, and Robert Asahina at Simon and Schuster—are Asian Americans. And in 1987 in perhaps the most dramatic instance of ethnic diversification, Sonny Mehta, a flamboyant British-educated Indian who had previously run Pan Books in London, was lured to New York to become president of Knopf.

To be sure, as Houghton Mifflin editor John Sterling disapprovingly informed me in 1988, "in adult trade publishing white males are still dominant." But it is also true that the ethnicity of those white males is now extremely diverse, and that while very few blacks have yet been admitted to responsible positions in the field, they are not totally absent either: Pulitzer Prize–winning novelist Toni Morrison was for many years an editor at Random House and Erroll McDonald is executive editor at Vintage Books.

In short, in contemporary publishing, as Alan Williams of Arbor House told me, "there is almost no ethnic group unrepresented," and in recent years women, too, have begun to reach the top in significant numbers. At the time John Sterling and I discussed the matter, in fact, the president of the entire publishing group at Putnam was a onetime specialist in subsidiary rights named Phyllis Grann,* and the roster of

---

* Ms. Grann's career history is not an unusual one for women in publishing. In the years immediately after World War II when paperbacks had not yet become as important a source of publishing income as they now are, sales of subsidiary rights were generally entrusted to an editorial secretary or very junior female editor. Subsequently, as these rights became far more important financially, women experienced in dealing with them tended to become more important as well.

---

top editors who had operated on my own books included Joni Evans, Betty Prashker at Crown Publishers, and Alice Mayhew at Simon and Schuster.

EVEN IF it signified nothing but the extension of more equal opportunity to yet another area of American life, the growing ethnic diversity of those who manage and market the nation's high culture would be of considerable importance. But in fact, it has had much broader implications and consequences than that. In particular, it has meant that the range of subjects, social viewpoints, and artistic traditions reflected in the high culture has greatly widened.

In so saying, I do not mean to imply that it is possible to establish some tidy and predictable equivalence between the ethnicity of culture managers and the art they find worthy of dissemination. As Houghton Mifflin's Sterling points out: "A relationship between who editors are and what they publish surely exists, but it is extremely hard to quantify." Indeed, it seems probable that in many, if not most, cases that relationship is an unconscious or at least unacknowledged one. Reflecting on the changes he has witnessed over nearly forty years in both the staffing of publishing houses and the books that they find acceptable, Alan Williams told me: "On the whole, I don't think it has been a matter of people saying 'let's open the doors of opportunity.' " Yet at the same time, Williams pointed out, it is obvious that "an editor can have greater openness to a work because of his or her own ethnic background." And along with editors, that clearly applies to art patrons, museum directors, theatrical producers, symphony conductors, and all the other pooh-bahs of the cultural establishment.

Equally clearly, the predilections of such people, whether conscious or unconscious, have great public importance. What the art museums and great collectors are prepared to buy and what publishing houses are prepared to publish inevitably influence in some measure what creative artists find it worthwhile to produce. And what a society's artists produce no less inevitably influences the way in which that society sees itself.

Consider, for example, the extraordinary degree to which the vision of the lone cowboy, tough, taciturn, and supremely individualistic, has shaped the way in which the American people perceive their own national character. Though not, to be sure, primarily a product of the high culture, the cowboy mystique is nonetheless essentially an artistic construct. As a matter of historical fact, the realities that spawned that mystique constituted only a small fragment of the American experience, a transitory phenomenon that effectively endured for only a few decades and involved only a tiny percentage of the population. Yet thanks to its unending glorification by artists ranging from sculptor Frederic Remington and novelist Owen Wister to massed battalions of Hollywood scriptwriters and directors, the cowboy legend has become so integral a part of the American psyche that even a quintessentially urban immigrant such as Henry Kissinger could invoke it as somehow relevant to his conduct of the nation's diplomatic business.

In a sense, too, the triumph of the cowboy myth serves to demonstrate another important fact about cultural trends—which is that they tend to be self-reinforcing. In the high culture as well as in pop culture, success breeds imitation. Driven both by the profit motive and the rarity of true originality, the creators, merchandisers, and patrons of the arts all follow fashion far more than most of them care to admit. The long period during which abstract expressionism dominated American painting, for example, surely reflected the fact that that was what critics, collectors, and galleries demanded as much as it did the inherent aesthetic and intellectual merits of this particular form of art. And the faddishness of the literary world is scarcely less marked. As editor John Sterling sees it, in fact, the publishing business "is very much like the stock market. We see that a stock has jumped and we all go buy it."

More precisely, perhaps, the publishing business appears to bear a distinct resemblance to the futures market—at least insofar as its attitudes toward ethnicity are concerned. Unlike pop culture, the high culture is not compelled as a matter of economic survival to appeal to the lowest common denominator of public taste; its basic market, in fact, is restricted to the more educated and, broadly speaking, more open-minded segments of society. As a result, the high culture, again unlike pop culture, does not merely stamp a seal of confirmation on changes that have already occurred in the national consensus on ethnic issues. Instead, it frequently serves as a kind of early warning system that registers emerging trends in ethnic relationships as well as a form of agitprop that speeds the general acceptance of those trends among the more influential members of the population. In short, the high culture both points to and helps to shape what the national consensus will ultimately become.

The precise degree to which all this is true seems to me to vary considerably from one form of artistic expression to another. It is not, for example, readily apparent that the changes in the way Americans have come to look at ethnicity in recent decades were either fore-shadowed or directly influenced by developments in our graphic arts. Conceivably, this may be at least in part a consequence of the fact that the most powerful postwar currents in American graphic arts have to a considerable extent been foreign in origin. It was, after all, primarily artists and intellectuals driven out of Western Europe by Nazism and World War II who so invigorated American painting that New York supplanted Paris as the world's artistic capital. And that change in the center of artistic gravity in turn has produced a continuing influx into this country of painters and sculptors who, like their predecessors of the 1940s and 1950s, are busily infusing American art with sensibilities primarily shaped by the traditions and concerns of Europe and Asia rather than those of the United States.

In purely professional terms, this latter-day immigration has un-deniably rendered American art more cosmopolitan if not pluralistic: the dominance of abstract art—and to a lesser extent of "modern" music—has greatly reduced adherence to self-consciously "American" themes of the kind favored by people such as Thomas Hart Benton and Grant Wood. And to the extent that use of such themes tended to foster, however unconsciously, a fundamentally WASP view of the world, it can be argued that their diminishing popularity has marked a step toward the deethnicization of American art and its impact upon the public.

The extent to which the graphic arts actually have had such im-pact, however, seems to me extremely hard to determine. It is probably not mere coincidence that it was an "ethnic"—Andy Warhol—who became the only avant garde American artist of our time to achieve full-fledged celebrity status. Perhaps, too, his success in doing so re-flected some degree of tacit public acceptance of the vision of Ameri-can society implicit in his works, a vision that scarcely embodied traditional WASP values. But that is speculation, and given the fact that so large a share of the general public is indifferent or actively hostile to contemporary art, the underlying reality, I suspect, is that our national attitudes toward ethnicity are at best only subliminally and peripherally affected by the creations of serious visual artists and musicians.

Serious writing, however, is quite a different matter; the work of novelists and playwrights in particular quite clearly, I believe, has a powerful and direct effect upon the public consciousness. That effect, to be sure, is more often than not relatively slow in making itself felt; the works of the ethnic authors I read in the late 1930s and early 1940s —Eugene O'Neill, James T. Farrell, Pietro DiDonato, Meyer Levin, Jerome Weidman, and Richard Wright to name just a few—had not yet significantly affected mass attitudes in this country by the time World War II erupted. But they did help to set the stage for the postwar years when, in a sharp departure from its previous history, the U.S. literary scene came to be characterized by one phase after another in which a particular ethnic or religious group essentially asserted its claim to full membership in American society.

Here again, what was at work (and still is) was a kind of delayed action fuse. "The line between assertion and acceptance," editor Alan Williams points out, "is an ever wavering one"—or to put it less neatly, the history of ethnic relations in America has been that the acceptance of any new group into the national mainstream occurs only after the members of that group have over a period of time insistently proclaimed their entitlement to such acceptance. Precisely for that reason, the various ethnic tides that have swept American writing in the last thirty to forty years have proved remarkably reliable indicators of looming changes in the general society—each new literary trend serving as a harbinger of the emergence of yet another group as a recognized recruiting ground for the American Establishment.

In retrospect, it seems fair to say that the first and most dramatic of these trends was in some sense heralded by the publication in 1948 of Norman Mailer's *The Naked and the Dead*. Mailer, of course, was by no means the first significant American writer of Jewish origin, nor has he as a novelist been chiefly concerned with the Jewish-American experience. He was, however, the first Jewish novelist to present himself as a contender for the heavyweight championship of American fiction, and rightly or wrongly, his rise to national stature tends to be associated with the appearance in the immediate postwar years of an astonishing array of major Jewish-American writers—a list headed by such names as Saul Bellow, Bernard Malamud, and Philip Roth.

This initial ethnic surge in American letters was remarkable for its speed and ubiquitousness. By the 1960s Jewish writers had undeniably supplanted white Southern ones as the nation's leading school of novelists; they had, in fact, come to dominate American fiction to such an extent that, as Norman Podhoretz recalls in *Making It*, that wayward WASP Gore Vidal was moved to complain that there was no longer room on any list of important contemporary American writers for more than one "OK goy."

Inevitably, the impact of all this upon the composition of the nation's literary life was enormous—a fact strikingly demonstrated in 1985 when serried ranks of the world's most eminent writers assembled in Manhattan for an International PEN meeting. In implicit confirmation of his status as the leading literary figure of the host country, Norman Mailer was in general charge of the proceedings. And judging from news accounts, the most vocal and attentively heeded members of the American contingent apart from Mailer were Saul Bellow, E. L. Doctorow, Cynthia Ozick, Susan Sontag, and Betty Friedan—all, like the champ himself, Jewish.

Yet despite all this—or rather, in a sense, because of it—the 1985 PEN meeting very probably constituted something like a last hurrah insofar as dominance of American letters by Jewish writers is concerned. For with so many of them now installed as deans (or doyennes) of the nation's literary establishment, the work of many Jewish-American writers has been transformed from a force for change to an integral part of the American literary heritage. Increasingly, in fact, the voices of change—and discontent—have come to emanate from other sources.

Logically enough, what has been happening in the literary world has paralleled in at least one respect the sequence of ethnic patterns observable in the academic one. By the 1970s and 1980s, more and more writers drawn from the two major components of the country's

Catholic population were taking their place alongside Jews in the ranks of important literary figures. In fiction, Don DeLillo and Mario Puzo— a novelist of serious account, *The Godfather* notwithstanding—have led a growing list of talented Italian-American practitioners. And more or less simultaneously there has appeared a new wave of Irish-American novelists—people such as William Kennedy, Thomas Flanagan, and John Gregory Dunne.

To a considerable extent, however, the increased prominence of Catholic writers on the contemporary literary scene has been obscured by a development that has partially overlapped the Catholic upsurge— and which was even longer overdue. To suggest that there was no black presence in American writing until very recent years would be patent nonsense; the careers of Richard Wright, Ralph Ellison, and James Baldwin alone are sufficient disproof of that. But what is undeniably true is that the 1970s and 1980s saw a vast multiplication in the number of black writers who succeeded in winning national recognition. A single statistic perhaps tells that story as well as anything else; of the twenty-nine Pulitzer prizes in letters awarded between 1982 and 1987, five were won by black writers—Rita Dove in poetry, Alice Walker and Toni Morrison in fiction, Charles Fuller and August Wilson in drama.*

How much greater the black role in American letters may ultimately become, and more specifically, whether black writers will ever achieve the degree of preeminence enjoyed by Jewish-American writers in the 1960s, remain to be seen. But even if that preeminence eventually comes about, it seems probable that black writers, like Jewish ones before them, will in due course find the members of other segments of society treading hard on their heels. Already, in fact, what could prove the beginning of yet another ethnic literary trend can be seen in the achievements of Asian-American novelists Maxine Hong Kingston and Bette Bao Lord and of playwrights Frank Chin and David Hwang.

---

* The success of *Fences*, the play for which August Wilson won his Pulitzer, was at least in part also a tribute to the talent of its black director, Lloyd Richards. Though perhaps not a literary figure per se, Richards plays a seminal role in the contemporary U.S. theater in his capacity as dean of Yale University's influential School of Drama.

LUMPING TOGETHER all writers of a particular ethnic background as I have been doing is, I think, fair enough up to a point; it seems a legitimate, if rough and ready, way to characterize from a sociological point of view the broad trends in American literary life since World War II. But in another sense it is clearly adding apples and oranges: writers of the same ethnic heritage obviously differ greatly in the extent to which they are preoccupied with that heritage. Ethnicity, in short, not only fails to play a central part in the works of a number of writers of non-WASP background but increasingly often is not necessarily even an important subordinate theme for them.

There are, indeed, a fair number of contemporary American writers who, without in any sense disavowing their heritage, resist identification as ethnic authors. A prime case in point, as I suggested earlier, is Norman Mailer, who in a 1962 essay in *Commentary* described himself as a non-Jewish Jew and who actively dislikes being categorized as a Jewish novelist. In a similar vein, Saul Bellow declared in an essay that he published in 1977: "I am often described as a Jewish writer in much the same way one might be called a Samoan astronomer or an Eskimo cellist . . . I have tried to fit my soul into the Jewish-writer category, but it does not feel comfortably accommodated there. I wonder, now and then, whether Philip Roth and Bernard Malamud and I have not become the Hart, Schaffner, and Marx of our trade. We have made it in the field of culture as Bernard Baruch made it on a park bench, as Polly Adler made it in prostitution, as Two-Gun Cohen, the personal bodyguard of Sun Yat-sen, made it in China."

What seems to me even more significant than the resistance some of our leading writers offer to ethnic categorization is the fact that for a growing number such labeling is simply not an issue. Though Mark Harris, Joseph Heller, and J. D. Salinger are all at least nominally Jewish, there is nothing that can be regarded as uniquely Jewish about the fictional worlds created by Salinger in *Catcher in the Rye*, Heller in *Catch-22*, or Harris in his brilliant baseball novel *The Southpaw*. Similarly, no one to my knowledge has ever seriously suggested that the novels of Philip Caputo are distinctively Italian-American in viewpoint, or that the French-Canadian experience in the United States is mirrored in those of Paul Theroux (who is, in any case, half-Italian by ancestry). Much as they differ in style and artistic concerns, all of these authors nonetheless have one thing in common: they reflect in their writing a generalized American culture and accord little or no priority to problems of ethnicity and assimilation.

Admittedly, this is a characteristic that up until now has been essentially confined to those non-WASP writers who trace their ancestry back to one of the major waves of nineteenth and early twentieth century immigration from Europe. By contrast, the great majority of black authors and the emerging cadre of Asian-American ones remain profoundly and explicitly preoccupied with their ethnicity. But the reason for this difference seems plain enough: the acceptance of Jews and Catholics as integral elements of mainstream American society has become so general that Jewish and Catholic writers no longer feel almost automatically compelled to serve in some fashion or other as ethnic spokesmen. It also seems a fair presumption that the degree to which black and Asian-American writers focus on their ethnicity will begin to diminish when a similar degree of acceptance is accorded their groups—and that, meanwhile, their ethnic assertiveness serves to accelerate the approach of the day when such acceptance becomes the national norm.

Anyone who finds that last statement unduly optimistic—as I know many will—seems to me to be overlooking one key fact: even the most aggressively ethnic of successful American writers today command a national rather than just an ethnic readership. This, in turn, means that no matter how parochial their own upbringing and background, the members of that small but influential minority of Americans who regularly read serious books now view their society through a literary lens that focuses on the complexity of our national heritage rather than on Anglo-conformity. If it ever truly was so, the American mind surely is no longer synonymous with the WASP mind. Over the last few decades our artists and intellectuals have decisively broken with that tradition—and at least partly as a result of their trailblazing the rest of us have embarked irrevocably upon the same path.

11

SOLDIERS, SPIES, AND THE STRIPED PANTS SET

At a Manhattan dinner party back in the mid-1960s, one of my fashionably liberal friends from the *New York Times* began to hold forth on what he saw as the irremediably retrograde attitudes of U.S. military men on racial and ethnic issues. When I demurred mildly, saying that I felt his views on the subject were somewhat out of date, he responded with incredulous laughter—which so annoyed me that I immediately offered to bet him a substantial sum that the United States Army would have a black chief of staff well before a black journalist occupied the top editor's office at the *Times*.

As of the spring of 1988, the day has not yet arrived when either my friend or I could collect on that bet (which he, in fact, declined to accept on the grounds that "it would be like taking candy from a baby"). But until he accepted a "political" job as President Reagan's national security adviser, at least one black officer, Lt. Gen. Colin Powell, was generally regarded as a hot prospect to become Army chief of staff within the next few years—and he may well yet do so. Meanwhile, the top editorial echelon at the *New York Times* includes no blacks at all. In short, it seems increasingly clear that my chances of eventually being able to say "I told you so" are a great deal better than those of my opponent in that dinner table argument so long ago.

Yet that fact, I am confident, has not essentially altered my friend's opinion of the major institutions responsible for the execution of the U.S. government's security and foreign policy decisions. Like many people who share his broad political and philosophical predispositions, he sees the nation's top diplomatic, military, and intelligence establishments as instruments of reaction, unrepresentative both in doctrine and leadership of the full spectrum of contemporary American society.

This, of course, is a perception with extremely far-reaching implications. Since they help to define as well as defend U.S. national interests, the officers of the armed services and the major intelligence agencies exercise both directly and indirectly an influence on American life out of proportion to their numbers. To begin with, they oversee the spending of a whopping share of the national income; in 1986, the U.S. intelligence budget alone was estimated at $25 billion. And the effectiveness or ineffectiveness with which these services perform has major bearing not only upon the way in which the United States is viewed abroad but upon our own national self-image; the CIA's disastrous venture at the Bay of Pigs and the demoralization that characterized so much of the Army in the last years of the Vietnam conflict were inevitably regarded by most Americans as cause for national shame. War and diplomacy, in other words, are too important to be left to the WASPs—or for that matter, any other single element of the American population.

For most of our national history, however, they pretty much were. At the beginning of World War II when I first became aware of such matters, it was still almost a foregone conclusion that any U.S. general or admiral would be either WASP or Irish-American by origin.* Simi-

---

* An apparent exception to this rule was the significant number of World War II U.S. officers of senior rank who bore German names, such as Eisenhower, Eichelberger, Spaatz, Kimmel, and Nimitz. But while two of Gen. Douglas MacArthur's top subordinates—Generals Walter Kruger and Charles Willoughby (né von Tscheppe-Weidenbach)—were actually

larly, the only notable non-WASP diplomat I can recall from those years was Robert Murphy, a Midwesterner of lower middle class Irish and German background who had begun his State Department career as a code clerk.* And in creating the nation's first serious foreign intelligence agency, another Irish American, William ("Wild Bill") Donovan, had drawn so heavily in his recruiting upon scions of the Eastern Establishment that cynics were moved to suggest that instead of Office of Strategic Services the acronym OSS actually stood for Oh So Social; a dedicated Anglophile, Donovan aped the class-conscious British practice of the time by enlisting for the OSS no fewer than forty-two members of the Yale class of 1943 as well as a clutch of operatives with names such as Junius Morgan, William Vanderbilt, Allen Dulles, James Jesus Angleton, Stewart Alsop, C. Tracy Barnes, and Joseph Toy Curtiss.

At the time very few people seriously questioned the propriety of such arrangements. Yet even then it should have been apparent that, given the basic thrust of American society, management of the nation's principal security and foreign policy bodies could not forever remain the monopoly of a privileged minority—and of course, it has not. Curiously, though, the speed and enthusiasm with which these various institutions embraced ethnic and social diversity tended to reflect quite directly how long each had been a solidly established arm of American government.

BECAUSE THE U.S. intelligence establishment in its present form is largely a post–World War II creation, it might seem that from the start it should have mirrored the general composition of the contemporary

---

of German birth, the great majority of Teutonic-sounding American commanders came from families that had long since been WASPified.

* A charming and highly intelligent man, Murphy nonetheless afforded striking proof that humble origins don't necessarily inspire broader social vision than privileged ones. I still recall my astonishment when at a luncheon he hosted in the late 1960s, Murphy joined that aristocratic paladin of the foreign policy establishment, former ambassador to Moscow George Kennan, in arguing that it was wrong for the U.S. to send black consular officials to South Africa or even to allow black U.S. navy personnel to go on liberty when their ships were in South African ports. "When you are a guest in somebody else's home," Murphy explained, "you follow the rules of the house."

American population more faithfully than the more tradition-bound leadership of the Foreign Service and the armed forces. And that assumption does, in fact, hold true for the largest and most secretive of American intelligence organizations—the ubiquitous but infrequently publicized National Security Agency (NSA). Ultimately responsible for the production and evaluation of all intelligence derived from communications, NSA has long since blossomed into a mammoth operation; from its sprawling headquarters in Fort George Meade, Maryland, it oversees the complex operations of a staff bigger than that of all the rest of the American intelligence establishment put together.*

A relative newcomer among government agencies—it was formally created by Harry Truman in 1952—the NSA basically traces its bureaucratic genealogy back to the Signal Intelligence Service established by the Army in 1930 under the directorship of perhaps the most brilliant cryptologist America has ever produced, Col. William F. Friedman. Since successful cryptanalysis rests upon highly developed mathematical and language skills, those were the talents Friedman sought in his subordinates, and as the son of a Rumanian-Jewish immigrant himself, he was profoundly uninterested in their social or ethnic background. Two of his first recruits, in fact, were graduates of New York's decidedly unfashionable City College—Dr. Solomon Kullback, who later rose to director of research and development for NSA, and Abraham Sinkov, a diminutive, bespectacled man of Russian-Jewish ancestry who began his career as a high school math teacher in Brooklyn and ended it as a major general in the United States Army.

Happily, the pattern set by Friedman proved enduring—a fact epitomized for me by the careers of three men who were serving in NSA's forerunner, the Armed Forces Security Agency, when I was attached to that organization during the Korean War. One of them, a graduate of Chicago's Loyola University named Louis Tordello, eventually became deputy director of the NSA and as such its de facto permanent chief. Another, Maurice H. (Moe) Klein, was for some years

---

* In his book *The Puzzle Palace*, which remains the most authoritative published work on the NSA, James Bamford reveals that as of 1978 there were more than 68,000 people entitled to membership in the agency's Federal credit union—and during the Reagan years that figure almost certainly increased.

---

entrusted with the highly sensitive post of director of personnel for NSA, and the third, a voluble Brooklynite named Milton Zaslow, ultimately emerged as the second-ranking professional cryptologist in the agency.*

But critical as the NSA's behind-scenes role in the gathering of secret information may be, it is, of course, the CIA that symbolizes U.S. intelligence to the man in the street everywhere in the world. And there, too, the recruiting pattern set by the institution's spiritual founding father proved to be remarkably persistent—a fact that among other things was to have fateful consequences for the prestige and power of the nation's traditional WASP elite.

In his authoritative book *The Agency*, John Ranelagh notes that when the CIA was established in 1947, one-third of its staff consisted of people who had previously served with Wild Bill Donovan's OSS. As a result, although its first four directors were all senior military officers, the tone of the Agency was set from the start by men whose characters had been shaped by the exclusive Ivy League and/or preppy Wall Street of prewar days. And in 1953, this state of affairs was, in effect, formally ratified when the most eminent of the OSS alumni, Allen Dulles, was appointed director, a post that he was to hold longer than anyone before or since.

Though he emphatically did not share Donovan's Anglophilia, Dulles was nonetheless by birth and breeding the very model of the Anglo-American patrician—a Princeton graduate and onetime Wall Street lawyer, grandson of one secretary of state and brother of another, tweedy in tailoring and upper-class avuncular in manner. Yet despite his presumably secure personal status, Dulles, so one of his subordinates later told John Ranelagh, "played the social game really hard." And while there may have been an element of personal bitter-

---

* Ironically, two of these three highly competent intelligence professionals were also ultimately responsible for winning the NSA rare and unwelcome public attention. In 1961, Klein was ousted from the agency for having falsely stated on a civil service form many years earlier that his law degree was from Harvard rather than the New Jersey Law School and that his mother had been born in the United States rather than Russia. A decade later, at the height of the Pentagon Papers flap, Zaslow incurred mockery for turning up to talk to officials of the *New York Times* with a pistol strapped to his chest and accompanied by a security agent who sported a revolver on each hip.

---

ness in that assessment, it is undeniably true that during the years of Dulles's directorship a disproportionate number of the senior positions in the CIA were occupied by conspicuously upper-drawer types such as Kermit and Archibald Roosevelt, William Bundy, Cord Meyer, and Richard Bissell.

To imply that these men and others like them owed their preeminence at the CIA purely—or even chiefly—to social background would, in my judgment, be grossly unfair. On the contrary, those whose careers I am most familiar with were people of intelligence, ability, and deep dedication to what they saw as the legitimate interests of the United States. But they were also "gentlemen"—a word that John Waller, who for a time was inspector general of CIA, once defined as denoting "somebody who doesn't buy clothes; he has them." And in many cases the gentlemen in question showed a distinct predilection for others of the same ilk when it came to choosing subordinates. Consider, for example, the standards that Frank Wisner, another former Wall Street lawyer, reportedly applied when recruiting staff for the CIA's covert action section. According to Robin Winks in his book *Cloak and Gown*, Wisner wanted "young men with high grades, a sense of grace, with previous knowledge of Europe . . . [and] an ease with themselves that athletic success can often bring. . . . Since foreign languages were important, this need further strengthened the tendency to look to Harvard, Yale, Brown, or Princeton. . . . But Williams, Swarthmore, Bowdoin, Reed, Berea—the smaller private colleges— were not overlooked."

To be sure, admission to the CIA was by no means confined to the children of privilege even in the Agency's earlier years. By the mid-1950s, CIA recruiters were active at Middlewestern and Western universities and at Catholic institutions as well as secular ones. (The Agency's interest in Catholic schools apparently reflected an assumption, perhaps valid at the time, that a strongly Catholic upbringing tended to foster a staunch brand of conventional patriotism.) But while performance rather than pedigree was the criterion at the working level, most of the top jobs at the CIA—those that really conferred power—continued to be held by members of the Eastern Establishment throughout the 1960s.

The extent to which this was true was driven home to me personally by two unrelated but similar glimpses that I got into the Agency's workings in the mid-1960s. The first of these occurred when, as part of my reporting for an article on Vietnam, I requested a nonclassified briefing on the CIA's view of what was happening there and found myself highly impressed by the officer who delivered it. He struck me, in fact, as someone who could scarcely fail to make it into the top ranks of the Agency, but when I said as much to the *Newsweek* Washington correspondent who had arranged the briefing, he chuckled sardonically. "Not a chance," he said. "One, the guy didn't go to an Ivy League school. Two, he's a French Canadian out of a Massachusetts mill town."

The second shoe dropped for me not long after when a wartime friend who had decided to make a career of intelligence work suddenly quit the CIA after more than a decade's service. During his last overseas tour, he told me, he had felt compelled to bring charges against his station chief for conducting an operation that was not only unauthorized but in my friend's judgment patently foolhardy. After a lengthy bureaucratic wrangle that carried the matter to the highest levels of the CIA, my friend was informed that his charges were totally justified —and that unless he agreed to drop them he had no future with the Agency. "So far as they were concerned, it was no contest," he told me bitterly. "I was just some Joe from a cow college in the Southwest; the other guy was Society with a capital *S* and had a president in his family tree."

But even then, though the fact had not yet become evident, the days of the ruling clique known to old CIA hands as "the Founding Fathers" or "the Knights Templar" were already numbered. In retrospect, it is obvious that the critical impediment to democratization of the Agency was removed in 1961 when, in the wake of the Bay of Pigs, President Kennedy not only sacked the CIA officer in charge of covert operations, a Groton and Yale product named Richard Bissell, but also forced the resignation of Allen Dulles himself. Ironically, however, the opportunity thus created went largely unexploited until the arrival in the White House of that improbable social leveler Richard Nixon. Long resentful of what he regarded as supercilious treatment at the hands of "Ivy League liberals" and "the Georgetown crowd," Nixon viewed the upper echelon of CIA officers with unmitigated dislike and as soon as he decently could, turned the directorship of the agency over to his own man, James P. Schlesinger.

As things turned out, Schlesinger, whose objections to the CIA operating style were founded on professional as well as political considerations, remained at the Agency for only seventeen weeks. But in that time he ousted some 1,500 people, the largest number of whom came from clandestine operations where the Ivy League old boy net had been strongest. And what Schlesinger had begun, his successor, longtime CIA careerist William Colby, relentlessly completed. A Princetonian himself but Catholic and decidedly not *Social Register*, Colby moved into the director's job with an insider's knowledge of where the bodies were buried and with the express intent of "kicking out the Eastern Establishment."

By the beginning of the eighties, thanks to Colby and Jimmy Carter's Annapolis classmate Stansfield Turner (who wiped out most of such remnants of the clandestine service as had survived the Colby era), the deed was done. Nothing could more clearly have revealed the impotence of the CIA's old guard than William Casey's attempt in 1981 to install as head of covert activities a hard-nosed businessman named Max Hugel, whose most notable previous foray into public service had been as New England campaign manager for Ronald Reagan. And while Hugel was quickly forced to resign by controversy over some of his past business dealings, Casey displayed equal—and more successful—eclecticism when he managed to enlist as the CIA's legislative counsel scrappy Stanley Sporkin, who in his previous incarnation as general counsel for the SEC had made himself the terror of Wall Street.

Since Casey's death and the advent of low-key Missourian William Webster as its director, the CIA appears to have once again achieved a measure of bureaucratic stability. Whether it constitutes a particularly effective instrument of national policy is debatable; the prolonged public washing of its dirty linen that began in the Nixon years has left its leadership gun-shy and for better or for worse, closer congressional oversight renders truly covert action by the Agency well nigh impossible. But whatever its other shortcomings, the CIA now attracts scores of thousands of job applications each year and draws its new recruits from a reasonably representative cross section of the nation's college-educated population. At long last, in other words, the Agency has become what William Colby once said he wanted it to be: "an American service."

DESPITE THE CHANGES it has undergone, the CIA today surely ranks as the branch of the U.S. government that is regarded with deepest suspicion by the general public. This, however, is essentially a post-Vietnam phenomenon; historically, that distinction belonged to the career diplomatic service. Even yet, in fact, the man in the street tends to think of Foreign Service officers as "cookie pushers," effete and supercilious sprigs of privilege given to such inherently un-American activities as wearing striped pants and making small talk over tea. And nowhere is this feeling stronger than among the professionally egalitarian politicans whom the voters send to Washington: as late as 1980 when it wrote a new Foreign Service Act, the Congress felt obliged to include in it a specific injunction that the U.S. diplomatic corps should recruit its officers from all segments of society in order to be truly "representative of the American people."

To a considerable extent the Foreign Service has only itself to blame for the suspicion in which it is held. At least until World War II the archetypal U.S. career diplomat was a WASP of "good family" born in the Northeast and educated at an Ivy League university. And well into the 1960s, it was still common to encounter, as I did on various journalistic ventures abroad, senior Foreign Service officers with names such as John Moors Cabot and Outerbridge Horsey (known to his familiars, so I learned, as "Outer"). Indeed, the competitive advantage that a privileged background affords a would-be American diplomat has not been totally eliminated even today: in a 1987 interview with the *New York Times*, Clarence E. Hodges, then the deputy assistant secretary responsible for equal employment opportunity at the Department of State, confessed that certain aspects of the Foreign Service examination process still appeared to favor applicants from families affluent enough to send their children to travel and study abroad.

Given the economic realities of contemporary American life, this fact obviously tends to have more impact upon some groups in our society than others. The most conspicuous evidence of this is that as of 1987 only 248 of some 4,000 career Foreign Service officers—which is to say just over 6 percent—were black. And of the service's 615 senior officers, blacks accounted for only 12, or less than 2 percent.

The other side of this coin, however, is that certainly since the 1970s ethnicity per se has not barred anyone from achieving senior rank in the Foreign Service. At the end of 1986 there were six blacks serving as U.S. ambassadors abroad, and a few years earlier there had been as many as twelve. When it comes to senior personnel other than blacks, no breakdown by ethnic background exists in State Department files, but here again it is clear that competence rather than heritage is the touchstone. Three U.S. ambassadors who in my view turned in outstanding performances in the 1970s and 1980s—Frank Carlucci in Portugal, Diego Asencio in Colombia, and Nicholas Veliotes in Jordan and Egypt—were respectively of Italian, Spanish, and Greek ancestry. John D. Negroponte, who rose to the rank of assistant secretary of state before becoming deputy to National Security Adviser Colin Powell, proudly proclaims his Greek Orthodox faith in *Who's Who*. And the career diplomat most heavily relied upon by Ronald Reagan, Brooklyn-born Philip Habib, is, of course, of Lebanese extraction.*

It is tempting to speculate that what all this reflects is not so much a change in the Foreign Service itself as the change that has occurred in the student bodies of the nation's more prestigious universities. Carlucci, for example, went to Princeton, Negroponte to Yale, Veliotes to Berkeley, and Asencio to Georgetown. But in fairness there seems to be more involved than that: Perkins, the first black American ambassador to South Africa, is a graduate of the University of Maryland, and Habib got his bachelor's degree at the University of Idaho. Educational as well as ethnic diversity, then, is increasingly the order of the day in the U.S. diplomatic corps.

What remains to be demonstrated, though, is that a diplomatic service more broadly representative of the overall American population will necessarily put a different spin on U.S. foreign policy than the old WASP diplomatic establishment did. So far as that is concerned, there

---

* Given the quasi-official role often played by ambassadors' wives, it should perhaps also be noted that as of 1986 two U.S. envoys holding important assignments—Winston Lord in Peking and Edward Perkins in Johannesburg—were married to women of Chinese ancestry.

---

is food for thought in the case of Terence Todman, a longtime career diplomat who in 1976 was named assistant secretary of state for Inter-American Affairs. In that job he so vigorously opposed the public sanctions that Carter administration human rights activists favored applying to oppressive Latin American regimes that in the end then deputy secretary of state Warren Christopher felt obliged to bundle him off as ambassador to Spain. What rendered all this perhaps a bit unusual was the fact that Mr. Todman happens to be black.

The Todman case, I believe, serves to underscore a comment made by Alan L. Keyes, who until he abruptly resigned from the post in September 1988 was assistant secretary of state for International Organizations Affairs and as such, the department's highest-ranking black official. Commenting on reports that he had quit in protest at racist behavior on the part of his immediate superior, Keyes declared: "The problem in the State Department is less racism than a kind of elitism—toward most people in this country. There is a feeling that the career bureaucratic elite know what's best for the country, and they are not really comfortable with democratic processes."

That statement, to my ear, has the unmistakable ring of truth. And it stands as a reminder that, indispensable as it may be to the general health of our society, the ethnic diversification of America's various leadership groups in no way guarantees the reshaping of our major institutions in a manner satisfactory to the nation's more passionate advocates of social and political change.

IT MIGHT, I suppose, be argued that the Foreign Service is too small an organization and too esoteric in its function to justify sweeping generalizations about the potential benefits of ethnic diversification. But the same can scarcely be said about an even older and more indispensable arm of government: the nation's 3-million-member military establishment.

By any objective standard, the most systematic and successful application of ethnic power sharing in the contemporary United States is to be found in the armed services—or more precisely, in the United States Army. No other American institution has made so much progress as the Army in bridging the oldest and most intractable of our ethnic divides—the gulf between white Americans and black ones. As one of the nation's leading military sociologists, Prof. Charles C. Moskos, wrote in *The Atlantic* monthly in the spring of 1986: "Today one is more likely to hear racial jokes in a faculty club than in an officers' club. And in an officers' club one will surely see more black faces."

This is a reality that, as I suggested at the beginning of this chapter, many white liberals find difficult to swallow and hence choose to ignore. In so doing, however, they are merely following in the footsteps of the nation's black political and intellectual leadership. When *Ebony* magazine published its 1987 list of the "100 Most Influential Black Americans," it included eleven clergymen, nine mayors, three particularly exalted Masons and Elks, and five sorority leaders. What it didn't include was a single black general or admiral—of whom there happened to be forty on active duty at the time. Perhaps in reaction to a *Wall Street Journal* article drawing attention to this curious omission, *Ebony*'s 1988 list did, in fact, include two generals. But one of them, Colin Powell, clearly got there on the strength of his appointment to a political job, and in any event the military men whom *Ebony* found worthy of mention were still outnumbered four to one by Masons, Elks, and sorority sisters.

To some extent, this reluctance to give credit where it is due doubtless reflects a high-minded view common among white as well as black progressives—the belief that the continued existence of armed forces, like that of prostitution, represents a deplorable accommodation to the baser human instincts. But to a considerably greater extent, I believe, it stems from two more cold-eyed attitudes almost universally held by influential black civilians.

One of these is the conviction that the U.S. military establishment consumes resources that would be better devoted to social programs of direct benefit to blacks yet implements national policies broadly inimical to black interests. The other is the view that blacks in the military have somehow sold out by meeting the standards of a fundamentally white power structure.*

---

* I am informed by Dorothy and Carl Schneider, the authors of *Sound Off*, a readable and uniquely comprehensive study of women in the U.S. military, that similar attitudes toward the armed services are held by some doctrinaire feminists. The difference, of course, is that in their rhetoric "white" is replaced by "male" and "black" by "female."

To the extent that they hold such views, though, black political leaders and social activists are clearly out of step with a considerable proportion of the nation's less privileged blacks. When I discussed the matter with him in 1987, Lt. Gen. Allen Ono, then the deputy chief of staff of the Army for personnel, told me: "I've had five assignments as a recruiter . . . With black families, I didn't have to prove that opportunity was available in the Army because they already knew that. They had brothers, nephews, or friends who had experienced those opportunities. And the same held true for Hispanics."

To say that the Army offers uncommon opportunity to underprivileged blacks and Hispanics is, of course, not to say that it is totally free of racism. Particularly among older personnel, off-duty relations between whites and blacks are not infrequently distant, and even among younger servicemen some informal social segregation survives: at a base with more than one enlisted men's club, whites will tend to do their drinking at one and blacks at another. And in purely professional terms as well, traces of discrimination, though almost never overt, appear to linger; most senior black officers remain convinced that a black still has to ourperform his white colleagues to achieve equal rank.

Yet, in a kind of reverse English, the fact that black personnel are held to stiff—even perhaps unfairly stiff—standards has one positive aspect. "Black officers," notes Charles Moskos, ". . . draw manifest self-esteem from the fact that they have not been the beneficiaries of [preferential] treatment." And none that I have encountered was disposed to challenge the estimate of race relations in the Army that was offered by its chief of staff, Gen. Carl Vuono, in 1987. "We're not perfect," General Vuono said, "but the institutional biases have been pretty well eradicated."

In a legal sense the eradication of those biases began long ago— with President Harry Truman's bold 1948 executive order forbidding racial segregation in the armed services. But as any bureaucrat knows, the effectiveness of even the most unambiguous government decree depends upon the diligence and enthusiasm with which it is enforced at the working level. And if further proof of that were needed, it could be found in the racial composition of the the various U.S. armed services nearly forty years after Truman issued his historic order. As of late 1986, the percentage of blacks in the all-volunteer Army was two and a half times as large as the percentage of blacks in the overall national population; it was also nearly twice as high as the comparable figure for the Air Force, and well over twice as high as that for the Navy.*

Up to a point, this disparity between the branches could perhaps be accounted for by the differing educational and technical demands made upon rank-and-file personnel in different services. But that rationale scarcely served to explain the even greater disparities in the racial origin of the most highly trained and professional personnel in the various services—the fact, for example, that 10 percent of all Army officers and 30 percent of all Army sergeants major were black while only 3 percent of the Navy's officers and 6 percent of its chief petty officers were.† The clear message inherent in those statistics is that from the 1950s on the Army outstripped not only industry and academia but its sister services as well in systematic recruitment, training, and promotion of black Americans.

Ironically, one of the first notable consequences of this groundbreaking effort was the birth during the Vietnam years of the widely accepted legend that the Army was deliberately using blacks as "cannon fodder." And while that charge was demonstrably untrue,‡ it was in a sense an understandable one: while black noncoms and junior officers were commonplace in the Army by the early 1960s, black officers of senior rank did not begin to be visible in significant numbers until the latter years of that decade.

The reason for that, however, was scarcely sinister. "You can't make a colonel or a general overnight," observes General Ono. "You have to grow 'em." And once the initial growing season for black officers was completed, the harvest became increasingly rich. As of 1988, somewhat more than one hundred black Americans had achieved the

---

* The actual percentage of black personnel in each of the services: Army—27%; Marines—19%; Air Force—15%; Navy—12%.

† Percentages of black officers and top-ranking noncoms in the other two armed services as of 1986 were: Marines—5% and 17.5%; Air Force—5% and 11%.

‡ In relation to total American casualties, the number of blacks killed in action during the Vietnam war hovered right around the percentage of blacks in the U.S. population generally.

rank of general or admiral in the armed forces. Of these, all but a handful were still living, and the great majority were Army officers. Indeed, of the forty black officers of one–star rank or higher on active duty at the end of 1986, a full three-quarters were Army generals.*

As the 1960s drew to a close, moreover, there was no longer any limit to the career aspirations that a young black Army officer could rationally entertain. By then, a number of black generals in the Army had commanded combat brigades and divisions—an almost indispensable stepping stone to the chief of staff's office. In the Air Force, blacks had not only led major strike forces but the North American Air Defense Command and the Air Force Systems Command.† But perhaps the officer most symbolic of the role now played by black Americans in the military was a less exalted figure, Brig. Gen. Fred A. Gorden. In mid-1987, General Gorden, himself a West Point graduate, was appointed the sixty-first commandant of the United States Military Academy. As such, he not only followed in the legendary footsteps of such men as Douglas MacArthur but had become—temporarily perhaps but in a very real sense—the keeper of the flame for the officer corps of the United States Army.

IT IS NO DOUBT inevitable that insofar as they give any thought at all to the ethnic makeup of their armed forces, Americans nowadays focus almost exclusively on questions of black and white. But in so doing they overlook another significant change in the nature of our military establishment: in the senior command positions once largely reserved for officers of WASP and Irish-American background, a remarkable degree of ethnic diversity has now become the order of the day.

The most conspicuous manifestation of this change occurred in June 1987 when Gen. Carl E. Vuono was appointed chief of staff of the Army. Personable and incisive with hawklike features and a college fullback's build, General Vuono is a onetime artillery officer who held

---

* The remaining quarter consisted of five Navy admirals, four Air Force generals, and one Marine general.

† As of 1988 the last of these organizations was commanded by Bernard G. Randolph, the third black to win the four stars of a full general—which is the highest rank normally granted U.S. officers in peacetime. His two predecessors: the Air Force's late Gen. Daniel ("Chappy") James and the Army's Gen. Roscoe Robinson, Jr., now retired.

---

combat commands in Vietnam and clearly falls into the category known in the Army as "a muddy-boots soldier." But he is also, as West Pointers frequently are, at least in the military context, a man of ideas, one of the most influential advocates of a post-Vietnam wrinkle in U.S. strategic thinking that emphasizes something called "the operational arc." Because of this combination of characteristics I was strongly reminded when I first met General Vuono of one of his most admirable predecessors as chief of staff, the late Gen. Creighton Abrams. Yet for all their similarities there was at least one difference between the two men: General Abrams, in the classic Army mold, was a WASP, a Yankee from Marblehead, Massachusetts; General Vuono is an Italian American from the Pennsylvania coal country.

To Vuono himself, the fact that he was the first Italian American ever to be chosen for the top uniformed job in the Army (or any other branch of the armed forces, for that matter) seemed of relatively marginal interest. "I wasn't particularly conscious of it," he told me. Then, with a faint smile, he added: "But I'll tell you who was: Italian-American organizations."

Thinking back to his youth, moreover, General Vuono conceded that perhaps the fact that his mother and father "had a sense there were things they couldn't belong to because they were Italian-American" may have had more impact on him than he recognized at the time. "That's possible," he said. "Maybe deep down that influenced my decision to go to West Point—that I felt that in the Army I'd be judged on performance alone.

"And that's the way it turned out to be," Vuono went on. One reason it turned out that way, he believes, is that "in the Army no single person determines your future; you're rated by a lot of people." That, he seemed to suggest, helped to counteract any particular set of biases individuals might hold. And in that he was implicitly seconded by his top personnel officer, Lt. Gen. Allen Ono. A Japanese American who came into the Army with an ROTC commission earned at the University of Hawaii, General Ono said he chose a military career because "I knew what the Army had given my relatives and friends— the most important thing being a chance to prove that they were loyal Americans." In the Army, he insisted, "what matters is performance. I don't think that being Japanese-American held me back at all. I've been given the same opportunities as others; assignments and transfers came my way in logical patterns and at logical times."

Carl Vuono and Allen Ono are clearly not unique in their response to the prospect of being judged solely on merit; by the time they were commissioned in the second half of the 1950s, white ethnics of every stripe abounded at the lower levels of the Army officer corps. And just as with blacks, the consequences of that diversification began to become apparent in the higher ranks of the Army in the 1970s and 1980s. "Just look around these offices," General Vuono suggested when I visited him in the Pentagon. "The generals I've got working for me include an Ono, a Weinstein, and a Schwarzkopf. And for a while I had a RisCassi working for me, too." *

Diverse as it already is, moreover, the cast of characters in General Vuono's Pentagon aerie promises to become even more ethnically variegated in years to come. Or that at least is the only conclusion it seems possible to draw when one looks at the wellsprings from which the U.S. armed forces now draw their potential leaders. Unlike European artistocracies, which have historically participated heavily in their nations' professional officer corps, Americans of privileged background have generally been only too happy to leave military careers to the children of the middle and lower middle class.† And today more than ever the service academies appeal primarily to what one Army staff officer described to me as "bright lower middle class kids—ones smart enough to make it in a topflight civilian school but not rich

---

* The last three of the officers to whom Vuono referred were respectively the deputy chief of staff for Intelligence, Lt. Gen. Sidney T. Weinstein; the deputy chief of staff for Operations, Lt. Gen. H. Norman Schwarzkopf; and the director of Joint Staffs, Lt. Gen. Robert RisCassi.

† A partial exception to this rule is to be found in a relatively small number of American families in which pursuit of a professional military career has become a tradition. In the past, a significant number of the sons of senior military officers chose to follow in their fathers' footsteps with the result that names such as Truscott, Patton, Grant, MacArthur, and McCain turned up in the armed services in successive generations. And not surprisingly perhaps, that same pattern has begun to be visible among the children of today's non-WASP senior officers: Generals Vuono, Ono, Weinstein, and RisCassi, for example, all have sons or daughters who hold commissions in one service or another and so do a number of black generals.

enough to pay that kind of tuition or poor enough to qualify for special treatment."

That, obviously, is a category which includes a great many white ethnics—the children and grandchildren of immigrants from all over Europe. But it also increasingly includes representatives of those groups officially proclaimed by the Federal government to be minorities. As late as 1968 fewer than one percent of the members of the entering class at West Point were black, and cadets from other non-white minorities were so few as to be negligible. By 1987, however, more than 15 percent of the 4,334 cadets attending the Military Academy were from such groups. Of these, 304 were black, 192 Hispanic, 152 Asian-American, and 19 American Indian. (Among the minority cadets were 71 of the 454 women enrolled at West Point that year.)

A similar but even more sweeping change occurred between the late sixties and the eighties in the Reserve Officers' Training Corps—and since ROTC supplies the Army with six times as many of its officers as West Point does, this was a portentous development indeed. Here the chief factors at work were the expulsion of ROTC from many elite campuses during the Vietnam era and the intensified determination of young Americans of privileged background to shun any relationship with the military whatever.

Because of these twin developments the armed services in general and the Army in particular have had little choice but to focus ROTC programs more heavily upon predominantly black colleges and those whose student bodies include a high percentage of youngsters from blue collar backgrounds. By the mid-1980s, in fact, one-fifth of all the ROTC officers commissioned each year were black. And those students at prestigious universities who did fulfill ROTC requirements, not infrequently by participating in programs at nearby institutions less sternly antimilitary than their own, tended not to come from the ranks of preppydom: of the three lonely members of the Yale class of 1986 who earned ROTC commissions, two were Asian Americans—and one of those was female.

What these facts imply concerning the future leadership of our country's armed forces seems to me abundantly plain. It can only be a matter of time—and not, as I suggested at the beginning of this chapter, too much time—before a black general makes a prophet of me by winning appointment as chief of staff of the Army. But that will only be the beginning: one day, perhaps in the first decade of the twenty-first century, the Army will have "grown" an Asian-American general —very possibly one of Vietnamese ancestry—who will be the logical choice for chief of staff. And eventually it is entirely conceivable— even, I think, probable—that the job will go to a woman.

That, of course, is a statement sure to expose me to derision from male chauvinists and extreme feminists alike. Surely, members of both factions will argue, no one can seriously believe that a woman will ever be allowed to serve as chief of staff of the United States Army. In reply, I can only echo the view of the current incumbent. "Maybe people don't think so now," General Vuono told me. "But then, fifty years ago nobody would have thought there could ever be an Italian-American chief of staff either."

12

HIGH SOCIETY BLUES

It was the sort of chic fund-raising gala in which *le tout Manhattan* delights. On a spring evening in 1988 some 1,300 high rollers resplendent in dinner jackets and designer dresses trooped in past the lions guarding the Fifth Avenue entrance to the New York Public Library to dine on apple-smoked turkey and admire ten tableaux featuring treasured items from the library's diverse collections. (One such display, created by restaurateur Warner LeRoy and entitled "A Glamorous Old New York Evening," somewhat mysteriously included what *New York* magazine offhandedly described as "an elaborate presentation of lobsters.") As all such affairs do, this one served twin purposes: since it enriched the library by some $1.5 million, it allowed the participants to enjoy a glow of virtue; yet at the same time it afforded them an opportunity to see and be seen by the likes of Brooke Astor, Lee Radziwill, financiers Felix Rohatyn and Henry Kravis, Texas tycoon Sid Bass, Norris (Mrs. Norman Mailer) Church, and couturier Oscar de la Renta.

As is their wont, the indefatigable band of society reporters and columnists who covered the so-called Ten Treasures Dinner spared few superlatives in trying to convey the wonder of it all. But when, in the interests of social history, I sought a firsthand account of the party from one of the few New Yorkers of my acquaintance who combines wealth, talent, and an impressive pedigree, the reaction I elicited was less than euphoric. "Well," he said disparagingly, "it was all in a worthy cause, of course. But the kind of people who turned out for that sort of affair mostly tend to be . . . well, you know, kind of glitzy."

The contrast between this gentleman's reaction and that of the journalists whose job it is to record the doings of Manhattan's upper crust reflects a perennial ambivalence among Americans about just what it is that confers superior social status in this country.

On one side of this argument are people such as Lewis Lapham, the editor of *Harper's* magazine and author of a work entitled *Money and Class in America.* Himself as unmistakably patrician as an American can get, Lapham argues that it is misleading to describe the holders of wealth in the United States as "upper class" since that phrase "implies a veneer of good manners that doesn't exist." To avoid falling into this error, he has coined the term "the equestrian class," which, as he explains, is "borrowed from the Roman usage" and includes "all those who can afford to ride rather than walk and who can buy any or all of the baubles that constitute proof of social status."

To be sure, Lapham does not contend that all money is equal; there are, he emphasizes, significant differences in psychology and lifestyle between "old money" and "new money." But in his scheme of things, it is money, old or new, that underlies any serious claim to superior social rank in the U.S.

This, however, is not at all the way things look to that indefatigable chronicler of the upper reaches of American society Stephen Birmingham. In *America's Secret Aristocracy*, which he published in 1987, Birmingham roundly asserts that "from its beginnings America's aristocracy had almost nothing to do with money at all." Rather, he insists, the hallmarks of the truly upper class American include very old family, deep respect for the demands of moral and financial probity, a strong sense of public duty, and a passion for personal privacy.

Both Lapham and Birmingham are obviously intelligent men, and both have clearly thought long and hard about the matter of class distinction in America. Nonetheless, I must confess that I have a great deal of difficulty in swallowing whole the position adopted by either of them. To begin with, it is manifestly not the case that the ability to buy the baubles that constitute proof of social status can by itself automatically confer such status upon anyone. There are all sorts of people ranging from Jimmy Swaggart and Sylvester Stallone to Joseph ("Joe Bananas") Bonanno and Hugh Hefner who have (or had) the wherewithal to buy almost anything yet do not enjoy exalted social status in most people's eyes. Either because of the way they acquired their money or their rejection of some of the traditional appurtenances of gentility, they remain conspicuously outside anything that could reasonably be described as a social elite. There are, in other words, at least some behavioral requirements that must be met by those who aspire to generally acknowledged social superiority.

Yet it is far more misleading to suggest that possession of upper class or aristocratic status has little to do with money. Mr. Birmingham to the contrary, aristocracy in America has from the very start of our history had almost everything to do with money. There is, in fact, probably no asset that depreciates faster in the United States than a claim to social status based upon ancestry and unsupported by wealth.

In terms of illustrious forebears, for example, there would seem to be little to choose between the first governor of Massachusetts Bay Colony, John Winthrop, and the founder of Providence Plantation in Rhode Island, Roger Williams. But in terms of American social rankings in the mid-1980s, the John Winthrop who was raking in money as an investment company executive in New York was plainly several cuts above the Roger Williams who was earning his living as a factory hand in Rhode Island.

An even more striking demonstration of the principle involved here is provided by two families that live in a small New England city with which I am familiar. Both of these families are descended from the same early eighteenth century regional dignitary, both still carry his surname, and the senior male members of both bear a strong resemblance to each other physically and in manner of speech. Yet while one of these families is part of the town's social elite, the other is not. And the reason for that at bottom lies in their relative financial circumstances: the family that is perceived as upper class lives in an elegant old home and sends its offspring to "good" colleges because it is, to use the local euphemism, "well fixed"; the family that is not so perceived has been headed for three generations now by skilled artisans and lives in the comfortable but homely fashion that such employment will support.

WHEN I SAY that the first of the two families I have just described is perceived as upper class, I do not, of course, mean to suggest that any of its neighbors would be so crass as to refer to it in those precise words. For that would violate one of the more peculiar unwritten taboos of American life. All of us are perfectly comfortable with the phrase "middle class," and both "underclass" and "working class" are now reasonably acceptable (though in the latter case the more delicate-minded still tend to prefer "blue collar"). But while conceding the existence of an underclass, a working class and a middle class would necessarily seem to imply the existence of a privileged group at the upper end of the social spectrum, most Americans shy away from the term "upper class"—primarily, I suspect, out of a vague feeling that to use those words tacitly proclaims acceptance of some kind of invidious and undemocratic value judgment.

To get around this dilemma, we Americans regularly resort to all sorts of Aesopian words and phrases—as I myself have repeatedly done in this book. One of the oldest and most commonly used of these devices is to fall back upon the word "society" as in such phrases as "high society" or "they're in society." But this, too, immediately starts one down a slippery slope since the real significance of the word "society" in this usage is almost as hard to pin down as quicksilver. Does it properly refer to people from long-established families whose members go to the same schools, belong to the same clubs, and tend to marry people from other such families—the sort of people, in short, who go to the trouble of being listed in the *Social Register?* Or is Society with a capital *S* instead composed in the effective sense of those who are rich, self-assured, and gregarious—the people in any community who lead the most opulent and highly publicized lives, give and go to the fanciest parties, and run things such as the Ten Treasures Dinner?

If you assume that the former is the case—that Society consists of the richies from old families—then the slope grows slippier yet. For Society in the United States, to fall back upon an old wisecrack, isn't what it used to be—and never was.

Perhaps the earliest evidence of this is to be found in a lament voiced in 1777 by Elizabeth Gray Otis, the daughter of a leading Boston merchant. Distressed at the fact that so large a number of those Bostonians "who were brought up in the most delicate manner" had gone into exile because of their Tory sympathies, Otis sniffed, "Those who never knew what it was to live in a gentle way are now the first people here . . ."

The parvenus who ultimately replaced the Loyalists as Boston's social elect bore such names as Adams, Cabot, Lowell, and Lodge. And within what in the broad sweep of history amounts to no more than the blinking of an eye, their descendants were echoing Otis's complaint. Little more than a century had passed, in fact, before that querulous patrician Henry Adams began to blame what he regarded as the demise of the old American virtues on the rise to national power of unscrupulous arrivistes. And in 1913, making less effort to find a philosophical sugar-coating for his snobbery, Adams's good friend, the first Sen. Henry Cabot Lodge, grumped that society had been too heavily infiltrated by "newcomers . . . very modern plutocrats."

And so it has gone as successive waves of interlopers have miraculously been transformed into birthright gentry. In 1954, Frank Crowninshield, the fastidious presiding genius of the original *Vanity Fair*, felt obliged to proclaim with an air of gloomy discovery that "there is no longer any real Society." And that, of course, is precisely what my wellborn New York acquaintance was implying nearly thirty-five years later when he turned up his nose at the "glitziness" of the guests at the Ten Treasures Dinner.

FUTILE AS the effort has invariably proved to be, those already ensconced in Society at any given point in American history have nonetheless characteristically fought a bitter rearguard action to prevent "climbers" from joining their ranks. This task, of course, has been greatly complicated by the fact that the United States lacks either a hereditary nobility or formally conferred titles of distinction such as the British knighthood or Italian *commendatore*. It may, in fact, have been partly because of the absence of such clearcut caste marks that the paladins of social exclusion in America early on resorted to ethnic discrimination as one of their prime weapons.

Historically, even eminently successful and cultivated Americans could confidently expect to be rejected by "real society" if they were black or, beginning in about the last quarter of the nineteenth century, Jewish.* And except for a few idiosyncratic parts of the country such as Maryland and Louisiana, the same generally held true for Roman Catholics. Indeed, as late as the beginning of the 1960s a member of Boston's Union Club (who proudly described that institution as "the second-best club in Boston") told me that had John F. Kennedy applied for admission to the Union prior to winning the presidency he almost surely would have been rejected because of his Roman Catholicism no matter how eminent his sponsors.

Inevitably, the resentment bred by such practices was intense and still remains so. Though they generally take refuge in the code word "preppy," many of the numerous Americans who proclaim a special distaste for George Bush are motivated, I strongly suspect, by their perception of him as a rich, snotty WASP and hence the epitome of the forces of bigotry. I also suspect that this does an injustice to Bush, who, whatever his other shortcomings, has not to my knowledge displayed signs of ethnic bias. But the strength and persistence of such hostility is not hard to understand. For on the Society scene WASP exclusionism is not yet by any means merely ancient history.

The most indisputable evidence of that—indisputable because it cannot be brushed away as social happenstance but patently reflects deliberate choices and agreed-upon policies—is to be found in the selection of members by the nation's more prestigious private clubs. These, for better or worse, are institutions that loom large in the lives of successful Americans. For those born to wealth and position, the hurly-burly of an unmannerly world can be mitigated by a stately prog-

---

* Until mass immigration of impoverished Eastern European Jews commenced, wealthy Jewish Americans were not routinely barred from membership in elite social institutions and quite frequently intermarried with their gentile social peers. The first truly conspicuous example of social anti-Semitism in the U.S., in fact, occurred only in 1877 when New York investment banker Joseph Seligman, a close friend of President Ulysses S. Grant, was turned away by the Grand Hotel in Saratoga Springs, New York.

ress from one social refuge to another—from the men's club, university club, or luncheon club to the country club, yacht club, or beach club. And for those on the make, clubs offer a stairway to status—a place where the favorable regard of the powerful can be won, alliances sealed, and fruitful business done in a discreet and gentlemanly way. (One would not, of course, be so tasteless as actually to bring any business papers into the club bar or dining room.)

Obviously, these benefits would diminish or even disappear if they were too indiscriminately shared, but even the most cursory survey of the club world in the United States as the second half of the 1980s began would have revealed scant danger of that. To start with, the number of elite private clubs that included any blacks at all in their membership was negligible.* And that was only the tip of the iceberg. In Atlanta, so often hailed as the symbol of "the New South," the Capital City Club not only still barred blacks as of mid-1986 but had, by its president's unabashed admission, no Jewish members "as far as I know." That same year, the Forest Lake Country Club in Columbia, South Carolina, an organization that had traditionally extended complimentary membership to the Army officer commanding nearby Fort Jackson, conspicuously failed to display such hospitality when that post was assumed by a Jewish officer, Maj. Gen. Robert B. Solomon. As for the members of the three most potent clubs in Palm Beach— the Everglades, the Beach, and the Bath & Tennis—they were, as of the early 1980s, forbidden even to bring Jewish guests to lunch or dinner. And all the way from Boston to Los Angeles there were still clubs that were devoid not only of black and Jewish members but of Hispanic and Asian-American ones as well.

Yet indefensible as all this was, it manifestly constituted the last desperate stand of an order that was passing; even in clubland, in fact, rigid ethnic discrimination began to erode significantly as the generation that had fought World War II increasingly assumed the reins of power in America. In 1959 an indignant speaker reported to a meeting

---

* Ironically, one of the most prestigious of the clubs that did include some black members, Manhattan's Century Association, became something of a symbol of another form of social exclusion: only under much-publicized legal pressure from the city government of New York did the Century in 1988 finally accept women as members.

---

of the American Jewish Committee that only one of "the top ten social clubs" in New York had Jewish members, and elsewhere in the United States at that time the picture was surely similar if not worse. By the late 1970s, however, it had already changed radically. Not only had the most select Manhattan clubs such as the Knickerbocker and the Links been opened to Jewish members, but Jews had also been admitted— albeit sometimes in only token number—to such other once "restricted" sanctums as the Meadow Club in Southampton, New York, the Chicago Club, the Detroit Club, Cincinnati's Queen City Club, the Minneapolis Club, Seattle's Rainier Club, and San Francisco's Pacific Union and Bohemian clubs.*

Often enough, to be sure, the initial steps in this opening-up process have been taken with visible reluctance and only under duress of some kind. But once taken, they have invariably proved irreversible and on occasion have had a kind of echo effect. Los Angeles' posh California Club, for example, sat on an application from physicist Harold Brown for six years and finally accepted him as its first Jewish member in more than half a century only in 1976 when he was on the verge of becoming Jimmy Carter's secretary of defense.† Ten years later, however, the club's 1,300 members not only included more than a dozen Jewish Americans but a handful of Asian Americans and Hispanics as well. And this example was not lost upon the Jonathan Club, the California's only slightly less prestigious rival for preeminence in the Los Angeles club world. Having seen its role model take the

---

* It is the Bohemian Club that sponsors the much-publicized summer revels of the mighty at Bohemian Grove, some seventy-five miles north of San Francisco. Drawn from all over the United States and from virtually every elite segment of society, the annual turnout of club members and guests at Bohemian Grove constitutes, in the opinion of sociologist G. William Domhoff, "significant evidence for the existence of a cohesive American upper class." My own view is that in so arguing Domhoff gives too much weight to the self-appraisal of Bohemian Grove participants. But assuming that he is right, the inescapable conclusion is that this cohesive upper class covers an ethnic spectrum ranging from Jewish Americans such as Walter Annenberg and yachtsman Emil A. ("Bus") Mosbacher to Arab-American lawyer and financier Najeeb Halaby.

† When the California Club was founded in 1877, 12 of its original 125 members were Jewish, but the virulent anti-Semitism that swept the United States in the 1920s subsequently stampeded the club into a "gentiles only" policy.

---

plunge, the Jonathan promptly proceeded to admit Jewish, Hispanic, and Asian-American members in similar number.

WHEN WE GAZE at the stars at night, we instinctively assume that the light we see is being produced even as we watch. Yet the reality, of course, is that what we are seeing originated long ago and simply took a great deal of time to come within our ken. In a sense, much the same is true of the current membership decisions of America's elite social clubs: it is only after a considerable interval that they come to mirror fully the forces of change constantly at work in high society as a whole. More specifically, the dilatory and uneven pace at which such clubs have accommodated to religious and ethnic diversity is at best a pale reflection of what has been happening elsewhere on the American social scene.

For much of the eighties, for example, the acknowledged queen of Manhattan fund-raising galas was author William Buckley's wife Pat who, though eminently WASP, is a Canadian by birth. On the cultural front one of the heaviest hitters during that same era was Ann Getty, a conspicuously loyal member of the Greek Orthodox Church and publishing partner of George Weidenfeld, Baron of Chelsea, a quondam Austrian transmuted first into a British peer and then into a fixture at elegant New York parties. But for all-round eclecticism there was no other pair on the New York scene to match Ahmed and Mica Ertegun. Ahmed, a pop music mogul with a whimsical taste for imposing the company of rock stars upon social ones, was born Turkish. Mica, one of the cofounders of New York's most socially "in" interior design firm, originally came to North America to escape the Communist rulers of her native Romania.

Less exotic but considerably more numerous among those New Yorkers whose doings were faithfully recorded by the society press in the last years of the eighties were couples in which one or both parties were Jewish. By 1988, in fact, investment banker John Gutfreund (pronounced "Goodfriend") and his wife Susan, a onetime airline attendant, had achieved such prominence that they were widely assumed to be the models for a society host and hostess satirized by Tom Wolfe in his novel *The Bonfire of the Vanities.*

A somewhat different brand of immortality was conferred upon retailing tycoon Milton Petrie when his wife Carroll marked his eighty-fifth birthday by inviting 176 of their friends to a dinner party held in the Temple of Dendur at the Metropolitan Museum of Art; so overwhelmed was the *New York Post*'s "Suzy" by the splendor of this occasion that she devoted the better part of two days' columns to it. But even that accolade could scarcely outweigh the one accorded Cecile Zilkha when *Forbes* magazine described her as a New York "socialite." To the ordinary citizen there might seem nothing remarkable about that in light of the fact that Mrs. Zilkha and her Iraqi-born husband, banker Ezra Zilkha, are, among other things, members of Long Island's exclusive (and pre-Zilkha, exclusively gentile) Meadow Club. In the eyes of the cognoscenti, however, the word "socialite" is often used with deplorable carelessness in the press; what lent it special force in this case was its use by a magazine whose publisher also owns the *Social Register.*

In honesty, though, it must be noted that the *Social Register* that Malcolm Forbes acquired in 1976 no longer was as reliable a benchmark of status as it had been in an earlier era. For living evidence of that no one served better than leading Manhattan hostess Gayfryd Steinberg. The daughter of a telephone clerk, widow of a convicted tax evader, and herself onetime manager of a New Orleans pipefitting company, Mrs. Steinberg could scarcely claim the kind of background that the *Social Register* requires of would-be listees. But with her marriage to corporate raider Saul Steinberg, she became the chatelaine of a 34-room Park Avenue duplex whose decor, as the *New York Times* once noted, ran to "Rubens in the drawing room, Renoir in the bath." Between this backdrop and judicious employment of her husband's wealth on the benefit circuit—among other things, she became archpatroness of the writers' organization PEN—Mrs. Steinberg acquired such status that in a survey entitled "The New American Establishment" that it ran in early 1988, *U.S. News & World Report* was emboldened to describe her as "the queen of nouvelle society."

In using the phrase "nouvelle society"—an appellation apparently coined by *Women's Wear Daily* publisher and self-anointed social arbiter John Fairchild—*U.S. News* was following what had become conventional practice in New York's society press. Underlying this practice was the fact that almost none of the socially prominent New Yorkers to whom I have alluded so far possessed either old money or ancient pedigree. And a number of them were illustrations of a remarkable new phenomenon: historically, the rule of thumb was that it took at least one generation and more often two for wealth to translate into superior social status for an American family; by the 1980s, however, the waiting time—at least in New York—had been reduced to very nearly zero.

This foreshortening of social history was outstandingly visible in the case of Gayfryd Steinberg, who, in terms of the society columns, made the ascent from nonperson to eminence in barely four years. But the all-time standing record for near-instant attainment of social prominence would appear to belong to Arianna Stassinopoulos Huffington, the author of highly controversial but also highly lucrative biographies of Maria Callas and Pablo Picasso. Greek-born and educated at Britain's Cambridge University, Arianna Stassinopoulos arrived in New York in her twenties armed principally with good looks, charm, and a finely honed talent for cultivating important friends. These qualities were sufficient to win her a series of devoted male escorts ranging from California's Gov. Jerry Brown to developer-turned-publisher Mortimer Zuckerman. And before long the company she kept won her the ultimate seal of approval—acceptability at Mortimer's, an Upper East Side Manhattan restaurant chiefly notable for the fact that in the 1980s it could, quite legitimately, have billed itself as the place "where the elite meet to eat."* But what really capped Ms. Stassinopoulos's social rise was the fact that when, at the age of thirty-five, she married Texas oil heir Michael Huffington, her wedding was given by no less a personage than Ann Getty and was staged in a fashion so regal as to prompt Henry Kissinger to observe that all it lacked was "an Aztec sacrificial fire dance."

Inevitably, however, people such as Mrs. Steinberg and Mrs. Huffington create a dilemma for professional observers of the social scene.

---

* Though its precise significance eludes me, it is a curious fact that a number of the restaurants favored by various New York in-groups over the years—21, Toots Shor's and Elaine's all leap to mind along with Mortimer's—have clearly owed their cachet to something other than distinguished cuisine.

While these newcomers obviously are not cast from the same social mold as the 65,000 families that populate the *Social Register*, they just as obviously do conform to the second of the two possible definitions of high society that I offered earlier—namely, those members of any community who lead the most conspicuously luxurious and privileged lives. It is, of course, precisely to deal with this dichotomy that social reporters resort to the phrase "nouvelle society" (or such alternatives as "the New Society" and "the New Order"). And in their efforts to keep the record straight, they not infrequently specify which participants at a given affair represent the New Society and which are entitled to be considered members of the Old Society.

There are, though, certain difficulties with this apparently tidy system of classification, the chief one being that of determining at precisely what point someone has made the leap from the New Society into the Old. The *New York Times*, for example, has on occasion bestowed Old Order status upon former CBS chairman William S. Paley, who is to all intents and purposes a first-generation tycoon; it has also applied the same label to retailing magnate Prentis Cobb Hale and his wife, a lady of recent Yugoslav and Czech ancestry. And while by one set of comparative standards that judgment may be justified, it is questionable whether either Mr. Paley or the Hales would be perceived as genuinely Old Order by most members of such historic New York clans as the Livingstones, Roosevelts, Van Rensselaers, Fishes, or even Vanderbilts.

The reality is that by the 1980s the distinction between Old and New, while still no doubt of subjective importance to those who privately continued to take such matters seriously, had ceased to have much practical effect in New York society. On July 4th, 1986, when Malcolm Forbes celebrated the 100th anniversary of the Statue of Liberty by throwing a birthday party aboard his yacht *Highlander* with its wine cellar, screening room, and Gainsborough paintings, he did not hesitate to invite the John Gutfreunds and Walter Annenbergs along with Brooke Astor and assorted Rockefellers. And the social mix was no less catholic in November of that year at the black-tie dinner-dance at the Plaza that marked the 60th wedding anniversary of John and Frances Loeb. Since Mrs. Loeb was born a Lehman, she and her husband between them represented two of the long-established upper class New York Jewish families profiled by Stephen Birmingham in *Our Crowd*, and as a result, it was only natural that their party was thronged with people bearing such blue ribbon names as Auchincloss, Roosevelt, Vanderbilt, Rockefeller, Dillon, Duke, and Lindsay. But also on hand for the festivities were former New York governor Hugh Carey and his wife Evangeline Gouletas-Carey, William Paley, Mr. and Mrs. Laurence Tisch, ex-senator and Mrs. Abraham Ribicoff, and Beverly Sills.

The reasons why such blending of Old and New has become the prevailing pattern in New York are not hard to see. For one thing, if the relative handful of Old Order WASPs whose activities still center on Manhattan were to dine and party only with each other, their social lives would soon come to resemble those of Western diplomats in Saudi Arabia for sheer tedium. For another, it is a price that must be paid to induce the possessors of new money to contribute both their cash and their clout to cases dear to the hearts of the possessors of old money.

What has come to characterize high society in New York, in other words, has been acceptance, however grudging, of the power realities of late twentieth century America. Perhaps the most authoritative appraisal of the new era was made by Louis Auchincloss, a man who is not only the preeminent fictional chronicler of the surviving WASP elite but who as a Groton alumnus, husband of a Vanderbilt, and partner in a Wall Street law firm undeniably is a charter member of that group himself. "The old ethnic barriers have broken down," Auchincloss told *New York* magazine's Denitia Smith in 1988. "Anti-Semitism is gone or has gone *deeply* into hiding . . . The old society has given way to the Society of Accomplishment."

SO FAR AS high society is concerned, it is easy—as it is in almost every other aspect of life—to argue that New York City is a special case. The trouble with this argument is that, in social terms, the same holds true for every other major community in the United States. Despite the advent of almost instantaneous communications and transcontinental transportation that is both rapid and relatively inexpensive, it was still impossible in the late 1980s to find in the United States as a whole the kind of uniform and elaborate social pecking order that exists on a nationwide basis in Britain.

There was, to be sure, one conspicuous exception to that rule: something approaching a national aristocracy began to develop in America in the late nineteenth century and became more of a reality with each passing decade thereafter. One major factor in this development was the emergence of fifteen or twenty Northeastern boarding schools as the accepted agencies for the indoctrination for children of the wealthiest WASP families throughout the nation. At institutions such as Groton, Andover, Exeter, Hotchkiss, and St. Paul's, Biddles from Philadelphia rubbed elbows with Bundys from Boston while Livingstones from New York, Laphams from San Francisco, Scrantons from Scranton, and du Ponts from Delaware all acquired the same social style.

Traditionally the links that these seminaries of status forged between children of privilege from all over the country were strengthened by subsequent shared experiences at a top Ivy League university or in the case of girls, at one of the Northeastern women's colleges known as the Seven Sisters. By the 1980s, of course, coeducation and the enthusiasm with which Ivy League admissions officers had assumed the function of social levelers had sharply reduced—though not totally eliminated—the accessibility of the elite colleges to any passably literate boarding school graduate of "good family." But for the scions of the aristocracy regardless of geographic origin there still remained another unifying force—one that as Lord Melbourne happily remarked of the Order of the Garter involved "no damned merit"; at resort communities such as Southampton, Newport, or Bar Harbor and Northeast Harbor in Maine, the grandees of St. Louis and Philadelphia could relax in the company of their peers from Long Island and Cincinnati.

Reinforced by the increased geographic mobility of all twentieth century Americans, this youthful commingling inevitably tended to foster a degree of fusion among the various regional aristocracies. Intermarriage between the leading families of a particular city or area has, of course, been commonplace in America since pre-Revolutionary times,* but in this century it has more and more become an interre-

---

* One evidence of this practice is the frequency with which U.S. blue bloods use names as a kind of substitute for the armorial quarterings of European aristocrats—a custom ex-

---

gional phenomenon as well. By the 1980s, it was no longer noteworthy to find close family alliances between the "best people" in Boston and Philadelphia, Rhode Island and New York, Connecticut and New Jersey, or Washington and San Francisco. For the truly old money in America, in short, social status had become readily transferable in a geographic sense. The most exclusive clubs in Boston and New York included nonresident members from New York and San Francisco, and a Houghton from Corning, New York, or an Alsop from Avon, Connecticut, could count on instant acceptance as a social peer by a Bingham of Louisville or a Pennsylvania Mellon.

To some, it appeared a natural consequence of this state of affairs that shortly after Malcolm Forbes acquired ownership of the *Social Register* he consolidated the thirteen separate city directories it had traditionally issued into a single large volume—and indeed the ostensible justification for this step was that cities such as New York, Philadelphia, and Boston no longer constituted independent social universes.

But while it might seem unduly cynical to suggest that publishing economics probably had more to do with the revamping of the *Social Register* than serious sociological analysis, it seems clear that the change rested on shaky assumptions. For, in reality, the members of the national aristocracy still constitute only a small fraction of the upper strata of U.S. society, and while their status has become geographically transferable, that of the majority of wealthy and successful Americans remains very much less so. Being chosen Queen of the Veiled Prophet's Ball undeniably confers distinction upon a debutante in St. Louis, but it does not automatically render the young woman an acceptable guest at the St. Cecilia Ball in Charleston. By the same token, membership in the Los Angeles Country Club will not in itself get an aspirant past the admissions committee of the Brookline, Massachusetts, establishment that Bostonians with ultimate hauteur title simply The Country Club.

---

emplified by such notables as Hamilton Fish Armstrong, Francis Drexel Biddle, Cornelius Vanderbilt Whitney, John Jay Iselin, Endicott Peabody Davison, etc. In general, a presumption of elite social status attaches to any American who shuns a simple middle initial and is habitually referred to by three full names, at least two of which are WASP surnames.

There are, in short, many Societies with a capital *S* in the United States—at least one for every community of any size and not infrequently more. One notable case in point is to be found in southern California where the descendants of great Spanish landowning families form a reclusive Society quite distinct from the WASP social establishment. In a different manifestation of essentially the same phenomenon, certain New England communities possess both a year-round Society and a weekend *cum* summer Society—and it is quite possible to belong to one but not the other.

All of the nation's numerous separate Societies do have one thing in common: they are composed of people who, as Irving Shapiro remarked of anti-Semites, "think you can't be somebody unless you exclude others."* But the grounds for exclusion from Society differ considerably from place to place. In Washington, for example, what prevails as in New York is a Society of Accomplishment—with the critical difference that in Washington accomplishment is interpreted to mean the attainment of high governmental status or assured access to top political and bureaucratic figures. In the absence of those qualifications, the possession of wealth, charm, or social prominence anywhere else in the United States is to no avail, a painful truth that Arianna Stassinopoulos Huffington apparently learned when her husband served briefly as deputy assistant secretary of defense during the Reagan administration. "It was a disaster," one Washington hostess told *New York* magazine's Julie Baumgold. "Michael was just a deputy assistant—they didn't get invited."

Yet what opens the best doors in Washington is socially irrelevant in nearby Baltimore and its more elegant suburbs; there the hallmark of top families such as the Fenwicks, the Colvills, and the Bonsals is horsiness, and one of the best tickets into high society is to ride as a gentleman (or nowadays gentlewoman) jockey in the Maryland Hunt Cup. And a little bit farther to the north in Philadelphia, one of the surest signs of social position is the possession of a summer home in Maine. "In some of these families," an irreverent young Biddle told

---

* William Dean Howells put the same point a bit more charitably when he observed that "inequality is as dear to the American heart as liberty itself."

me with a grin in 1985, "people are still talking about the Bar Harbor fire." *

Socially speaking, most American communities resemble Philadelphia or Baltimore more closely than they do New York or Washington—which is to say that inclusion in the highest levels of Society in such towns and cities is less apt to rest upon personal accomplishment than upon the antiquity, at least in local terms, of one's family and even more important, of one's family money. And as a general rule, it is safe to say that the greater the degree to which this characterizes a local social elite the less likely it is that the members of that elite play a truly influential role in the general life of the United States.

For me, that reality is epitomized by a prominent citizen of one of the several New England communities with which I have special ties. A scion of the seventeenth century founder of the town in which he lives, this gentleman has managed his very substantial inherited wealth with sufficient astuteness that he is both the largest individual taxpayer in town and one of its largest landowners as well. All this renders him in local terms a mogul, social arbiter, and a behind-scenes political power. But with every mile that he travels away from his home base his influence dwindles: in the state capital, he still carries some weight as a potential contributor to political war chests, but he would surely be outgunned by a politician who can deliver the vote in one of the state's thriving industrial centers. In New York, he would be dismissed as a rich rube and in the eyes of most Washingtonians he would be just another nonentity from outside the Beltway.

To put it baldly, while this man is undeniably a member of America's upper class, he is not a member of the nation's ruling class. And the same holds true for the great majority of those people who can legitimately be said to belong to the national aristocracy. Partly because of their passion for privacy—which presumably reflects reluctance, conscious or unconscious, to associate too closely with people of different background and/or ethnicity—relatively few members of the national social aristocracy have made truly major contributions to

---

* A conflagration that occurred in 1947 and devastated much of Mt. Desert Island where both Bar Harbor and Northeast Harbor are located.

---

the political or economic development of the United States in the last four decades.

At bottom, then, the social distinctions made by those who applaud or deplore the existence of what they describe as the Old Society in America are of importance only to those who choose to attach importance to them. But that is not to say that there is not a meaningful and potent class structure in America. Such a structure clearly does exist—and it is one that in certain respects has proved remarkably stable throughout our history and seems likely to continue so for the foreseeable future.

Though it is not something to which Americans often give much thought, it is a noteworthy fact that unlike the great majority of European countries the United States has never experienced a major political upheaval or massive redistribution of the national wealth resulting from class struggle. From the beginning of our history a relatively small percentage of the population has controlled a disproportionately large share of political and economic power in this country. What's more, in terms of the relative size of the population segments involved, the distribution of power and income in the United States has followed a pretty consistent pattern over the last two centuries.

What has changed, however, has been the identity of the individuals and groups that occupy the top rungs of the national ladder. The composition of that dominant minority has continually evolved in response to changes in the economic, social, and political climate as well as in the relative weight of various geographic regions of the country. Southern planters, New England merchants, New York financiers, Pennsylvania steel barons, Midwestern industrialists, Southwestern oilmen—all these and others have had their moments in the sun economically, and in political terms the progression has been no less diverse.

It is, of course, this kind of pragmatic adaptability that enables a ruling class to remain a ruling class. And in the end it is the members of the ruling class, not the members of a putative upper class preoccupied with matters of pedigree and ethnicity, that constitute America's true social masters.

13

THEM AND US

In an age when the linguistic landscape is already hopelessly littered with such cutesy creations as RATS, SANE, and SNAG,* any further proliferation of acronyms should in general be discouraged as a matter of lexicographical principle. But there is, in my opinion one instance in which an exception to this rule might be desirable: the time is now at hand when the term WASP probably should be replaced or at least supplemented by one that more accurately reflects the new ethnic character of the American Establishment.

To imply that any single acronym would suffice for the purpose may seem unrealistic. Yet when one considers what is clearly going to

---

* RATS, as technological sophisticates will recognize, stands for ram air turbine system. SANE, depending upon the context in which it is used, may denote either our own National Committee for a Sane Nuclear Policy or the South African National Antarctic Expedition. As for SNAG (Stop North American Garbage), it is a British organization dedicated to curbing the export of refuse by American cities to landfills in the United Kingdom. Honest!

---

be the makeup of our national elites in the years ahead it is not so at all. Just as people of Dutch, English, Scots, Scotch-Irish, French, and German blood fused into what came to be perceived as a unified group of privileged Americans known as WASPs, so today the members of that group are fusing with people of Jewish, Irish, Italian, Greek, Slavic, and other ancestries into what is plainly destined to become the "old stock" of tomorrow. The next phase in the formation of the American nationality—a phase toward which we are already rapidly moving —will see the breakdown of the old distinction between WASPs and white ethnics and the emergence of a privileged class that incorporates the genes of every major European immigrant group from the beginning of our history through the early decades of the twentieth century.

Inevitably, the operations of this genetic blender will color the way in which its products regard their own ethnicity. For those of particularly complex heritage, the precise mixture of strains that they represent will become what it already is for a substantial number of fourth- and fifth-generation Americans—a matter of little more than academic interest and in some cases, outright uncertainty. As time goes by, there will be more and more upscale Americans like the wealthy Philadelphian of my acquaintance who brushes aside the question of her ethnicity with the casual comment "Oh, I'm a mutt" or the elegantly turned-out New York matron whom I overheard telling a luncheon companion one St. Patrick's Day: "Green really doesn't become me and anyway I'm not Irish—or at least I don't think so."

For the next generation or two, however, what seems likely to be more common among the members of the emerging post-WASP elite is a rather selective and denatured form of ethnic identification. There are, I am convinced, strong intimations of the shape of things to come in the lifestyles of three eminently successful Americans whom I have come to know well. These men, whose names and exact circumstances I have altered somewhat in the interest of retaining their friendship, are themselves transitional figures, and the attitudes they manifest are even more visible in their children. Their case histories:

> John Grogan inherited a modest fortune from his politician father and has parlayed it into a much bigger one in the course of a career as a Wall Street broker.

The grandson of Irish immigrants, John has given his five children names like Seamus, Patrick, and Deirdre and has seen to it that all them were raised as nominal Catholics. The practical effect of these gestures, however, has been diluted by the fact that he was obliged to share custody of his first four children with two ex-wives, both WASP, and that all of his offspring have attended New England boarding schools and secular colleges. Though he himself is a prep school and Princeton product, John likes to describe himself as "just a dumb Mick" and is particularly prone to do so while playing golf at the tony Long Island country club to which he belongs.

Frank DeAngelis, the son of a stonemason from Calabria, acquired an accounting degree by studying nights at a local business college and now earns perhaps half a million dollars a year as a tax consultant and estate planner. He and his wife, who is of French-Canadian ancestry, have two children, both of whom got their early education at parochial schools but then were sent to Ivy League colleges. When the youngsters were in their teens, Frank made a point of taking them on a European trip that included three weeks in Italy. He freely confesses, however, that everyone in the family enjoyed London more than Rome or Naples, perhaps because none of them speaks any Italian except Frank—and his is vestigial. Recently, Frank's daughter, who is married to the son of one of his clients, a Jewish-American businessman, presented her father with his first grandchild. But Frank's son, who is a rising star in a Wall Street law firm and married to a WASP girl he met at college, remains stubbornly childless. Like a lot of other things that disturb him, Frank is inclined to attribute this disappointment to what he sees as the pernicious social and economic influence of "the goddamn liberal Democrats."

While serving in the Army during World War II, Arthur Bloom married a Louisiana girl of WASP and Cajun origin. This did not sit especially well with his Jewish parents, so instead of taking over the small department store they operated in a New York suburb, Arthur went into the business end of broadcasting and wound up a multimillionaire. Now retired, he spends a lot of time fishing and playing tennis with two longtime business associates, both gentile. Though he still likes to sprinkle his speech with Yiddish words and is a strong supporter of Israel, Arthur never goes to temple except for funerals. Both he and his wife dote on their daughter-in-law, an Austrian Catholic whom their son met while skiing in Europe.

One attribute that John Grogan, Frank DeAngelis, and Arthur Bloom have in common is obviously the fact that ethnic loyalties have not played a decisive role in the central aspects of their lives. Their choices of careers, wives, business associates, and schools for their children have all been made not on the basis of ethnic suitability but rather reflect their personal predilections and social and economic aspirations. To be sure, none of the three makes any attempt to conceal his ethnic background; on the contrary, each of them tends in some ways to flaunt it. But the ways in which they choose to do so are essentially peripheral, involving matters that affect the perimeters of life rather than its core.

Of necessity, I believe, this is the role that ethnicity will increasingly play in the lives of successful Americans in the future. In ever greater degree, the manifestations of ethnic loyalty will become leisure-time indulgences—the kind of nostalgic behavior practiced by people with transparently non-Scottish surnames who turn up at Highland games sporting clan badges and even kilts on the strength of the fact that their mother's maiden name was Campbell or that a couple of their great-grandparents were born in Glasgow.

A development that has both paralleled and reinforced this trend toward largely symbolic proclamations of ethnicity has been the declining importance of religion as a divisive factor in American life. This is not to say that the United States is becoming a nation of atheists; the great majority of Americans still profess to be religious, and a greater percentage of them claim to be adherents of one or another organized church than is the case in most other industrialized nations. Yet for all that, the extent to which religion affects the daily behavior of Americans has notably diminished in the last few decades.

Broadly speaking, the pattern that has emerged is this: wherever religious tradition or the exhortations of religious authorities conflict with the evolving American ethos, it is the American ethos that prevails. This is a tendency that has perhaps most strongly affected American Catholics: by 1977 there were 50,000 fewer Catholic priests and members of Catholic religious orders in the United States than there had been a decade earlier. And by 1987, a *New York Times*/CBS poll of American Catholics showed that, despite Vatican injunctions to the contrary, 64 percent of them favored the use of artificial means of birth control, 66 percent were prepared to sanction divorce and remarriage, and 80 percent believed that indulgence in premarital sex was not necessarily incompatible with being a good Catholic.

Among Protestants and Jews the evidences of the trend toward cultural rather than religious conformity were less dramatic but still unmistakable. One such was the volte-face performed by many Protestant clergymen and even more Protestant laymen in the 1970s and 1980s when in a rather striking manifestation of progressive revelation it was vouchsafed to them that the practice of homosexuality was not a sin after all. As for the Americanization of Judaism, that was apparent in many ways; one of these was the growing popularity of the bas mitzvah, a feminine equivalent of the bar mitzvah that was actually invented in the United States. Another was the readiness of American Jews to find a counterpart to Christmas in Chanukah even though the latter in strict Jewish religious observance is only a minor holiday.

In part, because the functioning of a free press serves willy-nilly to accentuate the negative, public attention in the 1970s and 1980s tended to focus upon developments that seemingly belied the notion of a decline in religious dogma in America—phenomena such as the resurgent aggressiveness of "born again" Protestants and the highly visible role that a vocal minority of Catholics played in the antiabortion movement.* But in reality these were essentially rearguard actions primarily conducted by diehards in the lower middle class and working class. On the upper rungs of the national ladder, such narrow orthodoxy was the exception. Far more prevalent among the members of the power elites was the attitude expressed by a wealthy Jewish American, Mrs. Charles D. Cole of Kings Point, New York, and Palm Beach, Florida, when her son Kenneth married Mario Cuomo's daughter Maria in October 1987. Asked about a *New York Times* story that reported that the newlyweds intended to raise any children they might have as Catholics, Mrs. Cole responded: "It might be true; it remains to be seen. In this day and age, you can't play God."

Indeed you can't—and with each passing year any attempt to do so was becoming less socially acceptable in the United States. Among the many privileged Americans who were already the products of religiously mixed marriages in particular, the disposition was clearly to wear religion as well as ethnicity far more lightly than their forebears had. The mere existence of such a group was in itself, of course, evidence that as an impediment to intermarriage ancestral religious loyalties no longer constituted a reliable reinforcement or substitute for the increasingly ineffective appeal to ancestral ethnic loyalties. And that, in turn, had a clear implication for the nation's future: the pace at which America's white population was merging into something like a single genetic entity was certain to accelerate still more in decades to come.

TO UNCOMPROMISING PARTISANS of equal opportunity the de-WASPification of the American Establishment is apt to seem at best cold comfort; what preoccupies them is the fear that it is destined to remain overwhelmingly white. And within limits that assumption would appear justified; as long as whites continue to represent a substantial majority

---

* The commonly held view that a great majority of American Catholics flatly opposes all abortion is mistaken. Among Catholics under the age of fifty who responded to the 1988 *New York Times*/CBS poll, 35 percent favored legalized abortion for anyone who wanted it, 48 percent supported abortion for endangered mothers and victims of rape or incest, and only 12 percent opposed it under all circumstances. Perhaps even more significant, 91 percent believed a woman could have an abortion and still remain a good Catholic.

of all Americans,* they can be expected to constitute a substantial majority of privileged and successful Americans as well.

Yet while racism still undeniably impedes the rise of Asian, Hispanic, and black Americans, they too are clearly benefiting from the reduced importance that elite groups place upon the ethnicity of their members—and of course, from the added impetus that government policies have given to this trend. Of the nation's leading nonwhite minorities, blacks have arguably faced more intractable discrimination than any other. Nonetheless, by 1988 a number of blacks occupied roles from which they would automatically have been excluded a generation earlier and in some cases, even a decade earlier. More than twenty blacks, for example, enjoyed six-figure incomes as partners in major New York law firms, and one of them, Richard D. Parsons, had been tapped to become the first black president of a large savings institution, the Dime Savings Bank of New York. Still another black lawyer, Reginald Lewis, had successfully put together a conglomerate with revenues of $2 billion a year. At the nation's biggest pension fund, TIAA-CREF, Chairman Clifton Wharton was responsible for the investment of some $60 billion. And breakthroughs of considerably greater public visibility had been made by Bernard Shaw, the senior Washington anchor for Cable News Network, and quarterback Doug Williams, who led the Washington Redskins to victory in professional football's Super Bowl XXII.

Even the most incurable optimist could scarcely argue that such individual triumphs reflected free access to high-status occupations for nonwhites. As of 1987 fewer than 1 percent of the partners in the nation's 247 largest law firms were black, and a study conducted in 1986 indicated that Asians, Hispanics, and blacks between them accounted for less than 9 percent of the senior managers at 400 of America's 1,000 largest corporations. In short, as of the late 1980s, talented and ambitious nonwhites faced essentially the same situation that talented and ambitious white ethnics had in the 1950s: though it was no longer impossible for them to win admission into the Establishment, it was extremely difficult for them to do so.

To some, it also appeared that the position of nonwhite strivers in

---

* As of 1987 whites accounted for more than three-quarters of the U.S. population.

the eighties resembled that of the white ethnic strivers of earlier times in yet another respect. Specifically, it was often charged that the price they had to pay for entry into the elite was acceptance of a latter-day version of "the brutal bargain"—in other words, the avoidance of any strong public display of ethnic identity in favor of careful conformity to the manner and mores of the dominant majority.

This again was a charge that while valid enough up to a point required careful qualification. For the most part nonwhite aspirants to elite status in the eighties *were* still expected to conform to the Establishment's tribal ways, but those ways could no longer accurately be described as WASPish or said to involve that dread syndrome "Anglo-conformity." Rather, what was required was conformity to upscale behavior patterns of indeterminate ethnic character.

For whites and nonwhites alike, the most reliable entry ticket was an MBA* or a degree from a "good" law school—or both. Once on their way up the ladder, nonwhites like whites were expected to wear appropriate uniform (more likely a suit influenced by French or Italian tailoring than one inspired by Savile Row) and to adhere to such rituals as the power breakfast, lunch at a suitably chic French, Italian, or Cajun restaurant, and regular workouts at an executive health club. And in the making of career decisions, it was remarkable how often ethnic concerns and personal advancement seemed to walk hand in hand. In 1988 when he decided to abandon law for banking, to cite one case in point, Richard Parsons explained to David Margolick of the *New York Times*: "Law has become less significant as an instrument for change . . . Financial guys are leading the parade now." Curiously, this was very nearly the same wording a young Italian American had used a couple of years earlier in explaining to me his reasons for switching from a $60,000-a-year position as an associate in a Wall Street law firm to a $150,000-a-year job at an investment banking house.

In short, the conformity that the Establishment exacted from non-

---

* At four of the nation's most prestigious business schools—Harvard, Wharton, Columbia, and Michigan—about 7 percent of the MBAs awarded in 1987 went to blacks. While still not proportionate to the number of blacks in the general population (nearly 12 percent), this figure nonetheless reflected the emergence of a large and growing black middle class.

whites as of the late 1980s was class conformity rather than ethnic conformity per se. In fact, certain displays of ethnicity were entirely permissible. (With evident amusement, the *New York Times* reported that one of his white law partners had picked up from Parsons the habit of referring to a particularly valued client as "my main man.") But there was a clear limit on how far such displays could be carried: they had to be compatible with easy association between people of diverse ethnic background. As Vaughn Williams, a partner in Manhattan's Skadden, Arps, Meagher and Flom, put it: "At a law firm you really do end up having not to forget that [you are black] but to put it aside."

Offensive as that necessity may seem to some, it is one with which as time goes by more and more Asian, Hispanic, and black Americans seem prepared to comply. And that fact, in my opinion, makes it inevitable that from year to year the American Establishment will come to include a larger and larger number of nonwhites—until at last there will be enough of them that their ethnicity will become no more noteworthy than that of their white colleagues.

IN A SOCIETY where the adjective "elitist" is widely regarded as one of the most damning that can be applied to any individual or institution, there are bound to be a great many people who will consider the changing ethnic makeup of the American Establishment as a matter of no more than marginal importance. After all, they will ask, what difference will it make to the man in the street?

In certain respects, the answer has to be that it will make little difference if any at all. Increased accessibility of elite status to nonwhites, for example, will not by itself remedy the problems of the black and Hispanic underclasses any more than the traditional accessibility of such status to WASPs eliminated poverty and ignorance among Appalachian whites. And that inevitably will strengthen the perception in many quarters that bigotry is the sole important barrier to the full participation of such disadvantaged groups in American life.

For that reason if no other it seems probable that even though ethnic loyalties and prejudices become more and more attenuated among successful Americans, they will remain strong in certain segments of the underclass and working class. In fact, as the increase of overt anti-Semitism among blacks in the 1970s and 1980s suggested, such attributes may become even more visible than before in certain elements of the population. For as far ahead as one can see, strong nuclei of ethnic separatism seem certain to persist at the lower levels of American society—though as a result of changed immigration patterns the most intractable of these will more and more consist of groups whose ancestral origins are in the Third World rather than Southern and Eastern Europe.

The persistence of ethnic separatism is a prospect that some of the more extreme partisans of cultural pluralism regard with unalloyed enthusiasm and actively seek to encourage. Whether out of vested interest in preserving an ethnic political base or philosophic opposition to cultural assimilation as a degrading process, such people promote a vision of the United States as a kind of loose federation of discrete ethnic blocs—a society whose "rules and goals and procedures," as Michael Novak put it, will be established in time to come by a coalition of defiantly unassimilated groups linked by "the solidarity of underdogs."

To those with a more traditional vision of American society, that seems a prescription for chaos. Though he was probably more influenced by narrow political calculations than anything else, House Speaker Jim Wright of Texas clearly voiced an apprehension shared by millions of his fellow citizens when in the mid-1980s he raised the specter of "a Balkanization of American society into little subcultures." And there was no shortage of evidence that seemed to lend plausibility to that concern—such phenomena as the emergence of a Havana-in-exile in Miami and a "little Odessa" in Brooklyn, the contention between black and Hispanic political leaders in some parts of the country, the entrenchment in various places of public bureaucracies clearly bent on the perpetuation of linguistic separatism, and the angry countercampaigns in California and Florida to enshrine English as the sole "official language."

Yet ominous as some of these developments might appear—the national experiences of Canada, Belgium, and India, for example, scarcely encourage optimism about the viability of avowedly multilingual societies—the threat of a culturally Balkanized United States has, I feel, been considerably exaggerated.

In part, this exaggeration has sometimes rested upon unwarranted extrapolation from local circumstances. Back in the 1960s an Irish-American editor of my acquaintance confided to me that he was twelve or thirteen years old before he realized that Luxembourg was not among the world's largest nations; the reason was that his childhood home in Chicago had abutted a neighborhood largely populated by "big, tough Luxembourgers" whose offspring regularly waylaid my friend as he was going to and from school. By somewhat the same token, anyone living in California, a state that in 1986 was home to 64 percent of America's Asian population and 35 percent of its Hispanics, might readily be excused for assuming that those groups loom larger on the overall national scene than they actually do.

This kind of skewed view is, I believe, enhanced by widespread ignorance of the true composition of the contemporary American population. Even if one were to accept the largest halfway supportable estimates for the annual influx of illegal immigrants, immigration into the United States in the latter half of the 1980s was running at a yearly rate equal to only one-third of one percent of the national population—or to put it another way, at considerably less than one-third the rate that prevailed in the first decade of the twentieth century. As of 1986, in fact, only 7 percent of the inhabitants of the United States were foreign born—which was substantially smaller than the comparable figure for Australia (20%), Canada (16%), or even France (11%). Perhaps even more significant, the nation's foreign-born population in 1986 was in relative terms less than half as large as it had been in 1910, a fact that inspired journalist James Fallows to ask somewhat plaintively: "Can we not accommodate an alien presence half as large as our grandparents did?"

Still another reality that is too often insufficiently appreciated lent added force to Fallows's question. As San Antonio's Mayor Henry Cisneiros once pointed out, even for the most recently arrived and least privileged members of U.S. society "all the things that shape the American way of life are indomitable." In an age of almost instantaneous and well-nigh universal communications, the behavior of the great majority of Americans increasingly reflects a response to a shared array of influences—technological, economic, and cultural. Rich or poor, white or nonwhite, we tend to be dependent upon the same computers, watch the same films on our VCRs, play the same video games, eat the same fast foods, root for the Dallas Cowboys, the Boston Red Sox, or the Los Angeles Lakers, and stoutly insist upon our right to due process (not to speak of undue litigiousness).

These and countless other ways in which American culture in the broadest sense imposes itself upon even the newest arrivals in this country can only be seen as evidences of that culture's enormous assimilative power. But it is of central importance that many if not most such manifestations of assimilation are either ethnically neutral* or have largely been drained of whatever ethnic content they originally had.

Among the nation's "old ethnics" this process of cultural convergence has in many respects gone very far indeed. In a popular "Italian" restaurant in my town, to cite a homely example, people of every ethnic background from WASP to Slavic wolf down pizza, pasta, and eggplant parmigiana prepared by a family of Greek origin. And earlier stages of the same process are clearly at work among many of the burgeoning number of Americans of non-European origin. One of the more striking evidences of that, to my mind, was supplied by media reporter Alex Jones in a story that the *New York Times* carried in June 1988. According to Jones, publishers seeking to tap the Hispanic-American market had discovered that Hispanics born in the U.S.—a group that now accounts for 75 percent of the steady growth in the nation's Hispanic population—tended to find English easier to read than Spanish.† On the strength of this discovery some forward-looking entrepreneurs had

---

* The extent to which this is the case is suggested by the fact that similar economic and technological developments tend to produce similar results in nations that have historically differed greatly from each other culturally. The fact that the Japanese have enthusiastically embraced Big Macs, Kentucky Fried Chicken, and Shakey's pizza does not, I believe, reflect Americanization of Japan any more than our own enthusiastic embrace of that epochal Japanese contribution to civilization, the VCR, reflects Japanization of America. In both cases the products in question simply met the lifestyle requirements of prosperous industrialized societies in which a high percentage of women had ceased to function exclusively as homemakers and the expectation of regular and relatively sophisticated leisuretime diversions had become virtually universal.

† One survey on the subject indicated that while Americans of Hispanic background generally retained an attachment to Spanish as a spoken language, English was the preferred reading medium in 57 percent of the Hispanic-American households that regularly purchased newspapers.

---

already launched Hispanic-oriented magazines published in English. But that, as Jones pointed out, finessed a critical question: would a teenage Hispanic girl who preferred to read in English necessarily want a magazine focused on other teenage Hispanic girls or would she choose to go straight to *Seventeen* or *Mademoiselle*?

The likeliest answer to that question in my judgment is that while they may not lose all interest in the Hispanic-oriented magazine, most such girls will sooner or later decide that *Seventeen* or *Mademoiselle* is a better mirror of the world in which they aspire to live. And that kind of decision, infinitely multiplied in a wide variety of situations, foreshadows the future role of ethnicity in the lives of most Americans regardless of social and economic status. In the decades to come, as historian John Higham has put it, "ethnicity . . . will have some meaning for the great majority of Americans but intense meaning for relatively few. Only minorities of minorities, so to speak, will find in ethnic identity an exclusive loyalty."

ONE THING THAT will surely help lead to the fulfillment of John Higham's prediction is the enormous appetite for success characteristic of so many Americans. Between the dictates of public policy and the changed ethos of the American Establishment, anyone who indulges in overt displays of ethnic prejudice and/or obsessive concern with ethnic identity will find it more difficult with every year that goes by to win admittance to the corridors of power. In a sense, it can be said that conformity to WASP style has been replaced as a requisite for advancement to the upper levels of American society by a more ecumenical imperative: the avoidance of behavior reflecting an inflexible and overriding commitment to the interests of any single ethnic group.

Already, as we have seen, this is a reality the nation's leading politicians must live with. Controversial as many of Jesse Jackson's economic and foreign policy views may be, none of them so damaged his cause in the 1988 presidential campaign as his inability to dispel the widespread belief that he was anti-Semitic. Yet at the same time nothing so tarnished the reputation of New York's Mayor Edward Koch as his naked attempt to make opposition to Jackson a test of ethnic loyalty for Jewish Americans.

In a number of other areas of American life the penalties exacted for unconcealed ethnic chauvinism are often less evident and less harsh than they tend to be in the national political arena. Nonetheless, the ethnic diversity now characteristic of the leading figures in business, law, education, communications, and many other areas of endeavor renders it ever more imprudent for anyone engaged in those fields to display either hostility or undue favoritism toward any ethnic or religious group. One reason for this, of course, is that in most mainstream American organizations such behavior is now certain to give personal offense to some of one's peers or more fatal yet, superiors. But another compelling reason is one exemplified by the experience of Colorado's Adolph H. Coors Co., which in 1987 in a radical departure from its arch-conservative traditions promised to spend $675 million over five years' time on contracts with black- and Hispanic-owned firms and donations to designated charities. The unconcealed purpose of this about-face: to induce various minority groups to end a long boycott of Coors beer that had seriously blighted the company's growth prospects.

The Coors case was, admittedly, a particularly dramatic one. But in virtually every major field of endeavor all across the United States the number of institutions that can hope to operate successfully without the support of a multiethnic clientele or constituency is continually diminishing. That, in turn, means that the number of career opportunities open to people unable or unwilling to eschew ethnic bias in their professional lives will steadily diminish as well.

Obviously there is a vast difference between ethnic equality imposed by fiat or economic pressures and the routine acceptance of such equality by people in their private lives. And where relations between whites and nonwhites are concerned, there are today many Americans —quite probably, a majority—who doubt that this gap will ever be bridged. In the face of three hundred years of discrimination and the failure of the civil rights movement to significantly alter the condition of the black underclass, many of the nation's ablest and most upwardly mobile blacks have despairingly concluded that white racism in America is ineradicable. And a similar despair characterizes a number of white Americans of good will. Even sociologist Nathan Glazer, who as late as 1983 held out hope that black Americans would ultimately come to see themselves as simply one more ethnic group "accepted by others and accepting themselves," sorrowfully informed me less than five years later: "I have changed my mind about that."

To suggest that such pessimism is excessive inevitably smacks of Pollyanna. Yet it is worth recalling that in 1934 in his book *Judaism as a Civilization*, the influential Jewish thinker Mordecai Kaplan took a view of American society very like that held by his black and Hispanic counterparts today. "The prospect of the Jew's attaining social and economic equality [in the United States] is . . . remote," Kaplan declared. And a similarly gloomy view concerning the outlook for their own groups was certainly prevalent among Italian, Greek, and Polish Americans who came to adulthood prior to the 1960s.

What seems to me to underlie all such negative thinking is the understandable tendency of people preoccupied with current injustices to give insufficient weight to the broad sweep of our national history. Somewhat paradoxically, I know of no one who has capsulized that process better than Nathan Glazer did in a conversation we had in 1987. "The boundaries of what is considered legitimate American identity," he said, "have kept on expanding. When Washington or Jefferson said this was a place of refuge for everyone, they were thinking in terms of Northern Europeans. Later on when immigrants of radically different origins arrived, the people who were already here were taken aback and said: 'Wait a minute! Did we mean *them*?' But after a while —usually, to be sure, quite a long while—they said: 'Well, yes, we really did mean them, too.' "

Unlike Glazer, I am not persuaded that there are any limitations on this process. Specifically, I do not believe that black Americans or any other sizable segment of the population can or will forever be relegated to outsider status purely on ethnic grounds. And I find the most convincing evidence for that view in the emergence of an American ruling class in which with each year that passes ethnicity becomes less and less of a touchstone, and the distinctions between "them" and "us" become more and more blurred.

As I made plain earlier, I am under no illusion that this transformation of the American elite will prove any cure-all for our social ills. In one form or another, there will always be inequities and injustices to be fought in this country, and ethnic bias will surely continue to be a source of conflict in some areas of American society for as long as the United States continues to attract and admit new population groups. But at the very least the fact that ethnic exclusivity is no longer the hallmark of those who set the pace in America constitutes a *sine qua non*—the establishment of a brand of leadership without which no search for a solution to any of our national problems could conceivably succeed.

SELECTED BIBLIOGRAPHY

HISTORY AND GENERAL ANALYSIS

Bailyn, Bernard. *The Peopling of British North America: An Introduction.* New York: Alfred A. Knopf, 1986.

Baltzell, E. Digby. *Philadelphia Gentlemen: The Making of a National Upper Class.* Glencoe, Ill.: Free Press, 1958.

Blumenthal, Sidney. *The Rise of the Counter-Establishment.* New York: Times Books, 1986.

Domhoff, G. William. *The Bohemian Grove and Other Retreats: A Study in Ruling-Class Cohesiveness.* New York: Harper & Row, 1974.

————. *Who Rules America?* Englewood Cliffs, N.J.: Prentice-Hall/Spectrum Books, 1967.

————. *Who Rules America Now?—A View for the '80s.* Englewood Cliffs, N.J.: Prentice-Hall, 1983.

Gans, Herbert J. Foreword to *Ethnic Identity and Assimilation* by Neil Sandberg. New York: Praeger, 1974.

————. "Symbolic Ethnicity: The Future of Ethnic Groups and Cultures in America." Included in *On the Making of Americans: Essays in Honor of David Riesman.* Philadelphia: University of Pennsylvania Press, 1979.

285

Glazer, Nathan. *Ethnic Dilemmas: 1964–1982*. Cambridge, Mass.: Harvard University Press, 1983.

————, and Daniel Patrick Moynihan. *Beyond the Melting Pot*. Cambridge, Mass.: The MIT Press and Harvard University Press, 1963.

Gordon, Milton M. *Assimilation in American Life: The Role of Race, Religion and National Origin*. New York: Oxford University Press, 1964.

Greeley, Andrew M. *Ethnicity in the United States: A Preliminary Reconnaissance*. New York: John Wiley & Sons, 1974.

Handlin, Oscar. *Race and Nationality in American Life*. Boston: Little, Brown, 1957.

Higham, John. *Strangers in the Land: Patterns of American Nativism, 1850–1925*. New Brunswick, N.J.: Rutgers University Press, 1955.

Jaher, Frederick C. *The Urban Establishment: Upper Strata in Boston, New York, Charleston, Chicago and Los Angeles*. Champaign, Ill.: The University of Illinois Press, 1982.

Kadushin, Charles. *The American Intellectual Elite*. Boston: Little, Brown, 1973.

Novak, Michael. *The Rise of the Unmeltable Ethnics: Politics and Culture in the Seventies*. New York: The Macmillan Co., 1971.

Podhoretz, Norman. *Making It*. New York: Random House, 1967.

Rovere, Richard H. *The American Establishment and Other Reports, Opinions and Speculations*. New York: Harcourt, Brace & World, 1962.

Schrag, Peter. *The Decline of the WASP*. New York: Simon and Schuster, 1970.

Silk, Leonard and Mark. *The American Establishment*. New York: Basic Books, 1980.

Sowell, Thomas. *Ethnic America*. New York: Basic Books, 1981.

INDIVIDUAL ETHNIC GROUPS

Alba, Richard. *Italian Americans: Into the Twilight of Ethnicity*. Englewood Cliffs, N.J.: Prentice-Hall, 1985.

Baltzell, E. Digby. *Puritan Boston and Quaker Philadelphia: Two Protestant Ethics and the Spirit of Class Authority and Leadership*. New York: Free Press, 1979.

Fallows, Marjorie R. *Irish Americans: Identity and Assimilation*. Englewood Cliffs, N.J.: Prentice-Hall, 1979.

Howe, Irving. *World of Our Fathers*. New York: Harcourt Brace Jovanovich, 1976.

Layburn, James Graham. *The Scotch-Irish: A Social History*. Chapel Hill, N.C.: University of North Carolina Press, 1982.

Lopata, Helen Znaniecki. *Polish Americans*. Englewood Cliffs, N.J.: Prentice-Hall, 1976.

Moskos, Charles C. Jr. *Greek Americans: Struggle & Success*. Englewood Cliffs, N.J.: Prentice-Hall, 1980.

Rippley, La Vern J. *The German Americans*. Boston: Twayne Publishers, 1976.

Rodriguez, Richard. *Hunger of Memory: The Education of Richard Rodriguez*. Boston: David R. Godine, 1981.

Silberman, Charles E. *A Certain People: American Jews and Their Life Today*. New York: Summit Books, 1985.

Vorspan, Max, and Lloyd P. Gartner. *History of the Jews of Los Angeles*. San Marino, Cal.: The Huntington Library, 1970.

Wilson, William Julius. *The Declining Significance of Race: Blacks and Changing American Institutions*. Chicago and London: University of Chicago Press, 1978.

Zweigenhaft, Richard L., and G. William Domhoff. *Jews in the Protestant Establishment*. New York: Praeger, 1982.

POLITICS, GOVERNMENT, AND THE MILITARY

Bamford, James. *The Puzzle Palace: A Report on America's Most Secret Agency*. Boston: Houghton Mifflin, 1982.

Broder, David S. *Changing of the Guard: Power and Leadership in America*. New York: Simon and Schuster, 1980.

Burch, Philip H., Jr. *Elites in American History*. Vol. 3, *The New Deal to the Carter Administration*. New York: Holmes & Meier, 1980.

Corson, William R. *The Armies of Ignorance: The Rise of the American Intelligence Empire*. New York: Dial Press/J. Wade, 1977.

Gabriel, Richard A., and Paul L. Savage. *Crisis in Command: Mismanagement in the Army*. New York: Hill and Wang, 1979.

Moskos, Charles C. *The American Enlisted Man: The Rank and File in Today's Military*. New York: Russell Sage Foundation, 1970.

Ranelagh, John. *The Agency: The Rise and Decline of the CIA*. New York: Simon and Schuster, 1986.

Winks, Robin W. *Cloak and Gown: Scholars in the Secret War, 1939–1951*. New York: Morrow, 1987.

FOUNDATIONS, THE PRESS, AND EDUCATION

Bagdikian, Ben H. *The Media Monopoly*. Boston: Beacon Press, 1983.

Hess, Stephen. *The Washington Reporters*. Washington, D.C.: Brookings, 1981.

Nielsen, Waldemar A. *The Big Foundations*. New York: Columbia University Press, 1972.

———. *The Golden Donors: A New Anatomy of the Great Foundations*. New York: E. P. Dutton, 1985.

Steinberg, Stephen. *The Academic Melting Pot: Catholics and Jews in American Higher Education*. New York: McGraw-Hill, 1974.

Wanniski, Jude, ed. *The Media Guide—1987*. Morristown, N.J.: Polyeconomics, Inc.

SPORTS

Bradley, Bill. *Life on the Run*. New York: Quadrangle/The New York Times Book Co., 1976.

Cosell, Howard. *Cosell*. New York: The Playboy Press, 1973.

Isaacs, Neil D. *Jock Culture, U.S.A.* New York: W. W. Norton, 1978.

Michener, James A. *Sports in America*. New York: Random House, 1976.

Rader, Benjamin G. *American Sports: From the Age of Folk Games to the Age of Spectators*. Englewood Cliffs, N.J.: Prentice-Hall, 1983.

Robinson, Jackie (as told to Alfred Duckett). *I Never Had It Made*. New York: G. P. Putnam's Sons, 1972.

Underwood, John. *Spoiled Sport*. Boston: Little, Brown, 1984.

Viannakis, Andrew et al. *Sports Sociology: Contemporary Themes*. 2d ed. Dubuque, Ia.: Kendall/Hunt Publishing Co., 1976.

ENTERTAINMENT AND THE ARTS

Adler, Richard. *Understanding TV: TV As a Social and Cultural Force*. New York: Praeger, 1981.

Burt, Nathaniel. *Palaces for the People: A Social History of the American Art Museum*. Boston: Little, Brown, 1977.

Davis, Kenneth C. *Two-Bit Culture: The Paperbacking of America*. Boston: Houghton Mifflin, 1984.

Friedrich, Otto. *City of Nets: A Portrait of Hollywood in the 1940s.* New York: Harper & Row, 1986.

Guttman, Allen. *The Jewish Writer in America: Assimilation and the Crisis of Identity.* New York: Oxford University Press, 1971.

Jarvie, I. C. *Movies As Social Criticism: Aspects of Their Social Psychology.* Metuchen, N.J., and London: The Scarecrow Press, Inc., 1978.

Meyer, Karl E. *The Art Museum: Power, Money, Ethics.* A Twentieth Century Fund Report. New York: Morrow, 1978.

Rosten, Leo C. *Hollywood: The Movie Colony, the Movie Makers.* New York: Harcourt, Brace, 1941.

Schickel, Richard. *His Picture in the Papers: A Speculation on Celebrity in America Based on the Life of Douglas Fairbanks, Sr.* New York: Charterhouse, 1974.

————. *Intimate Strangers: The Culture of Celebrity.* Garden City, N.Y.: Doubleday, 1985.

Schwed, Peter. *Turning the Pages: An Insider's Story of Simon and Schuster, 1924–1984.* New York: Macmillan, 1984.

Tebbel, John W. *Between Covers: The Rise and Transformation of Book Publishing in America.* New York: Oxford University Press, 1987.

Tompkins, Calvin. *Merchants and Masterpieces: The Story of the Metropolitan Museum of Art.* New York: E. P. Dutton, 1970.

SOCIETY, OLD AND NEW

Amory, Cleveland. *Who Killed Society?* New York: Harper & Bros., 1960.

Baltzell, E. Digby. *The Protestant Establishment: Aristocracy and Caste in America.* New York: Random House, 1964.

Baumgold, Julie. "The Picasso Wars: Arianna, Her 'Monster' Book and the Critics." *New York* magazine, June 13, 1988.

Birmingham, Stephen. *America's Secret Aristocracy.* Boston: Little, Brown, 1987.

Lapham, Lewis H. *Money and Class in America: Notes and Observations on a Civil Religion.* New York: Weidenfeld & Nicolson, 1987.

U.S. News & World Report. "The New American Establishment." Feb. 8, 1988.

INDEX